⬧ **W9-AOD-727**

Reading
WOMEN
Writing

a series edited by
Shari Benstock
and Celeste Schenck

The Unspeakable Mother: Forbidden Discourse in Jean Rhys and H.D.
by Deborah Kelly Kloepfer

ALSO IN THE SERIES

Autobiographical Voices: Race, Gender, Self-Portraiture
by Françoise Lionnet

THE UNSPEAKABLE MOTHER

Forbidden Discourse in Jean Rhys and H.D.

Deborah Kelly Kloepfer

Cornell University Press

ITHACA AND LONDON

First published 1989 by Cornell University Press.

After Leaving Mr. Mackenzie by Jean Rhys. Copyright © 1931 by Jean Rhys. Reprinted by permission
of Harper & Row, Publishers, Inc., and André Deutsch Ltd.

Good Morning, Midnight by Jean Rhys. Copyright © 1970 by Harper and Row, Publishers, Inc.
Reprinted by permission of Harper and Row, Publishers, Inc., and André Deutsch Ltd.

Quartet by Jean Rhys. Copyright © 1929, 1957. Reprinted by permission of Harper & Row,
Publishers, Inc., and André Deutsch Ltd.

Smile Please: An Unfinished Autobiography by Jean Rhys. Copyright © 1979 by the Estate of Jean Rhys.
Reprinted by permission of Harper & Row, Publishers, Inc., and André Deutsch Ltd.

Voyage in the Dark by Jean Rhys. All rights reserved, 1982. Reprinted by permission of W. W.
Norton & Company, Inc., and André Deutsch Ltd.

Wide Sargasso Sea by Jean Rhys. Copyright © 1966 by Jean Rhys. Reprinted by permission of W. W.
Norton & Company, Inc., and André Deutsch Ltd.

Unpublished manuscript material by Jean Rhys printed by permission of Francis Wyndham and
Special Collections, McFarlin Library, University of Tulsa.

Bid Me to Live by H.D. Copyright © 1960 by Norman Holmes Pearson. Reprinted by permission of
New Directions Publishing Corporation.

Collected Poems, 1912–1944 by H.D. Copyright © 1982 by the Estate of Hilda Doolittle. Reprinted by
permission of New Directions Publishing Corporation and Carcanet Press Ltd.

End to Torment by H.D. Copyright © 1979 by New Directions Publishing Corporation. Reprinted by
permission of New Directions Publishing Corporation and Carcanet Press Ltd.

Helen in Egypt by H.D. Copyright © 1961 by Norman Holmes Pearson. Reprinted by permission of
New Directions Publishing Corporation and Carcanet Press Ltd.

HERmione by H.D. Copyright © 1981 by the Estate of Hilda Doolittle. Reprinted by permission of
New Directions Publishing Corporation.

Palimpsest by H.D. Reprinted by permission of New Directions Publishing Corporation, agents for
Perdita Schaffner; the Estate of Hilda Doolittle; and Carcanet Press Ltd.

Tribute to Freud by H.D. Copyright © 1956, 1974 by Norman Holmes Pearson. Reprinted by
permission of New Directions Publishing Corporation and Carcanet Press Ltd.

Trilogy by H.D. Copyright © 1973 by Norman Holmes Pearson. Reprinted by permission of New
Directions Publishing Corporation and Carcanet Press Ltd.

Unpublished letters and manuscripts of H.D. copyright © 1989 by Perdita Schaffner. Reprinted by
permission of Perdita Schaffner, New Directions Publishing Corporation, and the Yale Collection of
American Literature, Beinecke Rare Book and Manuscript Library, Yale University.

Passages from "Diving into the Wreck" from *Diving into the Wreck: Poems, 1971–1972*, copyright ©
1973 by W. W. Norton & Company, Inc., and "Transcendental Etude" from *The Dream of a Common
Language: Poems, 1974–1977*, copyright © 1978 by W. W. Norton & Company, Inc., by Adrienne
Rich reprinted by permission of the author and the publisher, W. W. Norton & Company, Inc.

International Standard Book Number 0-8014-2306-6
Library of Congress Catalog Card Number 89-7182

Printed in the United States of America

Librarians: Library of Congress cataloging information appears on the last page of the book.

*The paper in this book is acid-free and meets the guidelines for permanence and durability of the Committee on
Production Guidelines for Book Longevity of the Council on Library Resources.*

For Arlene:

> *In the beginning were no words,*
> *and the words were with you,*
> *and the words are me.*

Contents

Foreword

As the editors of *Reading Women Writing*, we are committed to furthering international feminist debate. To that end, we seek books that rigorously explore how differences of class, race, ethnic background, nationality, religious preference, and sexual choice inform women's writing. Books sensitive to the ways women's writings are classified, evaluated, read, and taught are central to the series. Dedicated primarily although not exclusively to the examination of literature written by women, *Reading Women Writing* highlights differing, even contradictory, theoretical positions on texts read in cultural context. Of particular interest to us are feminist criticism of non-canonical texts (including film, popular culture, and new and as yet unnamed genres); confrontations of first-world theory with beyond-the-first-world texts; and books on colonial and postcolonial writing that generate their own theoretical positions.

Deborah Kelly Kloepfer's *Unspeakable Mother: Forbidden Discourse in Jean Rhys and H.D.*, the second volume in the series, reexamines an important area of recent feminist criticism—that of the mother-daughter dyad. Asserting that this area has been curiously marginalized, read either as women's *experience* of motherhood or daughterhood, or theorized through the mother's position as the absent referent of discourse, Kloepfer has situated her work at the intersection of these two perspectives. *The Unspeakable Mother* questions the Freudian notion that the mother-child relation can be theorized only through the oedipal model (from the position of the father), wherein the child's entrance into the symbolic—into language and identity—is purchased through the prohibition of sexual access to the mother's body. The "trope" of the absent mother whom the child represses in order to use language persistently presents itself. Kloepfer asks, "Why is the figure of the mother so central, so insistent, and so unbearable?" Her answer is that there are both linguistic and erotic components to the relationship with the mother: "She is *unspoken* both because representation requires her repression and because releasing her, in the economy of desire, is illicit (incestuous) and therefore *unspeakable*."

Reading the trope of the repressed mother, Kloepfer simultaneously rewrites the oedipal paradigm and writes a new form of feminist criticism: her text "shuttles" between women's experience of motherhood and the position of the mother as absent referent in discourse; it also shuttles between the works of two modernist writers, Jean Rhys and H.D., who shared a common literary project—the attempt to transcribe the ambivalent relation of mother-daughter *through* writing. The spatial field of this project is the textualization of the mother's body from the perspective of the writing daughter. If the androcentric and linguistic oedipal model insists on the abandonment of the mother (who, in the son's version, is first desired and then denied), an important strategy for the writing daughter is the reformulation of the oedipal story so that she can claim her place within the symbolic system. In Kloepfer's analysis, the new terms of the symbolic contract are based not on the daughter's castration but on mother-daughter incest, and the mother is a "site/sight of both seduction and danger." *The Unspeakable Mother* argues against any ecstatic return to lost (maternal) origins. Rather, it risks the "unbearable price" of reactivating her.

Reactivation of the mother, the effort to "speak the unspeakable," requires new ways of reading. Kloepfer discovers that the Rhys and H.D. texts she examines are pierced by "flashing things"—dreams, delirium, cremation, abortion, phantoms, curses, and masquerades—"liminal moments and figures that exist at the intersection of two spaces, replicating the textual struggling of semiotic and symbolic." Thus *The Unspeakable Mother* restages a kind of textual "incest," the struggling and mutual seduction of the central mother-daughter couple.

SHARI BENSTOCK
CELESTE SCHENCK

I came to explore the wreck.
The words are purposes.
The words are maps.
I came to see the damage that was done
and the treasures that prevail.
I stroke the beam of my lamp
slowly along the flank
of something more permanent
than fish or weed

the thing I came for:
the wreck and not the story of the wreck
the thing itself and not the myth
the drowned face always staring
toward the sun
the evidence of damage
worn by salt and sway into this threadbare beauty
the ribs of the disaster
curving their assertion
among the tentative haunters.

This is the place.
And I am here . . .

ADRIENNE RICH "Diving into the Wreck"

Acknowledgments

"I came to explore the wreck. / The words are purposes. / The words are maps," writes Adrienne Rich. I come, likewise, to *The Unspeakable Mother* as one returning to familiar but forgotten territory. Rich's sense of mapping is perhaps a useful analogy to a writing that might be an alternative to representation premised on loss, a topography of language and an enactment of being, "visible language" as H.D. calls it, language of the body, hieroglyphs, cryptograms, "songlines"—all these are purposes that blur the boundaries between presence and absence. We ourselves are the riddling, are the writing.

I feel very fortunate to come of critical age in a time when much struggling with resistant "word-stuff" has been done, when women have already taken enormous risks and made enormous sacrifices. The possibility of writing this book is due in large measure to previous work that opened a space where the unspeakable no longer need be disguised.

I am grateful to Lori N. Curtis, assistant curator of Special Collections at McFarlin Library, University of Tulsa, and Francis Wyndham, Jean Rhys's literary executor, for access to and permission to quote from Rhys's unpublished work. I am likewise indebted to Patricia C. Willis, curator of the Collection of American Literature at the Beinecke Rare Book and Manuscript Library, Yale University, and to Perdita Schaffner for permission to use portions of H.D.'s unpublished manuscripts. Some of the work in this book first appeared in journals; I thank *Contemporary Literature, Sagetrieb,* and the

National Poetry Foundation for allowing me to use all or part of the following articles: "Fishing the Murex Up: Sense and Resonance in H.D.'s *Palimpsest*," *Contemporary Literature* 27, no. 4 (copyright © 1986 by the Board of Regents of the University of Wisconsin System); "*Voyage in the Dark:* Jean Rhys's Masquerade for the Mother," *Contemporary Literature* 26, no. 4 (copyright © 1985 by the Board of Regents of the University of Wisconsin System); "Flesh Made Word: Maternal Inscription in H.D.," *Sagetrieb* 3, no. 1 (copyright © 1984 by the National Poetry Foundation); and "Mother as Muse and Desire: The Sexual Poetics of H.D.'s *Trilogy*," in *H.D.: Woman and Poet*, ed. Michael King (Orono: National Poetry Foundation, University of Maine, 1986).

No book appears without the life that precedes and surrounds it. I thank Claire Kahane at State University of New York–Buffalo for the earliest inklings of what my work would be and the insistence that I encounter the spaces of greatest resistance. To Ray Federman I owe not only respect and affection but the enabling belief that the line between narrative and scholarship is a negotiable boundary. I am deeply grateful to Rachel Blau DuPlessis—more than she knows—for extending herself beyond measure and for producing work that helped me understand my own desire to work. Susan Stanford Friedman's generosity, sound advice, and intelligence have touched me always at the moment of greatest need. In a vast conceptual framework, Shari Benstock has been an extraordinarily perceptive and supportive reader who saw obstacles—and solutions—I couldn't see. I am grateful on another level to Judith Bailey for editing the manuscript, word by word, phrase by phrase, with skill and grace. I am also astonished by what happens sometimes in darkness and silence: H.D. and Jean Rhys both spoke to me until I listened.

In a more private space, I remember Tracy Cogswell, whom I love beyond death; she knew the unspeakable and gave me dreams transposed. Arlene already knows this book is through her; I thank small voices and many colors, especially purple and white, for parts of the story. Finally, I thank George for humor, patience, and love and for watering me during drought; Sarah and John continue to give me hope and the immeasurable loyalty of childhood.

DEBORAH KELLY KLOEPFER

Buffalo, New York

THE
UNSPEAKABLE
MOTHER

"O careless, unspeakable mother"
H.D.

Prologue

The mother-daughter dyad has occupied a curiously marginal space in criticism, pushed aside or held under by "the narcissistic language of the son (or the female son) [which] acts as writing only to deny, repress, censure, and exploit that inaccessible place, no longer to be avoided, the mother's body" (Burke, 847–48). Considering the inescapability and intensity of this relationship, its repression in both literature and criticism as "the great unwritten story" (Rich, *OWB*, 225) deserves serious and repeated consideration.[1] Although feminist critics have begun to understand that Freudian psychoanalytic theory has slighted the significance of the preoedipal experience, the profound ambivalence toward the mother imbedded both culturally and individually has allowed continued insistence on the oedipal configuration as the key moment in the development of identity. As Juliet Mitchell has observed, even "revisionists" continue to main-

---

[1]Marianne Hirsch writes an excellent (if now somewhat dated) survey of mother-daughter criticism and theory in "Mothers and Daughters." Since I began to think about this issue, more critics have become interested in the implications of the mother-infant dyad in women's literature, particularly in terms of language; one good example is Joan Lidoff, "Virginia Woolf's Feminine Sentence: The Mother-Daughter World of *To the Lighthouse*," in which she writes of the rhythm between "relinquishing and preserving the lost world of the mother" (51) as "the novel itself becomes the mirroring mother" (49). The most important sustained work on the mother-daughter relationship and the role of maternal loss in the formation of the female speaking self, however, has been done by Margaret Homans, first in *Women Writers and Poetic Identity*, in which she explores the nineteenth-century writing daughter's ambivalence toward the mother, and then in *Bearing the Word: Language and Female Experience in Nineteenth-Century Women's Writing*, to which I refer periodically in this book.

tain "that the relation of mother and child cannot be viewed outside the structure established by the position of the father" (23).

One of the central points of *The Unspeakable Mother* is that decades before structuralism, poststructuralism, and deconstruction, women, partly through their absorption of modernism and partly through their private vision and despair, *were* viewing the mother-child dyad outside the structure of the father, even though what they viewed was often loss. Moreover, they were *writing*, working textually in this space in profoundly disturbing and startling ways, discovering, creating, and permitting intersections of language adequate to transcribe their split experience. Many critics, nonetheless, echo the sentiment that "to date, feminine discourse has almost no antecedents, and those few are primarily male" (Crowder, 141). This remark reflects a most bizarre lacuna in feminist criticism and critical theory, one I call into question here as I consider the textual implications of the early relationship with the mother and the asymmetrical psychosexual evolution of male and female children.

As a structuring device for this work, I offer a particular "trope": the censored, repressed, or absent mother, a figure missing, not surprisingly so, when we acknowledge that text constitutes itself on the premise of her absence. As Margaret Homans has observed, "Women's place in language, from the perspective of an androcentric literary tradition (and the psycholinguistic theory it generates), is with the literal, the silent object of representation, the dead mother, the absent referent" (*BW*, 32). I further suggest not only a linguistic but an erotic component to relation with the mother: she is *unspoken* both because representation requires her repression and because releasing her, in the economy of desire, is illicit (incestuous) and therefore *unspeakable*.

In reading this figure, I focus on the work of H.D. (1886–1961) and Jean Rhys (1890–1979), two modernist writers who shared a literary project: the attempt to transcribe the incredible ambivalence of relation with the mother and to manipulate "crude ornament of awkward word-stuff," which seems, initially, to be the only medium available.[2] First, however, I look at the critics' own struggles with

---

[2]Judith Kegan Gardiner discusses the difficulty women, particularly Rhys's women, have operating within discourse in "Good Morning, Midnight; Good Night, Modern-

"awkward word-stuff." Although a subtext is emerging in critical discourses that continue to rely on the father, the phallus, and the oedipal moment, those who employ this subtext write out of disparate and sometimes antagonistic linguistic, philosophical, and psychoanalytic contexts. One of my main goals in *The Unspeakable Mother* is to find a way to talk about the relationship of the mother and the writing daughter through a vocabulary that will accommodate the lexical shifting of the key writers who, speaking out of different disciplines, are really talking about why the figure of the mother is central, so insistent and so unbearable.

This issue calls on long epistemological and philosophical traditions while denying the possibility of reliance on these systems at all; as Alice Jardine has suggested, we are in a "vertiginous critical condition" (G, 31), one that seems simultaneously to demand and to abandon fluency in disciplines at the outer edges of what fluctuates between "literature" and "text." Most significant, current French theory has displaced Western psychology, metaphysics, and representation into the sphere of language.

The question of language seems to mark some invisible boundary not only in criticism generally but in feminism; it is one way of distinguishing "Anglo-American feminism," for example, from "French feminism." Despite the danger of polarizing these energies in a way disturbingly mimetic of other gendered polarities, I will nonetheless briefly "represent" the French-American split because it (even a fiction of it) is central to an understanding of the current critical dialogue, its rupture, and the usefulness of the dialogue to a reading of some powerful and disturbing women's texts.

American feminist criticism has been marked by several major trends. For some, the project has been to find a "female tradition."[3]

---

ism," where she explores how the patriarchy "denies [woman] the freedom of language and therefore the freedom to define herself" (239) and then despises her for it; Gardiner does not relate this pattern to the mother, however.

[3]Besides many important articles, three books remain cornerstones in this critical edifice: Sandra M. Gilbert and Susan Gubar, *The Madwoman in the Attic: The Woman Writer and the Nineteenth-Century Literary Imagination;* Ellen Moers, *Literary Women;* and Elaine Showalter, *A Literature of Their Own: British Women Novelists from Brontë to Lessing.* More recently, Gilbert and Gubar have published the first of three projected volumes of *No Man's Land: The Place of the Woman Writer in the Twentieth Century,* in which they tackle the "female affiliation complex" and "sexual linguistics," both part

According to Nelly Furman, in "The Politics of Language," "Feminist critics have tried to understand how social restrictions have shaped women's lives and their relationship to art and literature, and they have then proceeded to validate women's perceptions of life by restoring their writing to public view" (62–63). In part, then, feminist criticism has been a process of "recovery"; in another vein it has been "re-vision," to borrow Adrienne Rich's now-classic term, a way of rereading texts for the images of women found there. As Furman points out, however, "When feminist critics focus their interest on women's experience of life and its 'picturing' in literature, what is left unquestioned is whether literature conceived as a representational art is not *per se* a patriarchal form of discourse" (67).

Recent critical theory, particularly French theory arising from deconstruction, "has put into question the notion that writing merely 'represents' speech, thought, or experience" (Furman, PL, 64). Indeed, it questions the whole notion of representation and perceives language as the mark not of presence but of absence and dissimulation: "A text is not a text unless it hides from the first comer, from the first glance, the law of its composition and the rules of its game" (Derrida, 63). From this perspective, emphasis is not on the "self" but on the "subject," a linguistic identity constituted within language. As a further complication, French theory engages a decen-

---

of a complicated "voyage of dread and desire" (196). The authors operate out of the paradox of simultaneous matrophilia and matrophobia, viewing the mother as "a figure to whose primal relation with tradition the daughter obsessively directs her consistently ambivalent attention, at just the moment when it would seem that maternal potency ought to have healed daughterly dis-ease" (196). The problem in this expansive and important text is that the "oughts" and "shoulds" and "celebrations" often interfere with a consistent distinction between the "powerful *literary* mother" (the authors' real subject) and the biological or psychological mother. This failure leads to lexical shifting and apparent (although not always actual) contradiction. The issue of language/representation vs. literature is also periodically blurred, although Gilbert and Gubar are consistent in the point of view that contrary to "Kristeva's identification of the symbolic contract with the social contract . . . the female subject is not necessarily alienated from the words she writes and speaks" (229). Perhaps future volumes will address the central issue raised at the end of the first: "Isn't it . . . possible that the primordial self/other couple from whom we learn the couplings, doublings, and splitting of 'hierarchy' is the couple called 'mother/child' rather than the one called 'man/woman'? If this is so, isn't it also possible that verbal signification arises not from a confrontation with the 'Law of the Father' but from a consciousness of the lure and the lore of the mother?" (265).

tered subject, calling into question the very nature or possibility of identity. The French, however, rarely apply theory to women's texts, maintaining that "woman" is a position in language rather than a self who speaks her condition.[4] And as Margaret Homans carefully remarks of Lacan, this "narrative depends upon a disingenuous confusion of trope and material condition" (9).

The evolution or disruption of the "woman question" is not my subject here. Nevertheless, a few landmarks on that path may help us find what it means to talk about "the mother" in the context of critical theory. On one level, it seems possible to keep "woman" separate from "the mother"; some critics who write through the question of *fémininité* designate no maternal connotation for the "feminine," which is, however, clearly sexually connoted. Luce Irigaray, for example, writes against the conjunction of the phallus and the "I," arguing that the female body in its multiplicity—"ce sexe qui n'en est pas un"—is the space of rewriting, the space out of which all Western preconceptions of self and unity can be, must be reexamined and rethought and shattered through a *parler femme* in the "doubleness, contiguity and fluidity of women's sexual morphology" (Jones, IF, 86) and in "double or multiple voices, broken syntax, repetitive or cumulative rather than linear structure, open endings" (Jones, 88).[5] As Alice Jardine has pointed out, however, Irigaray has emphasized not feminine writing but the "feminine repressed" in male-written texts (G, 262).

In some ways Hélène Cixous is more explicit about the relationship between women and writing, positing *l'écriture féminine* focused on a linguistic eroticism. "Write yourself," she enjoins. "Your body must be heard" (TLM, 250). Yet Cixous's strong calls for inscription of the body leave unclear how this might be accomplished: "It is impossible to *define* a feminine practice of writing, . . . for this practice can never be theorized, enclosed, encoded—which doesn't mean that it

---

[4]Various women have been helpful to me in locating these issues. Among others, see Domna C. Stanton, "Language and Revolution: The Franco-American Dis-Connection," and Jane Gallop and Carolyn G. Burke, "Psychoanalysis and Feminism in France," both in *The Future of Difference*. Perhaps the most useful extended study is Alice Jardine's *Gynesis: Configurations of Woman and Modernity*.

[5]For a study of women's work which breaks the traditional female textual resolutions, see Rachel Blau DuPlessis, *Writing beyond the Ending: Narrative Strategies of Twentieth-Century Women Writers*.

doesn't exist" (TLM, 253). Even so, in a periodic reparation she attempts to articulate the "undefinable": "This is how I would define a feminine textual body: as a female libidinal economy, a regime, energies, a system of spending not necessarily carved out by culture" (CD, 53). I return to this remark at various points, for part of what I posit is that one of the unexplored "specificities" of feminine writing may hinge on the particular libidinal economy out of which a woman writes, which, it may turn out, has little to do with the (male) "desire" that mobilizes discourse.

> As soon as the question "What is it" is posed, from the moment a question is put, as soon as a reply is sought, *we are already caught up in masculine interrogation.* . . . And this interrogation precisely involves the work of signification . . . A work of meaning, "This means that." . . . And while meaning is being constituted, it only gets constituted in a movement in which one of the terms of the couple is destroyed in favor of the other. [CD, 45]

If desire is contingent on loss, any economy constituted out of that loss will necessarily form itself around a hole, a gap, a wound. "The couple" Cixous refers to might be read as female-male, signified-signifier, mother-child, the latter term of each constituting its identity at the expense of the former. It is not just the *female* body that concerns Cixous but the *maternal* one underlying her impulses. "Writing in the feminine," she says, attempting to define what she elsewhere describes as undefinable, "is passing on what is cut out by the Symbolic, the voice of the mother, passing on what is most archaic" (CD, 54). This process is not open only to women, although they do seem, in Cixous's vision, to have a kind of privileged access to it, perhaps in part because of the maternal connotations—the rhythm of childbirth and flow—which sustain the imagery of much of Cixous's work; women write "in white ink" (TLM, 251) through a "desire for the swollen belly, for language, for blood" (TLM, 261).

This textualization of the body is not, however, meant to reverse polarities and revalorize the feminine. To the extent that it appears to do so, it presents serious limitations (and misinterpretations) and opens itself to charges of perpetuating the image of woman as passive, illogical, unfocused, unpredictable. It is a question, says Alice Jardine, of the functioning of a "supplementary register," a reinsertion of the "feminine," not necessarily woman's body in the mor-phological sense that Irigaray understands but rather the space of privileged contact ("Pre-texts," 228). Monique Wittig (and others) makes an important distinction between "women" as social con-struct and "woman" as myth, process, and "imaginary formation" (50–51). It is in fact this distinction that has led to a male critical appropriation not of women's issues but of the issue of "woman," an appropriation that appears throughout history but comes into a par-ticular kind of focus through both Freud and deconstruction.

It is enormously difficult to "shorthand" French theory because of the complexity of its thought and its elaborate intersection with other critical and philosophic discourses. There is also a kind of built-in refusal to be reduced or explicated, partly a function of "deconstruc-tion" itself and partly the result of a rather petulant resistance on the part of, say, Jacques Lacan to participate in easy access, a kind of acting out of his disgust with the way Freudian theory has been popularized and picked apart. On the one hand, there seems to be an insistence in Lacan that his canon be taken as a whole, the gaps, splits, omissions, contradictions, and interstices being crucial to its functioning, that in fact the text has a life of its own, which cannot be sliced or torn into convenient passages. In part, this idea might be read as any text's desire for itself, for its own otherness. One always has the suspicion, however, that we are being confronted not by the text's desire but by Lacan's—some urgent need for mastery from the man who "discovers" (with great relief) that the mother and child cannot be considered out of the context of the father and that women "don't know what they're saying, that's the whole difference be-tween them and me" (*Encore*, 68, quoted in Jardine, *G*, 164). Reading a body of work punctuated with equally outrageous statements, one can readily understand Lacan's resistance to being "snipped apart." When we dismiss Lacan from connection with his work, however, what is left, almost by definition, is Lacan's *text*, a very different object. Roland Barthes has suggested that the literary (or critical) work is associated with "authorship," implying biography, inten-tionality, meaning, whereas the text "exists only as discourse. . . . In other words, *the text is experienced only in an activity, a production*" (FWT, 75). Nelly Furman summarizes, "Whereas the literary work has an author . . . the literary *text* is fatherless" (PL, 69), and this

fatherlessness is at the heart of what Alice Jardine calls "modernity"—"the recognition that delegitimation, experienced as crisis, is
the loss of the paternal fiction" (G, 67).

If we accept that the current critical crisis is the disruption of a
phallogocentric (textual) economy—the loss or calling into question
of unity, identity, self, syntax, logic, and meaning—we can see modernity as "a search for that which has been 'left out,' de-emphasized,
hidden, or denied articulation within Western systems of knowledge" (G, 36). In trying to locate these issues, it is necessary to
"interrogate [the dominant] discourse," as Josette Féral has suggested, in a criticism adapted to "disordering, deviation, and de-
railing" (DT, 46, quoted in Jones, IF, 94). We might try, for example,
to reach into the gaps or holes in the text while rendering them
fatherless, leaving the discourse to speak (to) itself.

So what do we hear when we listen? The voice of an invisible
"m/other text"? Silence? Snortings, mumblings, chants? Screaming,
madness? Pleasure? Death? Are we in the presence of the unrepre-
sentable, and if so, what marks the space where it is not? Perhaps we
enter not the space of absence but the space of the "simultaneously
present and absent" (Jardine, G, 124), a space in which *fort-da* no
longer/does not yet exist either as game or theory.

The interest of the contemporary critical text for feminist critics is,
Alice Jardine observes, that "this space, new place, is tenaciously
feminine" (G, 89); "all of the words used to designate this space (now
unbound)—nature, other, matter, unconscious, madness, hylé,
force—have throughout the tenure of Western philosophy carried
feminine connotations" (G, 88). Moreover, as this "space" has been
released or discovered or displaced in text, the feminine body "has
rematerialized as *isographic:* as *writing*" (G, 161).

This "putting into discourse of 'woman,'" however, presents
some conflicts, which Jardine outlines in her important work *Gynesis.*
A major problem lies, it appears, with the "woman-subject," who
"usually becomes a kind of 'filter' for questioning this space"; moreover, there is a warning against the "mystification produced by
imagining 'that there is *someone* in that filter'" (G, 89). The conflict is
perpetuated by Lacan's insistence that a woman is a woman "to the
extent 'that she cannot find herself' . . . ; she does not correspond to
a self-in-language: 'there is always something about and in her which

escapes discourse'" (*G*, 165). For Lacan female "subjecthood" is oxymoronic; the feminine, "woman," is that which disturbs and ruptures the subject and the symbolic.

Both prongs of current debate—"woman" and "self"—ultimately lead back to the mother, the first in the intersection of the female body with maternity and the second in the importance of the pre-oedipal relationship to the formation (or dis-integration) of the "I." In feminist criticism, the mother is read from both sides—mothering and being mothered.[6] My emphasis is on the daughter, particularly the writing daughter, and the implication of denied access to maternal voice and form. My focus, then, is not motherhood but the mother-child dyad, the expression or loss of which marks many women's texts and might, in fact, be read as one of the elusive specificities of women's work.[7] The daughter's relationship to and perception of the mother particularly interest me here, for while the male certainly has access to preoedipal experience, he experiences it differently from the female, and this gender asymmetry is crucial to what it means to write as a woman.

The most significant writer to address this issue in terms of its psychological implications is Nancy Chodorow, who illustrates that the oedipal "crisis" is less of a crisis for girls than for boys and that female children do not relinquish the mother—internally—with the same violence that male children do. The "intervention" of the father (phallus) in the mother-child dyad does not represent difference for the girl in the same way that it does/"must" for the boy. For the boy it is the mark of his difference from the mother; for the girl it is not. The phallus (its presence bringing with it its absence) is also the sign of the castration "contract" and therefore the mark of the incest taboo. But even this cultural premise is asymmetrical: incest, at least heterosexual incest, is less taboo for the girl; since she does not have the phallus, she "needs" something else to replace it (Chodorow suggests that perhaps she "wants" it not out of "envy" or desire but

---

[6]For discussions from the perspective of motherhood, see (among others) Judith Kegan Gardiner, "The New Motherhood"; Adrienne Rich, *Of Woman Born: Motherhood as Experience and Institution;* and Susan Rubin Suleiman, "Writing and Motherhood."

[7]Joan Lidoff makes a similar observation: "I suggest that both the relationship with the mother and the sense of self and reality that develop from it are formative for women's literary style" (44).

because she sees it as a way of access to the mother).[8] According to Freud, her normal response is to desire to bear the father's child, the child who will substitute for the missing phallus.

Hence we find the beginning of the "chain of desire" and the chain of signifiers at the center of Lacan's psycholinguistics—the presupposition that all systems of representation are based on absence, echoing the primal loss of the mother. We begin to see, then, the dependence of both androcentric culture and "phallogocentrism" on the loss or absence of the mother, the event that is both solicited and mourned, so that, as Terry Eagleton has written, "to enter language is to be severed from . . . the mother's body. . . . We will spend all of our lives hunting for it" (168).

This "lack" and its association with the mother are further developed by another important theorist, Julia Kristeva, whose occasionally intrusive Lacanian vocabulary might nonetheless be turned to advantage. For all her convoluted discourse and mining of epistemological systems, she, like Cixous, works through a space, the *chora*, which, "although it can be designated . . . can never be definitively posited" (*RPL*, 26). The *chora*, a term she borrows from Plato's *Timaeus*, is used "to denote an essentially mobile and extremely provisional articulation" (25), which, "as rupture and articulations (rhythm), precedes evidence, verisimilitude, spatiality, and temporality" (26). Its importance in the discussion here is its liminality as well as its archaic nature: "The *chora* is not yet a position that represents something for someone (i.e., it is not a sign); nor is it a position that represents someone for another position (i.e., it is not yet a signifier either)" (26). While it "is a modality of significance in which the linguistic sign is not yet articulated as the absence of an object and as the distinction between real and symbolic" (26), it is "generated in order to attain to the signifying position" (26). "Our discourse—" writes Kristeva, "all discourse—moves with and against the *chora* in the sense that it simultaneously depends upon and refuses it" (26). It is not surprising, then, that Kristeva connotes this articulation maternally: "The mother's body is . . . what mediates the symbolic

[8]I am extracting only those portions of Chodorow's work relevant to my discussion, leaping over many of her major contributions. For a fuller understanding of the implications of her work, see *The Reproduction of Mothering: Psychoanalysis and the Sociology of Gender*.

law . . . and becomes the ordering principle of the semiotic *chora"* (27).

Kristeva repeatedly relies on the two terms *symbolic* and *semiotic*, terms that many feminist critics have begun to employ in their work on the specificity of female or maternal language. She associates the symbolic with Lacan's name-of-the-father—the "inevitable attribute of meaning, sign, and the signified object for the consciousness of [the] transcendental ego" (*DL*, 134). The semiotic, on the other hand, is a "dissonance within the thetic, paternal function of language" (*DL*, 139) before sign, predication, and meaning, "unnamable, improbable, hybrid, anterior to naming, to the One, to the father" (*DL*, 133). It is tempting to read Kristeva a bit too ecstatically, to view the site of the mother in sacred, Eleusinian terms, the daughter's version of Bellini's representation (via Kristeva) of the mother: "a luminous spatialization, the ultimate language of a jouissance at the far limits of repression" (*DL*, 269). The semiotic is not (only), however, what it first appears to be—the working of "poetic language," of vocalization, rhythm, music, laughter—but (also) a "crisis" of "the *unsettling process* of meaning and subject" (125) at the edges of *jouissance* and also psychosis: "The occult, the esoteric, and the regressive rush in as soon as the symbolic surface cracks and allows the shadow of the . . . mother to appear—its secret and its ultimate support" (194).

The two most important Kristevan concepts for my work here are, first, that the mother, as either object or lack, is both dangerous and desired and, second, that this ambivalence is reflected in (or is the result of) the liminality of the psychological and linguistic space she occupies. Although language constitutes itself at her expense, depends on her absence (there is no need or desire to re-present presence), the maternally connoted semiotic surfaces as a register to discourse, a memory, an intonational " 'instinctual' breakthrough which is situated at the most intense place of naming—at the thetic place of an inescapable syntax that abruptly halts the maternal body's vague, autoerotic jubilation—recognizes its reflection in a mirror and shifts instinctual motility into logically structurable signifiers" (*DL*, 167). In one sense, then, as Lacanians insist, self and language are inseparable as "the entry into syntax constitutes a first victory over the mother" (*DL*, 189). But Kristeva consistently maintains that the "relationship of the speaker to the mother is probably one of the most important factors producing interplay within the structure of meaning" (137), and it is this idea of interplay which offers the most promise for reading the maternal subtext in women's work.

> To rediscover the intonations, scansions, and jubilant rhythms preceding the signifier's position as language's position is to discover the voiced breath that fastens us to an undifferentiated mother, to a mother who later, at the mirror stage, is altered into a *maternal language*. It is also to grasp this maternal language as well as to be free of it thanks to the subsequently rediscovered mother, who is at a *stroke* . . . pierced, stripped, signified, uncovered, castrated, and carried away into the symbolic. This is the text. [*DL*, 195]

1

The Blind Spot

In her unfinished autobiography, *Smile Please,* Jean Rhys recalls the Catholic school in Dominica she attended as a child, where the mother superior asked, "Who made you?" and a roomful of young girls recited the catechism. Rhys's chief memory is of

> a little girl who persisted obstinately in saying, "My mother!"
> "No, dear, that's not the answer. Now think—who made you?"
> "My mother," the stolid girl replied. At last the nun, exasperated, banished her from the class. [64]

This is a rather remarkable scene in several ways. Coming out of an unfinished autobiography, it is an emblem for women's abandoned narrative. It marks a (female) child's entry into discourse, her attempts to position herself in terms of her origins. The question "Who made you?" is a quivering matrix—the space of body, mind, desire, memory, rage, fear. To the woman who poses it, however, it is merely a formula, the incantation that will elicit the answer that knew itself before there was the need of the question. The nun is well taught by the patriarchal theology within which she lives; there are "right" questions and "right" answers, all of them revolving around a context in which the female is seen only in terms of her relationship with the Father and the Son. A little girl who persists in speaking out of her own experience rather than the father's text is an exasperating figure to be banished, someone who, like the nun herself, is exploited and excluded by a discourse in which she has neither body nor voice.

This scene resonates not only theologically but culturally, politically, psychologically, and linguistically; in a sense, it presents the three main "characters" with which I am concerned in this book: the motherless daughter, the daughterless mother, and a patriarchal text. The scene could be read as a kind of dream, that which is both repressed and desired, just as any text in its interplay between conscious and subconscious material might be read liminally. If we allow this scene to act as the nun's dream—indeed, as her nightmare—or the text's dream, we then might question its functioning, poke for its "blind spot," "the locus of greatest resistance . . . the heart of the dream, the crisis point crying, begging for analysis" (Gallop, FS, 37). The blind spot, as it turns out, is the mother, much as it was for Freud in another context. "It is as if," Iza Erlich suggests, "Freud could not bring himself to look closely at the mother, the figure his theory proclaims to be so central. Be it Dora's madly cleaning mother, Little Hans's beautiful, seductive mother, or the Rat Man's absentee mother, they all appear as silhouettes against the rich background of other relationships; other entanglements" (284). Thus, if we read psychoanalysis itself as Freud's dream text, his blind spot is the same as the Dominican nun's—neither can see the mother.

Little work, relative to the enormous possibilities, has been done on the thematic, syntactic, and linguistic implications of the semiotic and the reemergence of the archaic mother. The novels and poems I deal with in *The Unspeakable Mother* are filled with dead mothers, dying mothers, mad mothers, absent mothers, stepmothers, and surrogate mothers; they are also full of abortions, stillbirths, miscarriages, and infant death. The women who populate these texts can neither find mothers nor be mothers; at every turn, maternal contact is subverted. I suggest, however, that sometimes the mother is not actually missing but rather occupying a "blind spot" and that by repositioning ourselves as readers we can see from the vantage point of Rhys's obstinate, exasperating little girl, who insists on the interplay between the banished mother and the male text. Coincident with this maternal subversion, in either case, is the inability of these women to operate effectively within discourse. Their speech is ignored, misunderstood, or censored. Their writing (many of them attempt to posit themselves in texts within texts) is similarly edited, slashed, criticized, or suppressed.

This concurrent maternal loss and linguistic alienation implies that rather than just dealing with women's experience thematically, these women are also experimenting linguistically and that there is a direct encoding of the mother in relation to language. A dead mother is a trope for textlessness, a way of speaking the unspeakable, a way of inscribing a silencing, a failure, or a repression of the female speaking/writing subject. "Woman," who has no space in a patriarchal linguistic system, cannot adequately articulate her exclusion; instead, she represents her linguistic alienation through alienation from or violence to the maternal body: the mother's deathbed or her own abortions. The thematic violence toward the female body, however, is accompanied by the rupture of the discourse by the semiotic, a process that, while reconstituting the abandoned mother, turns the violence, textually, against the symbolic, which has both denied and desired her.

In both H.D. and Rhys, the maternal loss and rejection resonate both textually and biographically.[1] H.D. was her mother's only surviving daughter, her elder sister, Edith, having died in infancy. Her maternal grandmother had also lost a daughter, Frances, and her father had lost a child, Alice, by his first marriage. Thus, hers was a family of lost daughters, of whom H.D. believed herself to be "the inheritor" (*Gift*, 4). She was, by report, her father's favorite, especially since she was the only surviving girl child, but she was tormented throughout her life by the feeling that her mother preferred her elder brother, Gilbert.

H.D.'s mother, Helen Eugenia Wolle, daughter of the head of the Moravian Seminary in Bethlehem, Pennsylvania, was raised in a family deeply devoted to the teachings of a mystical sect. This heritage fostered in H.D. an early experience of mystical discourse through Moravian hymns and the language of the "Hidden Church," forced

[1]The nature of this work precludes my providing a lengthy biographical context for either writer. Primary resources for H.D. are Susan Stanford Friedman, *Psyche Reborn: The Emergence of H.D.*; Barbara Guest, *Herself Defined: The Poet H.D. and Her World*; and Janice Robinson, *H.D.: The Life and Work of an American Poet*. Also, much information can be culled from shorter critical works, detailed by Mary S. Mathis and Michael King in "An Annotated Bibliography of Works about H.D.: 1969–1985." Biographical work on Rhys remains sketchy and often contradictory. Besides Rhys herself in *Smile Please* and in collected letters, Thomas Staley, *Jean Rhys: A Critical Study*, and Teresa O'Connor, *Jean Rhys: The West Indian Novels*, seem to me the most reliable sources; Carole Angier's *Jean Rhys* is also somewhat useful as a chronology of events in Rhys's life.

after centuries of persecution to go underground and disguise its "secrets" in a language open only to the initiate. A significant aspect of Moravianism is its "attempt to down play the role of the father so as to create a culture based upon the ideal of sexual equality" (Robinson, 82–83).[2] It is also to be noted for its inclusion of women as initiates: "All members of the faith were permitted to know and use the symbolic language so that it could not be used against them" (Robinson, 83). Thus on one level, H.D.'s maternal heritage transmitted to her a mystical and poetic perception of symbols and language and the affirmation of women's access to them.

On the other hand, H.D.'s birth as a poet and her early artistic development initially involved a denial of her maternal heritage. Susan Stanford Friedman maintains in *Psyche Reborn: The Emergence of H.D.* that "while [Helen Doolittle] consistently signified in H.D.'s writings women's artistic potential, she also represented the woman whose talent had been thwarted and mind diverted by her identification with her husband, sons, and masculine culture in general" (140). Thus when H.D. left home in 1911 to follow her fiancé Ezra Pound (the engagement was later broken) to Europe, she was filled with ambivalence; she simultaneously (alternately) perceived herself as having abandoned her mother, as having been snatched from her, and as having been denied by her. It was a long and painful journey to the point where she could write, "The mother is the Muse, the Creator, and in my case especially, as my mother's name was Helen" (*ETT*, 41). This journey involved for H.D. a profound reexamination of the catechism, both cultural and psychoanalytic, until she could finally determine to what extent her mother made her and the extent to which she might remake the mother.

In 1933 H.D. began a series of sessions with Freud. Noting that Helen Doolittle had spent her honeymoon in Vienna, Freud told H.D. that she had come to that city "hoping to find [her] mother" (*TF*, 17). H.D.'s response to this is "Mother? Mamma. But my mother was dead. I was dead; that is, the child in me that had called her Mamma was dead" (*TF*, 17). H.D. instinctively tries to amend the articulation of her deepest conflict. It is *not* just the child Hilda who is

[2]My understanding of H.D.'s Moravian heritage as expressed in this chapter is from Robinson.

gone, however; in a very real sense, the dead mother does imply a dead *self* ("I was dead"), particularly a dead speaking self. As I suggested earlier, a dead mother is a way of narratively encoding a linguistic loss. It is only when H.D. comes to restore the mother that she herself can be reborn into her work. She begins analysis, however, in a state of estrangement both from her mother and from herself as speaking/writing daughter.

H.D.'s version of her sessions with Freud suggests that he focused considerably on her relationship with her mother. In *Tribute to Freud* H.D. writes of Helen Doolittle, "One can never get near enough, or if one gets near, it is because one has measles or scarlet fever. If one could stay near her always, there would be no break in consciousness" (33). It is significant that there is no "I" in this longing for maternal contact; woman as other cannot speak desire. Moreover, H.D.'s perception of a return to the mother, never near enough, as conceivable only in illness, suggests that such a "regression" is unhealthy or pathological.

That, in fact, is essentially how Freud perceived her "fixation": "the experience of 'no break in consciousness' between subject and object is a regression to infantile desire for union with her mother" (Friedman, *PR*, 131). Similarly he affirmed H.D.'s Scilly Isles experience, which she described as "the transcendental feeling of the two globes or the two transparent half-globes enclosing me" as "some form of pre-natal fantasy" (*TF*, 168).

In 1920 H.D. traveled with her companion Bryher to Corfu.[3] Freud considered this trip another manifestation of her desire to merge with her mother. "I was physically in Greece," she writes, "in Hellas (Helen)" (*TF*, 44). While there, H.D. had a vision, a series of light images projected on the shadowed wall of her hotel room, which I discuss at length in Chapter 6. For the moment, we need to know only that Freud translated these pictures or "writing" on the wall as H.D.'s "desire for union with [her] mother" (*TF*, 44), undoubtedly

---

[3]Bryher was the name used by Winifred Ellerman, a wealthy Englishwoman who, earlier taken with H.D.'s work, "rescued" her from the illness and breakdown following the birth of H.D.'s daughter, Perdita, in 1919. The two women became involved in an intense and complicated relationship that endured for more than forty years, a relationship on which much work remains to be done. See, for preliminary discussions, Guest and Friedman, *Psyche Reborn*.

connecting the oracle of Delphi seen in the vision, H.D. tells us, with "the shrine of Helios (Hellas, Helen)" (*TF*, 49). Both Freud and H.D. also associated Bryher with Helen Doolittle; that H.D. "shut off" before the last image appeared, requiring her companion to finish the "reading," seemed to bear on H.D.'s search for a mother-muse who would serve as a source of both mystical and poetic inspiration.

Freud also called this vision H.D.'s *only* "dangerous symptom." "I do not yet quite see why he picked on the writing-on-the-wall as a danger-signal," H.D. writes, "and omitted what to my mind were tendencies or events that were equally important or equally 'dangerous' " (*TF*, 41). What H.D. herself didn't "quite see" is that continuous relation with the mother, in Freud's scheme of "normal" development, is "dangerous," disruptive of the system. His purpose in her analysis would be, as Friedman suggests, "to help her recover and interpret the fragments of her dreams and visions so that the neurotic symptoms rooted in desire for union with her mother would disappear" (*PR*, 135) and so that she might pass beyond her preoedipal fixation and transfer her affection to her father. Freud interpreted H.D.'s attempt to join her mother as a neurotic fixation, and yet, Friedman points out, H.D. was able to turn this view around and extract from his "translations" only what would serve her purposes: "H.D. took Freud's theories, dismissed their evaluative framework, and developed his ideas in a direction ultimately antithetical to his own perspective" (*PR*, 137).

Although she was fascinated with his interpretation of dreams, she perceived them simultaneously in much more mystical ways, writing later to Viola Jordan, "I think people do actually come to us in dreams. I dream of my mother, simply confused dreams, mixed-up, that don't count—then one so clear and exact, with such perfect detail, that I KNOW that this time, I have actually been with her."[4] On 20 March 1933 H.D. recorded one such dream in which, trying desperately to return to her London flat, she encounters a man and a "rough boy" who bar her way and threaten her. "As I stood threat-

[4]H.D., letter to Viola Jordan, 30 July 1941, Collection of American Literature, Beinecke Rare Book and Manuscript Library, Yale University, New Haven, Conn., quoted in Friedman, *Psyche Reborn*, 137. I am grateful to Patricia C. Willis and Perdita Schaffner for access to this correspondence and for permission to reprint it in my work.

ened and terrified I call [*sic*], loudly, 'Mother.' I am out on the pavement now. I look up at the window of my flat. A figure is standing there, holding a lighted candle. It is my mother. I was overpowered with happiness and all trace of terror vanished" (*TF*, 174–75). This is hardly, one would argue, a dream of regressive fusion. Rather, it involves two adult women separated and threatened by men. It is both sexually charged and an invocation of Demeter and "the primal bond of protective love between mother and daughter" (Friedman, *PR*, 139).

Freud intended H.D. to "retrieve" her mother so that she might free herself of her fixation, adhering finally to the oedipal agreement. "Instead," Friedman suggests, "this identification and bond with her mother freed her to explore the meaning of woman's experience in a male-dominated world. . . . The spiritual reunion with her mother that she experienced in the realm of dream and vision helped to confirm art as a possible female destiny in a world that designated aesthetic genius and creation as the province of men" (*PR*, 137). Having access to a maternal image, to what Cixous might call the archaic mother, through dream and an exploration of the unconscious, H.D. was able to sense more clearly her place within language.

> To restore this bond as center of her artistic identity, H.D. used Freud's diagnosis of her desire for union with her mother to transform her mother from the wounded woman of the patriarchal world to an ideal mother-symbol who is free to nourish her daughter. Her mother's existence as her daughter's muse represents H.D.'s liberation of her mother from imprisonment in her Victorian context. In the realm of the imagination fed by the inspirational river of the unconscious, H.D. could re-create the image of the whole mother, the all-powerful Demeter who is prevented in the material world of the patriarchy from loving and protecting her daughter. [*PR*, 142]

During her evolution as a writer, H.D. begins to recover her mother, liberating her from her conventional self-sacrificing, Victorian context into a muse who births both her daughter and her word. As Rachel Blau DuPlessis has observed, however, "in claiming maternal love as the occulted element in our civilisation, . . . H.D. took several risks" (*H.D.*, 115–16), not the least of which was confronting the psychological and linguistic consequences of incest.

In a similar way Jean Rhys struggled throughout her work with the specter of her mother, Minna Lockhart Williams. Rhys was reticent about details and explicit confessions, unable to provide a record of personal analysis like H.D.'s *Tribute to Freud*.[5] Rhys's unfinished autobiography provides few specific memories of her mother, but it does make clear that Rhys, like H.D., competed with a sibling for her mother's affection; she writes in *Smile Please* about the arrival of the "new baby" after whose birth her mother "seemed to find [Rhys] a nuisance" (33). "She drifted away from me and when I tried to interest her, she was indifferent" (34). Rhys fantasizes about a time of intimacy—"there must have been an interval before she seemed to find me a nuisance and I grew to dread her" (33)—but it is difficult for her to seize more than a fleeting image in which her mother comforts her. "Gradually I came to wonder about my mother less and less," she says, "until at last she was almost a stranger and I stopped imagining what she felt or what she thought" (36).[6]

Although Rhys insists that she thinks about her mother less and less, she encodes her more and more into her texts as death and absence. Critics, for the most part, have noted the mother-daughter relationship, the *loss* of this relationship, only elliptically, largely ignoring the primacy of the preoedipal bond in Rhys's work, her "yearning for her mother, her desire for this present-absent figure," the damage caused by the "distant, inaccessible, depressed, rejecting mother," and the daughter's "deeper, regressive need for the all-encompassing maternal bond which she did not know" (Scharfman, 100, 102).[7] Despite Rhys's own denials, there is indeed in her work a

[5]Teresa O'Connor, in *Jean Rhys: The West Indian Novels*, is the first critic to use an important Rhys resource, the so-called Black Exercise Book, which Rhys sold to the University of Tulsa along with other manuscripts and papers in 1976. This book is a rich source of details of Rhys's early life and family relationships; as O'Connor describes it, however, it "is most difficult to follow. For the most part Rhys kept the journal in pencil and apparently often wrote in it while she was drunk. Most of the inclusions are fragmentary, almost incoherent and with virtually no punctuation; it is not quite clear at times whether certain inclusions are notes for fiction or whether Rhys was writing about fact—in some cases probably a combination of the two" (4).

[6]Passages O'Connor quotes from the Black Exercise Book reveal a much more severe indictment of the mother than the portrait of the distracted, negligent woman in *Smile Please*: "My mother who beat me ['whipped me severely' is inserted above the line] I was fond of but somewhere in my heart I despised her. (fol. 12)" (22).

[7]Besides Scharfman, in her important article "Mirroring and Mothering in Simone

hearkening for the mother's voice, a search for the mother's body, and an attempt to locate that "interval," the space of women's language, before it is filled with dread.

Rhys, like H.D., had available to her from earliest origins a maternally connoted sphere that eventually turned out, as we shall see, to validate to some degree her attempts to rewrite the oedipal myth. As a third-generation Dominican Creole, Minna Williams developed within a network of mystical religious cults—voodoo, obeah, chants, curses, zombies, and incantations. This maternal heritage, to which Rhys was highly attuned, despite her Welsh father and her immersion in Catholicism in the convent school, was a major influence throughout her work, serving for her a function similar to that of Moravian mysticism for the child H.D.[8]

Schwarz-Bart's *Pluie et vent sur Telumée Miracle* and Jean Rhys' *Wide Sargasso Sea*," O'Connor is the only critic I am aware of to emphasize Rhys's "early incorporation of her mother's rejecting voice, a voice that haunts all of Rhys's fiction" (31) and to stress "the 'negative motherliness' Rhys attaches to the island: the unsatisfying mothering she received as a child and her own identification, often unconscious, of the island and her mother" (10). Thomas Staley, for example, reads *Voyage in the Dark* as "the story of exile" (66) and believes it is focused on the split between the West Indies and England, but although he senses that the islands are associated with "vital qualities of life" and "one's natural impulses" (61), he does not make the connection between the geographical locus and the mother. Elgin W. Mellown mentions an "adjunct theme" having to do with "woman as creator." "These tortured women," he writes, "cannot reach maturity by giving birth to a child which, depending on them, will force them into adulthood" ("Characters and Themes in the Novels of Jean Rhys," 464), a Freudian echo of a woman's "normal" turning toward the father, who will fill her "lack" by giving her a child. No one has asked what this refusal of maternity in Rhys might suggest; maternity is simply considered something "tortured" women "cannot" achieve. Helen Nebeker does sense the importance of the mother, also reading through *Voyage in the Dark*, but she writes with a distracting Jungian myopia that insistently and arbitrarily "decodes" symbols and dreams in a quest to uncover the "truth" of Anna Morgan's psychosexual development and movement toward the discovery of her "SELF" (*Jean Rhys: Woman in Passage*). Although Nebeker suggests an underlying matrilinear impulse in Rhys, she argues onomastically rather than textually.

[8]Teresa O'Connor frames her text with Rhys's own framing texts, *Voyage in the Dark* and *Wide Sargasso Sea*, reading them closely and within the cultural and historical context out of which these West Indian novels emerge. Embracing so wide a scope is both a strength and, inasmuch as the reader is subject to recurring shifts in strategy, a weakness. O'Connor, for example, clearly finds the figure of the indifferent mother significant, but she views the "flawed relationships between parent and child" alternately as psychological constructs and as "microcosmic mirrors of the failure of culture and history" (197). Although sexuality and gender conflicts are also at issue, O'Con-

The interest and significance of H.D. and Rhys for feminist critics is that although it takes both women a lifetime to approach some way of discovering and then inscribing the *chora*, reconciling thereby the debilitating and sometimes maddening desire for and rejection of the mother, very early they instinctively insist on subverting the premise of language—that to write means to relinquish the mother. Two key scenes, one from *HERmione* and the other from *Good Morning, Midnight*, illustrate the conditions out of which H.D. and Rhys write. In the first, encompassing the events and entanglements following her failed semester at Bryn Mawr in 1906, H.D. writes a rather remarkable scene, which encapsulates the relationship among men, women, and language as reflected in her texts. Eugenia and Hermione, mother and daughter, allied rather uncomfortably with the sister/daughter-in-law, Minnie, sit facing Carl and Bertrand Gart, father and son, across the dinner table:

> Bertrand Gart picked up the salt cellar, was making a pattern with it and the pepper pot and his little pearl-handled fruitknife. He dropped the . . . knife, picked it up again and ran it along the edge of the damask wall-of-Troy pattern on the table-cloth. Hermione watched him, watched Eugenia, slid covert glances at Minnie. Minnie would be too immersed in soup to notice. "I'm sorry mother but you know I can't eat thick soup." Minnie would or would not say that, the soup wasn't so very thick. Celery was the salty thing that flavoured it. . . . Eugenia didn't like it. Eugenia hadn't noticed it. . . . Minnie was saying "It wasn't Jock's fault. It was Mandy's."
>
> Mandy was coming back. Don't, don't let Mandy hear you. . . . there was always that moment of waiting . . . Mandy hadn't heard her. "Cop-

nor situates childhood in "a time that predates sexual consciousness" (104). Whereas most of the "gaps" in O'Connor's fine work are simply reflections of the reasonable and necessary limits she has placed on her project, the major weakness of the book is her suggestion that "Rhys's ideal mother—the nuns and the black obeah women—are never attached to a man; they are outside sexuality and outside the continual triangles that occur and reoccur in Rhys's works. . . . [T]he nurture that all of her heroines seek . . . cannot occur in a world in which sexuality also exists" (178). The implications here are that being without a man implies being "outside" sexuality and that sexuality, for women, is necessarily heterosexual. Clearly, this formulation is the antithesis of what I am suggesting in *The Unspeakable Mother*: that longing in Rhys does occur outside of triangles and within dyads, specifically in the mother-daughter dyad. Although O'Connor's work and mine part ways over the issue of preoedipal sexuality, I consider her work enormously important, the first book-length "scholarship" on Rhys.

pard tells me the Copenhagen volume hasn't any more than the last series of Minnenberg's." "Minnenberg found his line *after* the younger Coppard." "Coppard had the elements but Minnenberg made the final constation." "Minnenberg simply picked up the thread where Coppard dropped it. He went on and on with the same pattern." . . . ". . . his thought applied on the plane of minus-plus. . . ." "Newton made gravitation accessible to the mob mind with his ripe apple. . . ."

"Mother, I said it wasn't Jock, but Mandy." "Shh-shh, don't let Mandy hear you." "If you would keep the salt in the oven, it wouldn't get so grey. . . ." "The usual demonstration wouldn't be applicable . . ." "I know it's Coppard's doing . . ."

. . . Hermione gave up following. It always ended in "after all" waving like a banner in the torn air. The air was torn, frayed by the sharp electric thought-waves of Gart and Gart facing each other across a narrow strip of damask. They hurl things at one another . . . like two arctic explorers who have both discovered the north pole, each proving to the other, across chasms of frozen silence, that his is the original discovery . . . There was no use trying to follow Gart and Gart into the frozen silence . . . "Mother you might make her." "I can't insist. . . ." "It's so odd your idea of servants. She ought to wear a white cap. . . ."

How long would mama stand it? Eugenia, Hermione knew, would go on, go on, go on keeping up a secondary line of dialogue with Minnie, for the moment Minnie was left to her own devices Hermione knew, Eugenia knew, Minnie would nag at Bertrand. [*HER*, 35–37]

This passage is incredibly rich in its replication of the very site of language. The women in this scene are "covert," "immersed"; they whisper and are suspended in "that moment of waiting," a "before" clearly juxtaposed to the male "after"—"after Coppard," "after all." In a space traditionally assigned to woman—the table, the serving of food, domestic details—woman, has been expelled. The damask has become a wall of Troy, a "chasm of frozen silence" over which the men leap, claiming authority, mastery through their words. They disparage the "ripe apple" (Eve's access to knowledge) as what has undermined the "plus-minus" system, the system of presence and absence in which what is absent is, as this scene enacts, the female body and voice. The women do have a "secondary line of dialogue," but it is still far from the semiotic register suggested by Kristeva, for it constitutes itself at its own repression. Unlike the semiotic, described as "a dissonance within the thetic, paternal function of language" (*DL*, 139), it is designed *not* to rupture; the mother tolerates the inane, exasperated exchange of her daughter-in-law, picking about the grayness of the salt and the maid's incompetence, in order to protect and maintain male discourse, the "dangerous *after* (logical, naming, castrating)" (*DL*, 189). At any expense, including her own annihilation, she must promote it without participating in it, must keep Bertrand from being interrupted and nagged, instead of rupturing through the fabric of meaning. To Hermione, this female mode offers nothing, worse than nothing, for it appears not as the *jouissance* of maternal access, not even as a rather limited "woman vibration" but as a prostituted corollary of the male system. The women who surround Hermione (and who surrounded H.D. at this point in her life)[9] use language to facilitate men's expression rather than to express or inscribe themselves.

Decades later, as I explore in Chapter 9, H.D. returns to the "wall-of-Troy pattern" in *Helen in Egypt*, where she revises the story of Helen, associated always with the mother; "I tell and re-tell the story / to find the answer" (*HE*, 84), the answer perhaps to the question "was Troy lost for a subtle chord, / a rhythm as yet un-heard, . . . a rhythm as yet unheard, / to challenge the trumpet-note?" (*HE*, 229). It is this rhythm that is missing from the dinner table conversation; it is this rhythm that will ultimately create Helen's palinode and retrieve the mother.

Jean Rhys produces an ancillary scene in *Good Morning, Midnight* involving Sasha Jansen, an almost middle-aged woman who wanders through Paris, in and out of liaisons with unknown men. The severance and emptiness of her life are reflected in her relationship to language, particularly to male language. In a strange, surreal scene early in the novel, Sasha thinks back on one of the first jobs she had in Paris. Mr. Blank, the boss of the London branch of the dress shop where she works, comes to inspect the French operation. He is suspicious of her from the beginning, not because she is incompetent, unstable, or apt to drink too much but because she cannot speak

[9]The scene recalls the Doolittle dinner table described by William Carlos Williams in a letter to Norman Holmes Pearson: "At a meal, usually supper, with every place at the table taken by children and others, if the alert Mrs. Doolittle detected in the general din that the doctor wanted to say something, she would quickly announce: Your father is about to speak! —Silence immediately ensued. Then in a slow and deep voice, and with his eyes fixed on nothing, as Ezra Pound said, just above, nothing nearer than the moon, he said what he had to say. It was a disheartening process." "A Letter from William Carlos Williams to Norman Holmes Pearson."

enough languages. Late in the afternoon he calls Sasha into the office and asks her to take a letter to the "kise." Without questioning him, she starts along the passage, working herself into a state of panic, disorientation, a "nightmare": "Kise—kise . . . It doesn't mean a thing to me. He's got me into such a state that I can't imagine what it can mean" (25). Margaret Homans discusses a theme in nineteenth-century women's fiction of "women characters who . . . carry messages or letters for other people, . . . usually men. . . . Like the mother of the Word, the woman who carries language from one place or state of being to another does not herself originate or even touch it and she gets nothing for her labor" (*BW*, 31). The women Homans describes, however—and this is perhaps a major difference between nineteenth-century and modernist fiction—though they may not understand the words they transcribe or deliver, respond to their exclusion less violently. Sasha, unlike George Eliot's women or Mrs. Gaskell's, becomes almost hysterical until she returns to find out Mr. Blank has meant *caisse*, the cashier, but has mispronounced it. Rather than demand an explanation, rather than name the word "nonsense," as the men do not hesitate to label her speech, she blindly participates in the ritual, and it never occurs to her to question the significance of the male word (Word). She is at this moment—as in so many other moments of the novel—both denied entry into the symbolic and trapped within it, rushing up and down steps, lost in the dress house, down passages "that don't lead anywhere," looking for a door with a mispronounced name.

Much of the language in women's mouths in these texts feels mispronounced as they try to deal with the "ungainly garments" of speech, the commonplaces, the "counters" of language. Hermione is maddened by "words said over and over, over and over. They were a stock company playing a road show, words over and over. . . . I'll never get out of this show" (40). In Rhys, many of the characters actually *are* show girls, as Rhys herself was; the many men they encounter "perfectly [represent] organized society" (*ALMM*, 22), in which Rhys's marginal women have no place. The women see the men as having a "mania for classification" (*Q*, 118), as participating in a patriarchal, bourgeois economic—and linguistic—code from which they do not deviate. Sasha Jansen calls her whole life a "cliché," significantly perceiving it not as, say, a prison or a swamp but in terms of language, as if what traps her is not society or nature but the Word. "Is it a ritual?" she asks as a man on the street approaches her with the same line other men have used before, the same line they use on women throughout Rhys's novels. "Am I bound to answer the same question in the same words?" (45–46). The ritual of going home with a stranger is not what provokes her despair at this point; rather, it is the triteness, literally, of the verbal exchange. Much like the mother of George Lowndes (the Pound figure) in *HERmione*, she feels she must speak "as if she had read it; little distinguished waxwork making a little speech, a little speech made up for it by someone else" (105).

A common denominator in these passages is that all this speech is from elsewhere, a catechism, "utterance[s] put into [their] head[s] from outside" (H.D., *BML*, 101). "George Lowndes is teaching you, actually *teaching* you words," says Eugenia Gart to her daughter, "telling you what to say" (*HER*, 95). The source of all this talking, however, is greater than just George Lowndes; it is the entire patriarchal, symbolic economy "outside" of female experience and design and far distant from the voice and rhythms of the maternal body.

What women in these texts seek is an "inside," a semiotic locus or *chora* or "woman's space." Margaret Homans observes about nineteenth-century women writers that "at the level of language their disconcertion of the categories of literal and figurative remains relatively limited when viewed from the perspective of the kinds of experimentation with language that . . . more recent writers have practiced" (*BW*, 16). Clearly, women like Dorothy Wordsworth and George Eliot and the Brontës are concerned with the figure of a "vulnerable or vanished mother" (16), but they tend to "thematize the position of women's language in a culture that does not admit it" (20) and, therefore, have no textual means available to inscribe "the pleasure in a nonsymbolic language" (20), even though "at the same time, their texts' literalizations of figures, in which the literal is sometimes preferred, constitutes a linguistic trace of a mother-daughter bond" (16).

Rhys and H.D. and many other neglected modernist writers move into language in new ways, "overwhelmed," like their earlier writing sisters/ mothers, "with a desire to know, but a desire to know more and differently than what is encoded—spoken—written," writes Kristeva. "If a solution exists to what we call today the feminine problematic, . . . it . . . passes over this ground" (*DL*, 164–65). As Claudine Hermann understands it in her essay "Women in Space and Time," "In order to avoid total annihilation, to escape man's habitual urge to colonize, [woman] must conserve some space for herself, a sort of *no man's land*, which constitutes precisely what men fail to understand of her . . . because she cannot express its substances in her inevitably alienated language" (169).

The result of the censorship and ridicule women are made to feel when they attempt to participate in the discourse of the males is the inability to retain a sense of this space, a space of the "inexpressible," which H.D. compares in *HERmione* to mercury rising in a thermometer: "What does it feel like when it can't rise any higher and is there, pulsing, beating to express degrees beyond the degrees marked carefully . . . on the glass tube? Mercury that felt expression . . . beating, pulsing; I am feeling degrees of things for which there is no measure" (59). Trapped within the careful markings of signification, women are "closed in," "suffocated," "smudged out," "beaten down," and "crushed," to use just a few of the expressions that appear throughout Rhys's and H.D.'s work to describe women's, particularly the mother's, place within the symbolic. The "space" they have lost is not a geographical locus but a space in language, an "in-between," where the semiotic register pulses beneath the "tin pan noises" (*HER*, 42) of male discourse.

2

Gazing for His Behalf

I shall break the trajectory of this study of how relationship with the M/mother influences a woman's relationship to discourse by a detour through *Jane Eyre*, a compelling text that repeatedly resists articulation. In a sense, *Jane Eyre* operates as a primal scene that critics circle round and round, both insisting on and retreating from its power, mining it for its defiance and its disturbing capitulation, its split of the female self into the Bildungsroman heroine and the enraged and repressed madwoman. It is almost irresistible in its mythic and archetypal resonance. It provides as well an incredible terrain of motherlessness and the search for surrogates, imitating in this sense the very basis of representation itself—loss of the referent and the attempt to replace it. It also offers a kind of framing device for *The Unspeakable Mother* because Jean Rhys returns to it in *Wide Sargasso Sea*, attempting not only to retell the story of the lost mother through a mother text but to reinvent the language available to do so.

However one comes at Brontë's novel, there is the unsettling sense of something working beneath the surface, some energy related to Jane's journey and to her story. Some of the most interesting critical work describes the movement of *Jane Eyre* as a movement into language, a novel in which a woman comes to find a place within discourse, a space in which she can finally tell her tale. In one sense this is an advantage, an acquisition of power denied her, the ability finally to articulate her life. But in another sense, even though thirty-year-old Jane Rochester is a self-conscious first person, well aware of her ability to monitor and manipulate narrative, her journey into language also traces a journey of loss, for Jane "trades" away other powers she does not have in language. At the heart of current feminist debate over the position of woman vis-à-vis discourse is this question of whether it is somehow a repressive and exclusive male structure to which she must capitulate or find alternatives or whether (these are not mutually exclusive) it is (also) a powerful system she must appropriate and turn to her own advantage.

From the first page of the novel, Jane's relationship to language is complicated and strained; Rosemarie Bodenheimer notes that almost all of her early attempts to express herself are thwarted.[1] When Jane asks what she has done to incur her aunt's anger, for example, Mrs. Reed answers, "Jane, I don't like cavillers or questioners. . . . Be seated somewhere; and until you can speak pleasantly, remain silent" (5). This is the cultural prescription for women. Like children, they must not complain or inquire, and if they cannot remain silent, they must speak "pleasantly"—that is, in ways that do not rupture or disturb social or sexual conventions. Thus, when Mrs. Reed "dares" Jane to "utter one syllable" (23), we find ourselves in a space traditionally occupied by women.

The question here relates to advantage as well as gender (although the two are clearly linked in the novel and in the world) in the sense that much of Jane's repression results not from her being female but from her marginality as an orphan in a patriarchal economy. Significantly, this position has an impact on her access to written text as well as on her ability to express herself verbally. In the earliest scene of the novel, for example, the child Jane slips into the breakfast room containing a bookcase, "possesses" herself of a volume, and hides in the window seat to read. Shortly thereafter, her abusive cousin John ferrets her out, issuing a culturally familiar mandate: "You have no business to take our books; you are a dependent. . . . you have no

---

[1]In "Jane Eyre in Search of Her Story," Rosemarie Bodenheimer takes up quite effectively the issue of "how Jane acquires and uses the power of speech and with whom" (387). Bodenheimer reads the novel as "a world full of fictions" in which Jane's history becomes "the story of an empowered narrator" (388) searching for a "fit audience" (389). Bodenheimer traces the "socialization" of Jane's narrative, her growing awareness of "the power of conscious control over sequence, diction, and tone," (391) and the tension between Jane's " 'internal' progress as narrator and the 'external' narrative" (392), which Bodenheimer reads in juxtaposition to a series of literary models offered in the secondary narratives of the text.

money; your father left you none. . . . Now, I'll teach you to rummage my book-shelves: for they *are* mine" (8). Adding injury to insult, he flings a book at her head, knocking her down; the entire household runs at the bleeding child, outraged by her "fury" and "passion," and carries her off to imprison her in the red room, where she falls unconscious.

In her position at Gateshead, as fatherless female child, Jane does not have the "right" to speak. At Thornfield, however, she is offered this "right," encouraged, indeed, by her new master, Rochester, who is initially less repressive of Jane's attempts to posit herself as a speaking subject than are the figures of her early life. One of his first impressions of her is formed by her spontaneous response to his question as to whether she thinks him handsome. "No, sir," she replies, impressing him with her ability to "rap out a round rejoinder" (115). Jane reports that he bids her talk to him: " 'Speak,' he urged. 'What about, sir?' 'Whatever you like. I leave both the choice of subject and the manner of treating it entirely to yourself' " (117). This exchange is followed immediately by a strange line: "Accordingly I sat and said nothing." It is the initial adverb that jolts; apparently she interprets his invitation as demanding refusal. In other words, the "subject" Jane seems to "choose" is women's silence, and her manner of treating it, similarly, is unspoken. This is not to say, however, that she refuses Rochester's challenge. Indeed, the entire novel might be read as her response to his invitation, but it is a response that circumvents "saying" and resorts to another kind of expression, retrieved, as we shall see, through the figure of the missing or displaced mother, a kind of expression that exerts more power, finally, than the language which initially seems to be the controlling system of the text.

Her early hesitation to parry with Rochester on the verbal turf he offers appears to derive at least partially from her sense that he operates in his most primitive and powerful moments within a strange and particular sphere of articulation from which she is excluded. When she approaches him outside at their first meeting, she observes that "he was pronouncing some formula which prevented him from replying to me directly" (99). After one of their long, early talks she says, "To speak the truth, sir, I don't understand you at all: I cannot keep up the conversation, because it has got out of my depth"

(120–21). Increasingly lost in Rochester's words and finding it "useless to continue a discourse which was all darkness to me," Jane prepares to leave the room, precipitating the following exchange: " 'You are afraid of me, because I talk like a Sphinx.' 'Your language is enigmatical, sir: but though I am bewildered, I am certainly not afraid' " (122).

Jane's bewilderment begins to give way to a kind of initiation in which she searches for some inkling of how Rochester—the Sphinx, the impersonator, the keeper of Thornfield's secret—both serves and severs language. "If he expects me to talk for the mere sake of talking and showing off," she thinks, "he will find he has addressed himself to the wrong person" (117).

In a sense, Jane is the "wrong person" because she has learned early on not to rely on language,[2] at least not the androcentric language of John Reed. Even when Jane usurps her cousin's book and hides to read it in the first scene of the novel, there is something else going on besides Jane's appropriation of text. She takes care to choose a volume "stored with pictures" (5), Bewick's History of British Birds, and she cares little for the letterpress (6); what compel her are the mysterious, shadowy images, "like all the half-comprehended notions that float dim through children's brains, but strangely impressive" (6).

This early intuition of the "spell" of the image is sustained as Jane begins to make her way in the world. At the oppressive Lowood School, though she is undernourished and deprived both physically and emotionally, Jane begins to gain some sense of her attraction to images and of the nature of her own gifts. In drawing class she discovers to her amazement a way to transfigure her world without passing it through the mediation of text: "That night, on going to bed, I forgot to prepare in imagination the Barmecide supper of hot

[2]Hermione Lee is one of the few critics who discusses Jane's art *in relation* to her language; see "Emblems and Enigmas in *Jane Eyre*." Lee notes the tensions of "a language which is always attempting to formalize and discipline strange, violent, and intense materials" (233), revealed to Jane and the reader in "signs" and "enigmas." Lee spends considerable time on Jane's "pictorial imagination" and on the "emblematic" nature of her portraits and imaginary scenes. She stresses the clumsiness of critical attempts to decode the three watercolors in Jane's portfolio, suggesting instead that they be read as "enigmatic emblems" of the tension in the novel between "formal, distinct procedures and inchoate, ambiguous materials" (242).

roast potatoes, or white bread and new milk, with which I was wont to amuse my inward cravings: I feasted instead on the spectacle of ideal drawings, which I saw in the dark; all the work of my own hands" (65). Jane's earlier proclivity for art begins to be transformed into a nourishing and liberating activity of her own. When the old housekeeper, Bessie, comes to say good-bye to Jane before she leaves Lowood, Jane ushers her into the teachers' parlor where one of Jane's landscapes hangs over the chimneypiece. Bessie is astonished by Jane's newfound ability, the talent that suddenly reverses Jane's inferior position in the family, freeing her to a certain extent from the perimeters of her past. "You will get on," says Bessie, "whether your relations notice you or not" (80). Whereas Jane fears early in the novel that she will "never get away from Gateshead till I am a woman" (20), she now discovers that she can "draw" herself out of her past in quite a literal sense. Instead of escaping into pictures, she begins to escape through them; the canvas becomes a passage through which she falls, like Alice, into her life.

As Jane begins to show her work to others, she discovers that her images are a source not only of her own pleasure but of power. There are two key scenes in the novel in which she reveals her drawings, significantly, to each of the men who threaten to absorb her—Rochester and St. John Rivers, the icy missionary, who informs her, "Your words are such as ought not to be used: violent, unfeminine, and untrue" (363).

St. John first discovers Jane's "true" powers when he sees a portrait she has drawn of Rosamond Oliver, the woman with whom he is secretly and torturously in love. "His tall figure sprang erect with a start," Jane reports; "he said nothing. I looked at him: he shunned my eye" (326). He pretends to have taken no particular notice of it, but Jane pushes him until he pronounces it "a well-executed picture . . . very graceful and correct drawing" (327). Janes sees instantly that the effect on him is more than he will allow, and she continues to bait him, promising to paint him a duplicate if he will admit the gift would be acceptable. In response, "He continued to gaze at the picture: the longer he looked, the firmer he held it, the more he seemed to covet it" (327). This is the one place where St. John wavers in his determination to become a missionary. "Now I see myself stretched on an ottoman in the drawing-room at Vale

Hall," he says, "at my bride Rosamond Oliver's feet: she is talking to me with her sweet voice—gazing down on me with those eyes your skilful hand copied so well. . . . She is mine—I am hers—this present life and passing world suffice to me" (328). This moment is a startling contrast to St. John's otherwise arrogant, dogmatic, and obsessive commitment to his religious calling. Even more compelling, however, is the connection between this scene and Jane as artist, for it is her drawing, more than the flesh-and-blood woman, which has tempted and seduced St. John and rendered him speechless, put him, momentarily, outside the fanatical discourse that structures his life. When he finally regains himself, reaffirming that his vocation is "dearer than the blood in my veins" (329), he has to cover the picture with a sheet of paper (331) to break the spell and extricate himself from its power.

It is clear that St. John is riveted by the image Jane presents to him; he quickly attempts to regain his composure by enclosing her work in a discourse which absolutely belies and negates its power: he tries to render it "well-executed" and "correct," words that speak to the surface, the elements of composition and technique, to control. St. John, however, finds it impossible to maintain this fiction; the vocabulary changes remarkably: he begins to "covet" it; he stretches into a space of sweetness, voice, gaze reduced finally to only a dyad which suffices. What has happened, I suggest, is that the image has drawn him back into a preoedipal moment in which not only "she is mine/I am hers" but "she is me/I am her." St. John's response reflects the incredible conflict of that space—at least the conflict that arises once it has been split—the concurrent terror and seduction, the need to deny it and the desire to enter it.

When Rochester first encounters Jane's work shortly after her arrival at Thornfield, he finds her sketches and drawings "peculiar" and disturbing and is at first reluctant to believe that Jane executed them without the aid of a master. When she presents him with her portfolio, he examines the contents and then removes three paintings for closer scrutiny.

These pictures were in water-colours. The first represented clouds low and livid, rolling over a swollen sea: all the distance was in eclipse; so, too, was the foreground; or, rather, the nearest billows, for there was no land. One gleam of light lifted into relief a half-submerged mast, on which sat a cormorant, dark and large, with wings flecked with foam: its beak held a gold bracelet, set with gems, that I had touched with as brilliant tints as my palette could yield, and as glittering distinctness as my pencil could impart. Sinking below the bird and mast, a drowned corpse glanced through the green water; a fair arm was the only limb clearly visible, whence the bracelet had been washed or torn.

The second picture contained for foreground only the dim peak of a hill, with grass and some leaves slanting as if by a breeze. Beyond and above spread an expanse of sky, dark blue as at twilight: rising into the sky was a woman's shape to the bust, portrayed in tints as dusk and soft as I could combine. The dim forehead was crowned with a star; the lineaments below were seen as through the suffusion of vapour; the eyes shone dark and wild; the hair streamed shadowy, like a beamless cloud torn by storm or by electric travail. On the neck lay a pale reflection like moonlight; the same faint lustre touched the train of thin clouds from which rose and bowed this vision of the Evening Star.

The third showed the pinnacle of an iceberg piercing a polar winter sky: a muster of northern lights reared their dim lances, close serried, along the horizon. Throwing these into distance, rose, in the foreground, a head,—a colossal head, inclined towards the iceberg, and resting against it. Two thin hands, joined under the forehead, and supporting it, drew up before the lower features a sable veil; a brow quite bloodless, white as bone, and an eye hollow and fixed, blank of meaning but for the glassiness of despair, alone were visible. Above the temples, amidst wreathed turban folds of black drapery, vague in its character and consistency as cloud, gleamed a ring of white flame, gemmed with sparkles of a more lurid tinge. This pale crescent was "The likeness of a Kingly Crown"; what it diademed was "the shape which shape had none." [110–11]

These are provocatively elemental pictures, full of water, earth, air, sky, and ice. (They are also temptingly full of analogues to people in Jane's life, and various critics have been unable to resist correlating and decoding the cormorant, the corpse, the colossal head, the Evening Star.)[3] The fascination of these pictures is twofold: first, they

[3]Most critics who have read through these paintings have been severely limited by the attempt to "decode" the pictures through analogues in either Jane's or Brontë's life. In "From Portrait to Person: A Note on the Surrealistic in *Jane Eyre*," Lawrence E. Moser, S.J., reads through what he calls the surrealistic aspect of the paintings, starting with the premise that "art of necessity mirrors the artist's personality . . . and tends violently towards a complete revelation of the self" (279). Reading for "internal," "external," and "actual," "meanings," he interprets the cormorant as Jane, the corpse as Helen Burns, the Evening Star as Jane, and the third painting as an allusion to Miss Temple's departure from Lowood. This essay, which maintains that "only by

are, as Rochester notices immediately, surreal and otherworldly, compelling in their premonitory strangeness; second, aside from their content, their position in the text suggests a certain significance, both in their careful selection for observation and in the interval in the discourse which they offer, a kind of gap or split, to which I shall return.

I would like to focus on the second picture, the ambiguous central figure, not so much in terms of whom or what she might "represent" but because she is the only one whose eyes compel us. The corpse offers only an averted glance. The Arctic head shows us "an eye hollow and fixed, blank of meaning but for the glassiness of despair." The gaze of the Evening Star, however, is the only detail of all the paintings on which Rochester focuses his attention, drawn into the encounter against his will: "These eyes in the Evening Star you must have seen in a dream. How could you make them look so clear, and yet not at all brilliant? for the planet above quells their rays. And what meaning is that in their solemn depth? . . . There,—put the drawings away!" (111). Like St. John, Rochester is captivated by the eyes; like St. John, he must literally, physically, extricate himself from the encounter, break, as it were, the gaze.

---

cleaving to [Rochester] can [Jane] in any true and meaningful sense rediscover herself" (281) is not particularly useful in a feminist context. M. B. McLaughlin, in "Past or Future Mindscapes: Pictures in *Jane Eyre*," considers Jane's work "the rather bad paintings that one might expect of a sixteen- and seventeen-year-old school girl who has undergone several periods of traumatic loss" (24), disputing the claim of Thomas Langford, that the paintings are "prophetic." Although he quite rightly suggests the strain of attempting "specificity in interpreting the pictures" through arbitrary symbols, McLaughlin nonetheless falls into the same trap: the first picture represents the death of Mr. Reed, the second is an "idealized portrait" of Miss Temple, and the third somehow blends Brocklehurst and Helen Burns. Thomas Langford has addressed the issue of the paintings twice. In "The Three Pictures in *Jane Eyre*," he offers the thesis that the paintings are indeed prophetic visions corresponding to the major sections of Jane's life and of the novel. He associates the first painting with Helen Burns, the second with Thornfield and Jane's own awakening "womanly instincts," and the third with St. John Rivers. In "Prophetic Imagination and the Unity of *Jane Eyre*," he elaborates on his earlier thesis, interpreting the pictures as "symbolic summary of the narrative, including both past and future events" (229). Gilbert and Gubar, who touch on many aspects of the novel, explore the paintings briefly as predictive of strains in Jane's and Rochester's relationship (*The Madwoman in the Attic*, 357). In *Charlotte Brontë's World of Death*, Robert Keefe offers yet another interpretation of the paintings, focusing on their connection with death, guilt, and punishment and on a "potentially hostile female presence" (101).

The "gaze" is central to understanding what is going on in this text; Brontë returns to this word at significant points in the narrative. St. John "gazes" at the portrait of Rosamond Oliver, and the portrait "gazes down" on him. The gypsy gazes, the madwoman gazes wildly, the apparition of the Moon Mother, Jane reports, "gazed and gazed and gazed on me" (281). These moments are in contrast to others in the novel when intense looks are reported but not in terms of a gaze; Mrs. Reed, for example, does not gaze but "surveys" Jane with a "severe eye" (22).

The gaze, then, *le regard*, is a particular kind of looking, both alienating and embracing.[4] In Lacan's theory it is related to lack, a primal separation that the subject must accept or solicit in order to constitute itself. D. W. Winnicott, on the other hand, using Lacan's "Le Stade du miroir" as a point of departure, discusses the mother's face as a "precursor of the mirror," the gaze as the space in which the infant both sees and is seen not as the division of self but as a kind of giving back of the self in what promises to be "a significant exchange with the world, a two-way process in which self-enrichment alternates with the discovery of meaning in the world of seen things" (113). The usefulness of the regard emerges in its ambiguity, in its reflection of the primal tension between split and merger and, I would add, between symbolic and semiotic. As Maurice Blanchot allows in *The Gaze of Orpheus*, "Seeing implies distance, the decision that causes separation, the power not to be in contact and to avoid the confusion of contact" (75). The initial seeing "nevertheless becomes an encounter" (75), an encounter with "the split, which had been the possibility of seeing" and which "solidifies, right inside the gaze, into impossibility" (75).

It is in this space of impossible encounter that the gaze offers a primary lesson of both relation and perception. In *Jane Eyre* it operates on two levels, first in terms of relationship with the mother and then in terms of how Jane translates the mother's lessons into her art. The "spell" of Jane's pictures issues from this maternal connection; the mother, missing in the text, shows up in the gaps, the splits, the

[4]Ronnie Scharfman also discusses the mirroring relationship, particularly through Sartre and Lacan, as an alienating replication of the divided or illusory nature of the self (90).

places where the discourse is interrupted by the gaze.[5] The gaze, in its tension between possession and severance, between merger and distance, replicates the always conflicted preoedipal "moment," the intersection where the mother is both self and other, the simultaneous seduction and terror of losing oneself in her.

This play between the two impulses in *Jane Eyre* is enacted in several key scenes. The first, in the red room, is precipitated, we should recall, by Jane's being stripped of her book—taken out of the patriarchal discourse. She finds herself suffocating in deep red damask, confined in a space, significantly, of "broken reflections" (11) where she is unable to recognize herself in the mirror. Even though many critics, and Jane herself, attribute the spell of the room to its having been her uncle's death chamber, *the text* says something different. The room is clearly associated with the first manifestation of the mother. The terrifying and hallucinatory light that appears to Jane during her confinement is not the ghost of her Uncle Reed but a sense of the mother, as Brontë confirms during the Moon Mother scene at Thornfield, which she situates within a "trance-like dream" that transports Jane back to the red room: "The light that long ago had struck me into syncope, recalled in this vision, seemed glidingly to mount the wall, and tremblingly to pause in the centre of the obscured ceiling" (281). The prenatal connotation of the red room is suggested in the "epilogue" to Jane's fit.[6] When she emerges from unconsciousness, Jane reports, "I heard voices . . . speaking with a hollow sound, as if muffled by a rush of wind or water: agitation, uncertainty and an all-predominating sense of terror confused my faculties. Ere long I became aware that some one was handling me; lifting me up and supporting me" (15). This scene reads like a birth-

[5]Herman Rapaport takes up the issue of the "encrypted mother" in "*Jane Eyre* and the *Mot Tabou*," where he explores the disembodied voices in the novel and, working through Lacan and Nicolas Abraham and Maria Torok, suggests that there is a kind of concealed script, or *mot tabou*, a chiming "sound-shape" that echoes in the text, which he works from Eyre into "mère." From here he makes quite a leap, suggesting that "who speaks" in the novel is "the collective mother" whose "lack" opens the "hole in the real," preparing the way of "those psychotic voices" (1102–3).

[6]Robert Keefe is one of the few to suggest a connection between the light in the red room and the mother. Helene Moglen also alludes to the red room as "a terrifying womb-world from which [Jane] is born." "*Jane Eyre*: The Creation of a Feminist Myth," in *Charlotte Brontë: The Self Conceived*, 111.

ing—a rush of water, agitation, terror—the child pulled upward. When Bessie reports to the apothecary who comes to check on Jane that "she had a fall" (19), he responds, "Fall! why that is like a baby again" (19). Indeed, it is profoundly like a baby, for when Jane is "borne" upstairs, she is thrust back into a preoedipal and preverbal state.

This "first" mother, however, fails; like Jane's "real" mother, she disappears too suddenly, without any transition or warning, leaving the daughter both engulfed and abandoned. The red room does prepare the way for the reappearance of the mother in another version, when the gleam is not bewildering but "such as the moon imparts to vapours she is about to sever" (281). "Immeasurably distant" and "yet so near," this figure who gazes and gazes at Jane reproduces the narrative and psychological tension between merger and severance. Her words, however, the very fact that there are words, extricate Jane from her regard: "My daughter, flee temptation!" she encourages; to which Jane answers, "Mother, I will" (281).

The mother offers her the freedom to flee, to separate both from Rochester and herself. But almost more important than the flight is the object to be fled, temptation. If we think of temptation as the loss of boundaries, the state in which obstacles, barriers, borders cease to exist, to be perceived or obeyed, then what the mother offers her is the chance to acquire boundaries.[7] This is not, contrary to many readings, a moral injunction to leave the bigamous Rochester. It is both an admonition and permission for Jane to seize her "whole life." To understand what the mother "means," however, Jane has to

[7]For an intermittent discussion of Jane's struggle with ego boundaries, see Helene Moglen, who remarks on Jane's self-abandonment in the red room and in her relationships with St. John and Rochester. She also alludes to but does not fully develop the series of Jane's "symbolic 'separations'" (140), starting with Bessie and ending with St. John Rivers. Moglen is not basically concerned with Jane's relationship to either narrative or art but rather with her insight into unresolved "psychosexual relationships" within a patriarchy. Ruth Bernard Yeazell also takes up the issue of boundaries, exploring the tension in the novel between engulfing love and independence. See "More True than Real: Jane Eyre's 'Mysterious Summons.'" Gilbert and Gubar discuss a "frightening series of separations within the self—Jane Eyre splitting off from Jane Rochester, the child Jane splitting off from the adult Jane, and the image of Jane weirdly separating from the body of Jane—" (Madwoman, 359). For a more general discussion of women's ego boundaries, see also Nancy Chodorow, The Reproduction of Mothering.

emerge from the "trance"; it is only then, she reports, that she can speak.

What we have in these two scenes, then, is a psychological sketch—the mother of earliest infancy transformed into the gazing mother who tempts and finally severs. In the novel Jane ultimately makes a choice, a choice facilitated by the mother herself, who offers her separation and language. For a time, however, Jane hesitates, retaining the option not to emerge from the gaze, not to speak, in her painting.

It is this rhythm of loss and access which so disturbs Rochester in Jane's paintings. Each of the three paintings he removes from her portfolio serves a particular function, but the common element is the tension between engulfment and boundaries, reflected in the psychological tension of the narrator and in the juxtaposition of the images to the surrounding text. "I daresay you did exist in a kind of artist's dreamland while you blent and arranged these strange tints" (111) says Rochester, keying into the sphere and power of these pictures, the pulse between blending and arranging, between relinquishing and setting boundaries.

It is this pulse, then, that is more useful than rather arbitrary interpretations of the bird and the drowned woman in the first painting. It is a picture composed of fixed forms—a mast, a bird, a beak, a bracelet, a corpse—in juxtaposition to a rolling, swelling, billowing space of "no land" where things are in danger of washing apart, sinking, submerging. Alone, this painting suggests the struggle of Jane's psychic life. Paired with the third painting—which rigidly asserts, in an echo of the Arctic zone depicted in Bewick's *History of British Birds*,[8] "reservoirs of frost and snow," "firm fields of ice" (6), a landscape where stone and glaciers appear "still" and icy, all carefully frozen, contoured and fixed—the two suggest the poles operative throughout the novel.

Both paintings share an image of death, the first through the corpse and the second through the allusion to Milton's "shape which shape had none." The suggestion is that either alternative—relin-

---

[8]A number of critics have explored Bewick as a source for Jane's paintings, among them L. Duin Kelly, "Jane Eyre's Paintings and Bewick's *History of British Birds*"; Jane W. Steadman, "Charlotte Brontë and Bewick's *British Birds*"; and Hermione Lee, "Emblems and Enigmas in *Jane Eyre*."

quishment or relentless maintenance of boundaries (or of the symbolic)—is fatal. As worked out through Jane's relationship with the
missing mother, Brontë's quest, much like Rhys's and H.D.'s, is to
find passage through a psychological and linguistic space contoured
by creating or abandoning distance. It is the rhythm of these paintings which is central to an understanding of the novel; the schoolgirl
Jane prefigures not the characters or script of her life but the working
of her own unconscious.

The sea and the Arctic serve as flanking panels to the central figure
in this curious triptych, the Evening Star, whose gaze Rochester
cannot bear. The figure itself is split antithetically, its softness and
duskiness subverted by a wildness and madness evocative of Bertha
Mason. The "dark and wild eyes" and the "streaming hair . . . torn
by storm or electric travail" read like the description of Bertha just
before she hurls herself from the burning roof of Thornfield, waving
her arms, her long black hair "streaming against the flames" (377).
But this wildness participates in the "faint lustre" that rises and bows
in a vision reminiscent of the Moon Mother. The importance of this
portrait, I think, is its duality, two faces, two figures joined by some
elementary principle, a kind of Janiform (Janeform) being associated
with both facets of the gaze. It serves then as a fulcrum not only
artistically but psychologically.

It also seems to prefigure the night Bertha appears in Jane's room.
"Just at my bedside the figure stopped: the fiery eye glared upon
me—she thrust up her candle close to my face, and extinguished it
under my eyes. I was aware her lurid visage flamed over mine, and I
lost consciousness: for the second time in my life—only the second
time—I became insensible from terror" (250). The elliptical reference
here, clearly to the red room, creates, with the Moon Mother, another triptych: the "swift-darting beam" (14) recalled from childhood, the lurid visage over the bed at Thornfield, and the gleaming
"white human form" (281) emerging from the moon. The "lineaments seen through the suffusion of vapour" in the painting encompass, then, for Jane, three versions of the mother.[9]

[9]For a discussion of Jane's relationship to women in the novel, particularly to the
series of surrogate mothers from Bessie to the Great Mother, "the matriarchal aspect of
her psyche" (102), see Adrienne Rich, "Jane Eyre: The Temptations of a Motherless
Woman," in On Lies, Secrets, and Silence, 89–106. See also Helene Moglen, who ad-

The appearance here of Bertha Mason is crucial to a reading of Brontë's text, and later women's texts as well, for it prepares the way for what in modernism will become an elaborate and dangerous detour on the oedipal journey. Bertha Mason has escaped, we remember, from the "third story," the "story" that is off limits, out of bounds, the "mystery" that periodically "[breaks] out, now in fire and now in blood" (185), much as the "thoughts too deep to remember" in H.D.'s *Helen in Egypt* "break through the legend . . . like fire / through the broken pictures / on a marble floor" (259). "What crime was this," Brontë asks, "that lived incarnate in this sequestered mansion, and could neither be expelled nor subdued by the owner?" (185). The crime, I suggest, is the violation of another "story," which would disrupt the "normal" passage from the suffocating preoedipal mother to the mother who "penetrate[s] the sable folds and wave[s] them away" (281). Bertha, the crime incarnate, is formed by neither mold; she is savage, wild, primitive, and no matter how Rochester tries to enclose and repress her, to claim "you may think of her as dead and buried—or rather, you need not think of her at all" (187), she is impossible to erase. She takes Jane's wedding veil "from its place," gazing at it "long" until she throws it over her own head and turns to the mirror (249). Strangely, it is at this precise moment of distortion and disguise that Jane reports, "I saw the reflection of the visage and features quite distinctly" (249).

Bertha operates here as the forbidden story, the one that becomes clearest when she displaces the controlling text by forcing us to screen the mirror, by forcing us to operate in an "in-between" that rips and tramples the wedding veil and yet relies on it, a space where the mirror is functional but deformed, the space in which her savage sexuality is revealed. If we accept Bertha through the series of red-room revisions as an aspect of the mother, we see the terror she suggests: incest. Jane, however, although severely disturbed by the encounter, does not question its reality. She demands of Rochester, "Now, sir, tell me who and what that woman was?" (250), perhaps the central question of the novel, the question Rhys tries to answer

---

dresses Jane's attempts to "discover herself anew in the images of women" (133) and through "the mother within" (132). Also useful in several regards are Gilbert and Gubar, *The Madwoman in the Attic*.

finally in *Wide Sargassso Sea*. Rochester evades her, trying to convince her that it was all a dream. He finally can offer only this, the tenuous framework of the son's entire psychological, cultural, and linguistic system: "Since I cannot [explain . . . the mystery of that awful visitant], Jane, it must have been unreal" (250).

When Rochester looks at the Evening Star, the picture that disturbs him most profoundly, he sees what he has spent his adult life trying to deny: Bertha's appeal and her horror and his inability to separate the two. Jane's painting fascinates him, asserting itself as a presence alien in space and time. "Where did you see Latmos?" Rochester asks, alluding to Selene, the moon, who, in order to possess the shepherd Endymion, casts him into a slumber from which he cannot awaken. The Evening Star, then, takes away Rochester's power to speak, to signify; it is a presence removed from the discourse in which he takes his power.

So. Where does all this leave us in an understanding of *Jane Eyre?* It is perhaps now useful to return to one of the initial suggestions of this chapter—that Jane's apprenticeship as narrator, her journey into language, traces a journey of loss in which Jane trades away a power that has provided her with a control she does not have in language. At the end of the book, after Jane's marriage to Rochester, all references to her art vanish.[10] In part, her powers cannot be sufficiently realized because within her role as narrator, Jane's paintings and drawings must be rendered to us, ironically, as text. What we see is what we are "told"; the "interval" of the image, then, becomes another discourse, can never escape language, as Jane herself finally trades her brush for the word. It is also no accident that Jane's art stops with Rochester's blindness. It is when he can no longer see her work, gaze at it, be fascinated by it, that its power ceases and it disappears. Jane becomes, she tells us, Rochester's vision: "never did I weary of gazing for his behalf" (397).[11] But in gazing for him,

[10]In "Narrative Distance in *Jane Eyre:* The Relevance of the Pictures," Jane Millgate reads Jane's paintings as "measurements of narrative involvement" (319), focusing on her increasing ability "to distinguish between actuality and her own imaginative vision" (317). Millgate reads the sudden disappearance of Jane's artistic life as her letting go of "compulsive self-expression" in exchange for "human communication of a peculiarly intense and passionate kind" (319).

[11]For a different reading of Jane's powers of storytelling in Rochester's behalf see Bodenheimer, "Jane Eyre in Search of Her Story."

she unfetters him from the power of the gaze. Rochester "sees" through her but through an "eye" mediated by language—"never did I weary of . . . putting into words the effect of . . . the landscape before us," (397) Jane tells us; "We talk, I believe, all day long" (397).

Her closed portfolio becomes, then, a kind of cloistered space, a room in the attic of discourse, in which Jane shuts away the subversive mechanism associated with a realm outside of discourse—the liminal gaze of the mother, her luster and her wildness. Jane has acquired the necessary credentials to narrate her life, but she has relinquished the space of a "story" very different from the tale told by the governess/narrator.

This "other" story, despite Jane's "capitulation," keeps rising up from below the surface of the text; it is the same story the stolid little girl tried to tell the Dominican nun and which Rhys tries to tell or enact in *Wide Sargasso Sea*. It takes its power from the incredible danger of telling it and the incredible seduction of returning back inside the space from which it is told. It is the story that gives birth to the self and threatens to destroy it, the story that emerges from "the place where the subject is both generated and negated, the place where his unity succumbs before the process of charges and stases which produce him" (Kristeva, *RPL*, 28).

It is the story in which the sister, Bertha, breaks through the story told to Rochester by her brother, who tries to suppress the truth of the mother and her madness and how his sister has "copied her parent" (*Jane Eyre*, 257). It is, then, through this copy, also the story of the mother, the story of earliest relation with her, loss of her, desire for her, and of rage and fear, fear of finding her, fear of not. To "tell" her is somehow to kill her; to refuse to tell is to die. *Jane Eyre* is a useful opening text because it sets forth the terms of loss—the orphan turned governess, the motherless daughter attempting to fill the space of motherlessness, the sister trying to usurp the brother— and establishes through the powerful subtext the incredible dilemma of articulating the mother, which clearly precedes Freud, modernism, and contemporary feminism.

We might leave the text, I think, not with the image of Mrs. Rochester and her baby but with the reminder that although in the end Jane opts for the word, abandoning the "fix" of the image, Jane's early sense of language as a screen for something deeper, darker, more enigmatic, more primal, is never resolved. The subtext of her "bewilderment," however, is perhaps more significant than the "ending," so I offer as an alternative to the oedipal resolution Brontë chooses one of the pivotal moments in the novel, the early scene in which Rochester impersonates a fortune-teller.

Jane is summoned to the library, where she finds "the Sibyl" seated in the chimney corner, reading and muttering to herself. This scene juxtaposes the elements central to feminist reading: woman as outsider, both by gender and estate, surrounded by the texts that both define and alienate her. Brontë replays here the opening scene, wherein Jane is psychologically and physically punished for trespassing into books.

In this incredible revision, the gypsy woman closes her book and gazes at Jane steadily; there is much cryptic and elliptical conversation about Jane's life and Rochester and his impending marriage to Blanche Ingram; the importance of the scene, however, is not what is said but the effect it has on Jane, who finds herself "wrapped in a kind of dream," "involved in a web of mystification" as a result of the gypsy's "strange talk, voice, manner" (175). "Where was I?" she asks. "Did I wake or sleep? Had I been dreaming? Did I dream still?" (177).

It is language that bears much of the strange effect of the gypsy-disguised Rochester. Jane's description of the Sibyl almost identically echoes Rochester's response to the paintings. It is in this scene that we begin to see the reason Rochester's language has from the very beginning seemed so mysterious and enigmatical to Jane. It is related to the fact that the gypsy will "have no gentlemen . . . nor . . . any ladies either, except the young and single" (170), and to the fact that Jane calls her "mother." What is operating here, I suggest, is a kind of "mother tongue," Kristeva's semiotic, a register to discourse that at its most powerful in the novel operates not separate from but within the symbolic, a discourse contingent on both language and image, on what is seen and unseen. Dressed as an old woman, a "Mother Bunch" (168), Rochester has, as it were, brought the "maternal" to the surface, inverted the discourse, so that text no longer castrates but gazes.

Brontë is manipulating powerful material here, although just when one "wants" her to "do" something with it, it begins to slide: at the very moment it begins to surface, this material most stubbornly refuses articulation. What does this conflation of semiotic and symbolic, where the father/lover impersonates the mother, mean? It is really a staggering moment in the novel and in women's literary history if we know how to read it, even though "reading" becomes an inoperative concept when one is pulled back by the desire to be released into the scene, simply to experience the gypsy's gaze; the incredible incongruency of context, then, is washed back into a scopic field where *incongruent* is not a functional term. This very state of conflict—the desire to impose order on the scene, to "read" it, to provide it with a kind of syntax and simultaneously simply to enter it, to allow it—offers an alternative Brontë abandons: the possibility of conflating the gaze and the sign into a maternally connoted language that both speaks and dreams, dreams a dream in which the blind spot becomes the gaze. Moreover, the master/lover/mother offers an erotic component to both the encounter and the discourse that appears, I suggest, when the mother's disposition is discovered and allowed and translated into text.

In the ensuing chapters, I look at the ways in which writing daughters have both refused and solicited this encounter with the mother and how both her loss and her presence insistently rupture the discourse of their texts. The conflation of the maternal aspect of Bertha, her sexuality, and her role as the silenced sister/daughter provides a paradigm through which to consider what Susan Friedman has called the "gendering of modernism" as I examine how twentieth-century women such as Jean Rhys and H.D. have reworked the oedipal journey textually, encompassing both desire and language and the fragile, violent slippage between them.

3

Orestes' Sisters

Jane Eyre, as we have seen, is a text determined by the cultural conditions out of which Brontë wrote and yet, nonetheless, is almost a century ahead of later women's writing that "begins" to explore the inscription of ambivalence and the interplay of subtext and surrounding discourse. Brontë, however, did not or could not develop the connections between the image and the preoedipal or the text and the symbolic as modernist women such as Rhys and H.D. often do. Jane's mother is lost when Brontë's novel begins, whereas one of the features of later novels is the liminality of the mother; the preoccupation is often not with her absence but with the *event* of her absence. Often, for example, we see the mother, textually, at the moment of her disappearance, just as she slips into death or madness, as though we catch both her and the daughter "in the act." A central question of this chapter is the nature of "that act" and the psychological and textual purpose it serves for the writing daughter.

In both Rhys and H.D., as I have suggested, there is always an alternation between desire and rage, the urge to claim the mother and the struggle to escape from or reject her. Although both instincts operate in each woman's work, I shall begin by setting up the interplay through one scene from H.D. and one from Rhys, not to characterize the totality of either woman's experience but to set the borders of women's fiction in general. In other words, I extract these two scenes to formulate a model of thinking about *the writing daughter's* relationship to the mother.

"Paint It To-Day" (written in 1921, unpublished), H.D.'s first novel, together with "Asphodel" (dated 1921–1922, unpublished) and *HERmione* (written in 1927 under the title *Her*), form a kind of trilogy or palimpsest structured around H.D.'s involvement with the young Ezra Pound, her friendship with and sexual attraction to a woman named Frances Gregg, and her relationship with her mother. In "Paint It To-Day" H.D. takes on the relationship of mother and daughter for the first time in any sustained way, sketching the obsessive story to which she will return time and time again. Here she seizes on the concurrent threat and attraction of nursery talk, bodily rhythm, and the maternal, which, long before the developed writer H.D. claims them as a liberating trope, seem to her restrictive, repressive, a selling out to a cultural prescription of what a woman's role should be.

The unevenness of "Paint It To-Day" makes it, in some ways, H.D.'s least successful effort to "tell the story"; on the other hand, the nerves are daringly close to the surface, giving the text, at least parts of the text, an astonishing raw power. The H.D. figure who later turns up as Hermione is here called Midget; the Pound figure, later called George Lowndes, is referred to cryptically as "the youth."

> When she was nineteen, she had parted with the youth, having gained nothing from him but a feeling that someone had tampered with an oracle, had banged on a temple door, had dragged out small curious, sacred ornaments, had not understood their inner meaning, yet with a slight sense of their outer value, their perfect tint and carving, had not stolen them, but left them, perhaps worse, exposed by the road-side, reft from the shelter and their holy setting. [447][1]

H.D. seems to see herself here, as she was prone to do at various times, as both oracle and temple. The imagery is of rape and violation, being stripped of small, sacred ornaments, which can be read not only sexually but in terms of her poetry; the passage reflects H.D.'s ambivalence about both Pound's physical advances and his appropriation of her early work. But there is also the sense here of H.D. herself as ornament, stolen from some other temple—an image

---

[1] Since my original work on this material, using the unpublished typescript at Beinecke Library, four chapters from "Paint It To-Day" have been printed in the H.D. Centennial Issue of *Contemporary Literature* 27 (Winter 1986): 444–74. To facilitate access, I have made reference to passages from the text as they appear in the journal.

of abortion, daughter reft from the mother's body, left exposed, torn from shelter and from a "holy setting." This is the vision of the mother as Demeter we will see again in *HERmione*.

Juxtaposed to this image of the mother as temple, dominating it, in fact, which is the particular interest of "Paint It To-Day," is a fantasy of matricide, the only overtly aggressive act toward the mother I am aware of in H.D.'s work. Midway through the novel Midget realizes that "she had never in all her life as far as . . . she could in any way recall it, said to her mother 'I can't' " (470); she had never rebelled. As her thoughts wind out, she first imagines telling her mother what she really thinks, trying to explain to her what she has always felt:

> There was another speech. That speech she could not rehearse in words. That speech was a hot wave across her brain. A fear possessed her, a fear that if they did not let her go, something terrible and tragic would eat out her heart and close over her head and beat her back, back into the present. . . . There were no words to this speech. A fear possessed her that suddenly she might find words to this speech, that she might shout or sing those words, and that they would break, those good and simple people, shrivelled to ash, before her utterance, or that they might seize her and bind her down forever. [472]

To speak to the mother—to *speak the mother*—Midget senses that she will need a speech for which there are no words, a speech associated with sense and rhythm, a hot wave. H.D. here sets up not a polarity between speech and no-speech but a dichotomy between speech and "another" speech, a subtext that the words readily available to her do not serve to translate. Moreover, as she contemplates the route of access to it, she is overcome with fear, first, not that she will be thwarted (that comes later) but that she will succeed, that she will somehow find "those" words, or "worse" that she already *has* those words, the power of which would shrivel both her parents. She is intensely ambivalent about this power; she wavers, unsure what it would mean to break from syntax into "utterance," "shouts," or "singing." The part of her that recedes from it perceives it as something punishable—she will be torn and seized and bound for having found it. And reactivating this "speech" prior to "words," maternally connoted as the *chora*, or semiotic, *is* punishable. It is at the heart of the castration contract which transforms the mother's body and its subversion of the symbolic into the "forbidden."

In this section of the novel, Midget still buys into the androcentric script; the two "good and simple people" are suddenly polarized, and it is the mother who emerges as the enemy, the traitor, as Midget imagines herself as Orestes, poised over her with a knife.

> How did Orestes feel when he held the knife ready to slay his mother? What did Orestes see? What did Orestes think? . . .
>
> What did Orestes feel? Something unnerved him. Not the present. Things, as the present drew them, were dire and evil and to be combatted. What of the past?
>
> "Your mother has betrayed your father," spoke the present to Orestes. "Your mother, your mother, your mother," the present said to Midget, "has betrayed, or would betray, through the clutch and the tyranny of the emotion, the mind in you, the jewel the king your father gave you as your birthright. Look," said the present, "and choose. Here is a knife, slay your mother. She has betrayed or would betray that gift." [473]

In this passage, H.D. lays out the tarot of her ambivalence, an arcanum of Emotion, Intellect, Daughter, Jewel. This is her earliest and most polarized working through the cards from which she feels she must *choose*, unable as yet to accept contradiction and multiplicity in her family, herself, or her work. H.D.'s father, astronomer and scientist, is cast here as the giver of her birthright; although she disappointed him in his sphere, failing at Bryn Mawr, never able (never fully wanting) to succeed in the space of his and her brother's success, she nonetheless perceives this space of intellect as necessary for her poetry, a poetry to which the mother's "emotion" is insufficient. For the daughter's gift to be released, then, for her to create not children but words, the mother must be slain.[2]

Yet even at the moment of her imminent death, the mother subverts the daughter's intent, working her way back through childhood memory; what *of* the past?

> The soul of Midget spoke words unrehearsed and unexpected to the mind of Midget. "Do you remember those frangipani fruits she used to get you? She redressed that hopeless doll many, many times when any other mother would have flung it on the dust heap. What of that birthday when she put morning-glories through the string of every birthday parcel and addressed each of the eight separate parcels with a separate pet-name? What of that wonderful convalescence from scarlet-fever when you found on your pillow—" "Stop," said the mind of Midget.

[2]Judith Kegan Gardiner makes a similar point, which veers in another direction in "A Wake for Mother: The Maternal Deathbed in Women's Fiction."

Knowing that she was defeated, she turned to rend the object of her downfall. [473]

It is emotion that would betray the mind, those unrehearsed and unexpected words that allow the mother to "win" through fruits and fabrics and pet names even as Midget plays out her resolve.

What is especially significant here, however, is that H.D. enacts this fantasy through Orestes, fulfilling the oedipal odyssey through the son; he is the one who must align himself with the father and kill the mother to enter culture and language, which are constituted as revenge for the mother's "betrayal" through her "lack." But this "'cultural myth' of Lacanian psycholinguistics" (Stimpson, ix) is not/does not have to be the daughter's story. Midget "plays out" the brother because in the model she chooses (not by accident), the sisters offer no better alternative. Clytemnestra, we remember, also had two daughters: Iphigenia and Electra. The first represents the daughter obliterated, sacrificed to assure male victory. Indeed, the murder of Agamemnon, which Orestes seeks to avenge by killing his mother, is Clytemnestra's vengeance for her daughter's death at Aulis. Beyond the obvious fact that to align herself with the sacrificed daughter is a kind of suicide, Midget cannot "be" Iphigenia for two reasons. Several years before "Paint It To-Day" H.D. tried this connection when she translated Euripides' Iphigeneia in Aulis. That translation shows an incredible ambivalence in two passages. In the first, H.D. writes

> It is not for me, the day,
> Nor this light of sun.
> Ah mother, mother,
> The same terror is cast on us both. [CP, 81]

She cannot be Iphigenia, first, because she represents an alliance with the powerless woman, not the Demeter figure H.D. longs for but the mother who cannot protect or save her daughter. Several stanzas later H.D. continues:

> O I am miserable:
> You cherished me, my mother,
> But even you desert me.
> I am sent to an empty place. [CP, 82]

Even though Iphigenia's underlying fate is the same in both passages, each carries a different emphasis: the first on weakness, the second on betrayal. Iphigenia, in H.D.'s view at this point, offers only two alternatives: she must either reject the mother to avoid "the same terror," the same fate, or, loving her, run the risk of being deserted, the mother turning, as H.D. felt Helen Doolittle did, to the father and the son.

Electra, who, rather than become a victim, aligns herself with her dead father through her brother and turns on her mother, presents H.D. with yet another troubling model. As Midget realizes, "She was defeated. She was not Orestes. She was a girl. Yet she was not Electra, the sister, who waited, though her heart was breaking to help Orestes. She was not Electra. She was not Orestes. Had she been one or the other, she would have won" (474). Electra does not slay the mother; she waits. H.D. knows that she is "not Electra" but the only apparent alternative is to be the brother, which she also "is not." In this myth, then, the myth out of which H.D. operates, partially, for years—out of which many women operate—to be the daughter means to be sacrificed or to sacrifice the mother or to be (impossible) the son. When H.D. gives Electra the voice to speak of Clytemnestra years later in a poem in *A Dead Priestess Speaks*, she reformulates the conflict once again: "To love, one must slay, / how could I stay? / to love one must be slain, / then how could I remain" (*CP*, 378). There is not a model in this "family romance" for a daughter who loves the mother or who rejects or slays the father or his word.[3]

Jean Rhys's characters are victims in a sense H.D.'s are not. They are abused, abandoned, powerless, and passive. Their mothers go mad or disappear or die as they watch helplessly. In contrast to the scene from "Paint It To-Day" in which the daughter attempts to do away with the mother in order to survive, Jean Rhys writes a scene in *After Leaving Mr. Mackenzie* (1930) in which a daughter struggles to survive through access rather than escape.

Julia Martin, a young woman living in Paris, has just been disposed of by her latest lover, Mr. Mackenzie, and is trying to find some way to stay financially afloat. Julia's existence abroad has been

[3]For further development of this idea, see, again, DuPlessis, *Writing beyond the Ending*.

marked by a series of unfortunate affairs, "disconnected episodes which made up her life" (179). All the men she encounters exploit her both sexually and linguistically, holding power over her body and her language. The evening of her final encounter with Mackenzie in a café, for example, she meets a man named George Horsfield; rather than go to bed with him, for once, she follows him home and attempts to tell him the story of her life: "She spoke as if she were trying to recall a book she had read or a story she had heard and Mr. Horsfield felt irritated by her vagueness, 'because,' he thought, 'your life is your life, and you must be pretty definite about it. Or if it's a story you are making up, you ought to at least have it pat'" (50). Within the confines of male discourse, story, narrative, must be "definite," whereas Julia comes out of vagueness, even about the events of her own life, which appear to her distant, shadowy, as if she is recalling a text with which she is not entirely familiar. Julia's attempts to translate her (female) experience into a male system are doomed to failure, and yet Julia, having as yet no access to the voice and body of the mother, has no other system or disposition to call into play.

After her failure with Horsfield and Mackenzie, her inability either to talk or to make love successfully, Julia decides to return to London, ostensibly to make contact with a rich male friend who might help her out. Julia's ten days in London form a central "space" or hiatus in this novel, which operates around sexual exploitation and economic exchange. For this brief time, she finds nights in men's beds replaced by a visit with her sister and her dying mother.

Julia's mother, Mrs. Griffiths, Brazilian by birth, has been transplanted to England, where she is "sickening for the sun" (105). Although Julia weaves "innumerable romances about her mother's childhood in South America" and has asked "innumerable questions," her mother has always answered "inadequately or not at all, for she was an inarticulate woman" (105). Julia remembers a time when

her mother had been the warm centre of the world. You loved to watch her brushing her long hair; and when you missed the caresses and the warmth you groped for them. . . . And then her mother—entirely wrapped up in the new baby— . . . from being the warm centre . . . had gradually become a dark, austere . . . woman, who, because she was worried, slapped you for no reason that you knew. So that there were times when you were afraid of her; other times when you disliked her.

Then you stopped being afraid or disliking. You simply became indifferent and tolerant and rather sentimental, because after all she was your mother.

It was strange sitting there, and remembering the time when she was the sweet, warm centre of the world, remembering it so vividly that mysteriously it was all there again. [106–7]

Rhys evokes here a world of preoedipal images and sensations— warmth, hair, caresses, groping, sweetness, mystery—a world that is inexplicable because it exists in a presence prior to the need to represent its loss. The mother that Rhys describes, however, despite her association as the "centre" of a typically Rhysian maternal geography, has to a certain degree already been inauthenticated, long before her imminent death: Julia "had been accustomed for years to the idea that her mother was an invalid, paralysed, dead to all intents and purposes" (72). When we read Julia, like Sasha in *Good Morning, Midnight*, as a woman absolutely encased in loss but particularly in her absence as a signifying subject in the discourse that engulfs her, we can trace her own absence to the absence of the mother, the repressed object for which the meaningless signifiers stand in, the "invalid" woman who, even when alive, is to all intents and purposes dead to the daughter.

Nonetheless, when Julia returns home to her mother's deathbed, her investment in the final encounter is great.

She felt too nervous to talk. The meeting with her mother was very near; yet she was still unable to imagine or realize it. Supposing that her mother knew her or recognized her and with one word or glance put her outside the pale, as everybody else had done.

She felt a sort of superstitious and irrational certainty that if that happened it would finish her; it would be an ultimate and final judgement. [96]

What Julia wants from her mother here is not yet entirely clear; Rhys writes instead about what Julia is afraid of—that the mother will judge her as the men have. Moreover, she establishes this judgment in terms of language itself. "With one word" the inadequate, inarticulate woman in the bed could put her daughter "outside the pale," reproducing the rupture of the mother-child dyad through language.

There is another kind of subversion going on in this central section, embodied in Julia's younger sister, Norah, who has taken possession of the household and acts as intermediary to the mother. Norah is shocked when she sees Julia after three years; she is suspicious of her sudden appearance, her precarious financial situation, and her request to stay at the flat, which Norah refuses. Although Norah accurately assesses Julia's state of affairs, Julia is undone by her sister's coolness and wariness: "'Oh God!' said Julia loudly. 'But it wasn't money I wanted'" (75). What she wants is access to the "warm centre of the world," but the fetid sickroom over which Norah has gained control is not that space. It is instead a distortion, a reversal, where the overwrought but imperious Norah becomes a kind of surrogate mother both to Julia and to her own mother, overseeing the dying woman in a "crooning and authoritative voice. 'Don't cry, my darling. Don't cry, my sweet. Now, what is it? What is it you want?'" (100).

In a sense Norah embodies the two faces of the childhood mother Julia describes—the caressing, warm woman who shifts, becoming dark and austere, the woman who slaps you for no reason that you know, the woman you are afraid of and come to dislike. Norah, similarly, "had a sweet voice, a voice with a warm and tender quality. This was strange, because her face was cold, as though warmth and tenderness were dead in her" (71). Like the inexplicably ambivalent "real" mother, Norah alternately feels "a fierce desire to hurt [Julia] or to see her hurt and humiliated" (102) and yet is overcome with reluctance to let her go: "She hated her, but she felt more alive when [she] was with her" (106). Norah is in fact a desperately unhappy woman, whose "life had been slavery" (104). Besides her hopes for a small inheritance, she cares for her mother because "everybody always said to her: 'You're wonderful, Norah, you're wonderful. I don't know how you do it.' It was a sort of drug, that universal, that unvarying admiration—the feeling that one was doing what one ought to do, the approval of God and man. It made you feel protected and safe, as if something very powerful were fighting on your side" (104). This scene in a sense replicates the opening scene in the Catholic school, Norah filling in for the mother superior

and Julia for the exasperating child. Each, in her own way, is sacrificed to God and man against the backdrop of the dead mother. And
just as the mother superior intrudes between the child and the
mother, Norah mediates between Julia and Mrs. Griffiths, warning
Julia that her mother won't know her.

Finally arrangements are made for Julia to come to the flat, and
when Norah decides to allow a visit, Julia sees, significantly, not her
mother but "her mother's *body*" (97, my emphasis) in a transformation
concurrent with a transformation in language. Julia enters the room
which smells of disinfectants and rottenness and which is quiet,
"quiet and shut away from everything" (98). This silence Julia finds
to be "the best thing in the world." Rhys writes, "It seemed as if she
had been sitting there for many years and that if she could go on
sitting there she would learn many deep things that she had only
guessed at before" (98).

Back in her mother's presence, Julia's language is reduced: she is
too nervous to talk, and when she does finally attempt to speak she
can only whisper "soundlessly," "There's something I want to explain to you. You must listen" (98). Like Midget, Julia wants to tell
her mother something crucial but finds there are "no words to this
speech." When Mrs. Griffiths's eyes open suddenly, Julia puts her
face up next to her and says "in a frightened, hopeful voice: 'I'm
Julia, do you know? It's Julia' " (98). The mother does not know, or at
least cannot formulate that knowing in discourse. She looks at Julia
"steadily" for a moment and then "nothing was there" (98).

But in fact something *is* there; it is just not what Julia anticipates.
Mrs. Griffiths "mumbled something in a thick voice, then turned her
head away and began to cry, loudly and disconsolately, like a child"
(98–99). Norah rushes in, hearing the cries, as Julia insists her mother
knew her for a moment, that she said something that sounded like
"orange-trees." "She must have been thinking of when she was in
Brazil," Julia says, plunging her back into the topography always associated with the body of the mother in Rhys's work. Norah, acting as
her mother's interpreter and censor, denies that her mother's cries—
which turn, as the scene progresses, into "snorts" and "whimperings" and "howlings"—"mean" anything. To Norah, these are just
random sounds she makes. But as she and Julia stand by the bed,
Norah, relating a story to illustrate how her mother's words no longer

signify, begins to laugh "in a high-pitched, hysterical way" (100), which Julia begins to imitate. As she laughs, she finds she cannot stop, "and she went on laughing, holding on to the foot of the bed and staring at her mother. Then she saw her mother's black eyes open again and stare back into hers with recognition and surprise and anger. They said: 'Is this why you have come back? Have you come back to laugh at me?' " (100).

This is a really remarkable scene in its conflation of opposing forces, the collision of symbolic and semiotic, the desire for signifying mother and the desire for the body before language which both "calls" Julia and rejects her. The laughter at this moment is an interesting intrusion into the text. According to Kristeva,

> Chronologically and logically long before the mirror stage (where the Same sees itself altered through the well-known opening that constitutes it as representation, sign, and death), the semiotic disposition makes it start as riant spaciousness. During the period of indistinction between "*same*" and "*other*," infant and mother, as well as between "subject" and "object," while no space has yet been delineated (this will happen with and after the mirror stage—birth of the sign), the semiotic *chora* . . . relieves and produces laughter. [*DL,* 283–84]

Significantly, H.D. reaches toward this same association in the last section of *Palimpsest,* where she writes of Helen Fairwood, "Her laugh again unexpected to herself, rang out. Uncanny. . . . The laughter utterly herself . . . was of long past vanished languages. . . . The laughter merged and made one of all the selves" (212).

The cadence of Mrs. Griffiths's bodily rhythms as she lies dying, her whimperings and mumblings, clearly pull Julia back into a maternal sphere anterior to syntax and signification, a long-vanished past where Norah breaks the laughter and Julia disappears into it. But ironically, it is at the very moment of the *chora* that the mother seems to identify the daughter and to shift into anger and language, although it is a language projected onto her by the child. Julia believes the mother is saying, through her gaze, "Don't laugh at me," but what Rhys is doing here is imbedding the struggle between rupture and representation. In Rhys's novels the daughter seldom knows what is true or what is available or what the mother or she herself wants.

At first, Julia does not identify with her mother's strange, dislo-
cated, intonational sphere of sound but, banished from the room by
Norah, sits outside her mother's door, covering her ears with her
hands "to shut out the cries" (101). She has come to be recognized, to
hear her name, but the mother fails her. And after the mother dies,
Julia finds no relief: "She was bewildered, as though some comfort
that she had thought she would find there had failed her" (124).

Julia has a strange experience at her mother's funeral, however, in
the chapel of the crematorium, where, significantly, the mother's
body is consumed. At that moment, Julia

> was obsessed with the feeling that she was so close to seeing the thing
> that was behind all this talking and posturing, and that the talking and
> posturing were there to prevent her from seeing it. Now it's time to get
> up; now it's time to kneel down; now it's time to stand up.
> But all the time she stood, knelt, and listened she was tortured because
> her brain was making a huge effort to grapple with nothingness. And the
> effort hurt; yet it was almost successful. In another minute she would
> know. And then a dam inside her head burst, and she leant her head on
> her arms and sobbed. [130]

Rhys explores here the notion of a "thing" behind talk, beyond lit-
any, beyond posturing—a thing or space associated with the mother
which "talk" prevents her from contacting. Curiously, H.D. uses
almost identical terms to describe Hermione's sense, after her conversation with another woman, of "something" behind language: "It
wasn't exactly what she said . . . it was the thing back of the thing
she said . . . that mattered" (*HER*, 193; H.D.'s ellipses). For Julia, it is
torturous yet compelling, and as she reaches the moment of most
intense contact, Rhys once again describes the experience in language similar to H.D.'s description of "another speech," Midget's
sensation of "a hot wave across her brain." Rhys writes: "Julia had
abandoned herself. . . . At the same time, in a miraculous manner,
some essence of her was shooting upwards like a flame. She was
great. She was a defiant flame shooting upwards not to plead but to
threaten" (131).

This is an astonishing passage in Rhys. Her women never perceive
themselves as "great"; they are desperate and pleading creatures,
totally nonthreatening to anyone but themselves. This "miraculous"

moment in which Julia *becomes* a defiant flame occurs in conjunction with the burning of her mother's body as if she is both what consumes her and what is consumed with her. This is a moment of great power, associated with Julia's sense that there is something "behind all the talking." It is one of the most striking examples of the way in which Rhys encodes the dead mother both as a trope for textlessness and as an inscription of the "other side" of language, a space in which women, through the syntactical equivalent of snorts and howls, might find the means to signify within and to subvert the symbolic. The epiphany of the crematorium does not last—"the flame sank down again, useless, having reached nothing" (131)—but the sense of what that flame suggested recurs later in the novel and is developed more fully in later novels.

One night after her mother's death, for example, Julia arranges to have dinner with George Horsfield, who has himself returned to London. When he takes her back to her boardinghouse, she begs him not to leave her, and so he sneaks noiselessly up to her room. In this scene the roles are reversed: unlike Julia's Uncle Griffiths who talks "eagerly, as if the sound of his own voice laying down the law to his audience of females reassured him" (133), the male here is stripped of language and even sound, forced to suppress voice and speech, to pass silently through the darkened halls to escape detection; "he mounted noiselessly after her. She was invisible in the darkness, but he followed the sound of her footsteps, placing his feet very carefully, so that they made no sound" (150–51). The second night, he attempts to pass her on the staircase; as he touches her, she becomes hysterical, screaming over and over, "Who's that? Who's that? Who touched my hand?" (164). This scene echoes the deathbed scene where Julia touches her mother's hand; it conflates the contact of their bodies and the words the mother couldn't speak or know. Julia becomes, in a sense, the mother and at the same time the daughter in relation to her; after she begins to calm down she says to Horsfield, "I thought it was—someone dead catching hold of my hand" (165). Once again Rhys makes the connection between mother and daughter initiated at the funeral; it is significant that Julia finds this second contact with her mother at a moment when the male is reduced to silence, stripped of language.

Again, however, the moment does not last; it disappears when

Horsfield regains his voice, and Julia wavers between the symbolic—
sign and predication—and her mother's touch. In this curious state
of suspension Julia returns to Paris and takes up her life where she
left it, wandering aimlessly without friends or money.

One night she finds herself at the edge of the Seine where a
policeman approaches her, afraid she is contemplating suicide. She
assures him that she is not, then asks him what the shadows are in
the river; "'It's a tree, the branch of a tree.' Julia thought: 'That's
what *you* say.' . . . The shadows seemed not to be on the surface, but
to be struggling, wriggling upwards from the depths of the water"
(184). While the figure associated with law keeping and codes projects onto the water an identifiable (and rather phallic) form, Julia
perceives not a shape but a process operating within the depths.

This scene is very like an early poem of H.D.'s, "Hermes of the
Ways," which represents, as Shari Benstock has observed, the same
"dual effort of supposition and subversion" (324):

> The boughs of the trees
> are twisted
> by many bafflings;
> twisted are
> the small-leafed boughs. [*CP*, 38]

If we attempt to read this image as Julia attempts to read the reflection of the same image, we encounter a "twist," the way in which
representation becomes both "baffled"—balked or deflected—and
baffling—perplexing, bewildering. The policeman baffles the shadow for Julia, ironically, by attempting to represent it. He "reads" the
water through a system which reflects identity and structure, while
she, baffled in her project to find the "thing" *behind* all the talking,
which almost surfaces at her mother's funeral, works beneath the
surface toward a kind of subtext.

Benstock also notes that this stanza from "Hermes" "finds its
structure in chiasmus" (324), a reversal of words in an otherwise
parallel structure. There is another word—chiasma—which refers in
anatomy to a crossing or intersection, particularly that of the optic
nerves, and in genetics to a crossing over or exchange of chromatids.
That the masculine form of the noun refers to rhetoric and the feminine to the body, reproduction, and vision is a strange and sugges-

tive coincidence, which helps us understand how "bafflings" become not an impediment to women writers but rather a mode of
"crossing over."

When Julia leaves the policeman, in fact, she does cross over,
entering a café where she finds herself staring at the woman behind
the counter.

> When she spoke to the customers, her voice was very soft and her eyes
> were big and dark. She was a slim woman with full, soft breasts.
> Julia had a great longing to go up to the woman and talk to her. . . .
> She sat thinking: "If I could talk to her, if only I could go up and tell her
> all about myself and why I am unhappy, everything would be different
> afterwards." [184]

Julia senses here the need to locate herself outside the "law," turning
instinctively to a place where there is sustenance, offered by a
woman with full breasts. It is important that Julia seeks talk as well as
nurturance; if she could tell this woman about herself, "everything
would be different," but the impulse is clearly related not to the
woman herself, unknown to Julia, but to her body.

Within the confines of this novel, the connection between authentic language and the female, maternal body is never complete, but
there is an important movement sketched in the juxtaposition of two
scenes, one at the beginning of the novel and the other at the end. In
the first, Julia has just received a letter informing her that her al-
lowance from her former lover, Mr. Mackenzie, is being terminated.
Not knowing how she is to manage, she wanders into a café, where,
filling up with "a heat, which was like the heat of rage" (20), she
notices a blotter and pen in front of her. "She opened the blotter and
began to draw little flags on the paper. As she drew she was watching the face of Mr. Mackenzie, which floated, wearing a cool and
derisory smile, between her eyes and the blotter" (20). These are
ambiguous little drawings suggestive of signal flags perhaps, an
alternative code, or of the white flag of defeat; in either case, they are
disrupted by the strange image of Mr. Mackenzie, decapitated, im-
posing himself between Julia and the page, flooding her with a
sudden "sensation of such dreary and abject humiliation . . . that
she would have liked to put her arms on the table and her head on
her arms and to sob aloud" (20). She abandons her "doodling" and

turns instead to a letter asking for more money. She begs and abases herself, realizing as soon as she writes it that "that sort of letter was never a bit of use, anyhow" (21).

At the end of the novel appears a variation of this scene. Julia enters another café, full of "talking and gesticulating men" and "subdued" women (186). She orders a drink and a blotter, intending to write to Horsfield, "but when she took up the pen she made meaningless strokes on the paper. And then she began to draw faces—the sort of faces a child would draw, made up of four circles and a straight line" (186–87). By the end of the text, she can no longer even draft the sort of letter she knows is "no use"; she writes only two words on the paper: "*Doucement, doucement,*" words that might be spoken to comfort a child. Both the system of signs and the face-of-the-father have disappeared as Julia moves back into the gaze, a face reproduced over and over by a child.

Rhys cannot yet sustain this movement, however. Julia ends up, just as she began, in an encounter with Mr. Mackenzie, asking him for more money, participating in a replication of the linguistic economy in which the object of exchange is the mother. The last lines of the text are these: "The street was cool and full of grey shadows. Lights were beginning to come out in the cafés. It was the hour between dog and wolf, as they say" (191).[4] The idiom that Rhys chooses here (in French: *entre chien et loup*) is an interesting echo of an earlier reference to organized society in which Julia has "no place and against which she [has] not a dog's chance" (22). Just as she began, trapped inside a cliché, she ends inside another one, enclosed in language as *they* say it. The idiom, however, also suggests indefiniteness. It is the hour *between* dog and wolf, when neither is clear, when perception and signification are in question, a space between domestication and the wild. This "in between," to which Rhys herself is clearly drawn, is where the critic Hélène Cixous locates the space of women's writing:

> To admit that writing is precisely working (in) the in-between, inspecting the process of the same and of the other . . . to admit this is first to want

[4]Strangely, H.D. uses a similar image to record Hermione's impression of George Lowndes's response to her description of "the thing back of the thing": " 'Wh-aat was the thing back of the thing that mattered?' [he says.] A wolf face; a wolf's face was looking at Her" (*HER*, 193).

the two as well as both, the ensemble of the one and other, not fixed in sequences of struggle and expulsion . . . but infinitely dynamized by an incessant process of exchange from one subject to another in a multiple and inexhaustible course with millions of encounters and transformations of the same into the other and into the in-between, from which woman takes her forms. [CD, 254]

4

Between Corpse and Song

Jean Rhys's fiction, as we have seen, operates around an economy of loss—loss of language, loss of homeland, loss of economic and sexual power, and loss of the mother. It is a fiction of barter and exchange where what women "want"—to echo Freud's famous query—is never "there," is instead displaced or represented in some kind of substitute. One of the most interesting novels in this regard is *Voyage in the Dark*, the very history of which reflects a series of substitutions and displacements. Although published in 1934, four years after *After Leaving Mr. Mackenzie*, it was actually written before any of her other four novels and stored in a suitcase for almost a decade.[1] In some way, then, from the very beginning, this "least engaging" (Abel, 161) of Rhys's novels, the most neglected by critics and yet Rhys's own favorite, was repeatedly deferred, delayed, suppressed, and ignored.[2] When in fact it came to print, Rhys's pub-

[1]The source of this information is Helen Nebeker, *Jean Rhys: Woman in Passage*, 43–46. Nebeker quotes from two letters from Diana Athill, Rhys's editor at André Deutsch, who reveals the then little-known chronology of Rhys's first four novels and attempts to explain why Rhys packed the manuscript away for six or seven years, "feeling sick whenever she saw it" (44). Teresa O'Connor identifies this "manuscript" as the exercise books Rhys showed to Pearl Adam, the wife of the British correspondent for the *Times* in Paris, in the early twenties before Ford Madox Ford published Rhys's first story in the *Transatlantic Review*. O'Connor's work sheds light not only on the history of the manuscript but on the contradictions in reports of both facts and chronology, an issue that is always evident in Rhys scholarship and in Rhys's own conflicting memories. See *Jean Rhys: The West Indian Novels*, 54–57.

[2]Abel is apparently not alone in her assessment of *Voyage in the Dark*; it is the novel in Rhys's canon which has been least often and least carefully explored. Plot summary

lishers at Constable, disapproving of the morbid ending, insisted that she rewrite it. Thus the framing context of the text, as well as the text itself, reflects the kind of loss and trading that permeated Rhys's artistic and personal life.

A reading of *Voyage in the Dark* can reveal the textual strategies Rhys uses to fill the gap left by the mother. Rhys was much less conscious of herself as a writer than H.D., who saw herself always, to some degree, in the literary, cultural, and mythic context through which she wrote. Rhys's novels often unfold in a space independent of the surrounding literary zeitgeist, in, as one of her characters reports, "cafés where they like me and cafés where they don't, streets that are friendly, streets that aren't, rooms where I might be happy, rooms where I never shall be, looking-glasses I look nice in, looking-glasses I don't, dresses that will be lucky, dresses that won't, and so on" (*GMM*, 46). The polarity, alienation, and chance contained in this passage resonate, as we have begun to see, throughout Rhys's work, in which women prostitute themselves and drink too much, caught between the financial security men seem to offer and the physical and psychological price the women must pay in return. Rhys's texts—except for the sections centered in her maternally connoted homeland—are barren, forlorn, haunted, and severed, punctuated with silence and despair. They convey an eerie quality as though one read them during a solar eclipse or through tinted glass. There *is* of course, as I have suggested, a major eclipse in her work, the space vacated by the mother, a mad, spectral, distracted, or dying figure around whom constellate some of the most significant thematic and linguistic moments of Rhys's texts.

As we have seen, the diseased, delirious, or transplanted "real" mothers in Rhys are inscribed at the moment of their disappearance, imitating in narrative the process through which the mother is removed from language. Each of Rhys's five novels deals to some extent with the search for surrogates, and it is not surprising that these surrogates are divided into two major categories determined by

---

has been the mode applied by various critics who seem uncomfortable in the presence of Rhys's work and who (consequently) end up judging or dismissing her women. Peter Wolfe, for example, writes, "Single women who live alone do not always become prostitutes or drunkards. Anna might have supported herself honorably. Somebody with more fiber would not have slid so easily into her groove of sameness" (117).

their relationship to speech: "alienating" substitutes like Norah who stand in more for the father than the mother and "true" surrogates associated with an island heritage (Rhys's novels are all intensely autobiographical) and with, not coincidentally, another kind of language.[3]

Quartet, Rhys's first published novel (1928), is to large degree an exorcism of her relationship with Ford Madox Ford, who took her under his wing and into his bed in the midtwenties when she was first beginning to publish her work. The novel centers on Marya Zelli, a young woman befriended, seduced, and eventually cast off by an art dealer named Heidler. *Quartet* is the novel in which women—both Marya and Heidler's wife, Lois, who has been forced to condone the affair—are most clearly under stifling male control, a novel in which women are "for sleeping with—not for talking to" (*ALMM*, 172).[4] It is, not coincidentally, this novel in which maternal loss is least inscribed, mentioned only in one line of the novel, in which Marya reports, in a detached way, that her mother is dead. Where the male structure is most repressive, the mother is most repressed, for as we begin to see again and again, the absent mother is the cornerstone of the phallogocentric system.

There is a kind of substitute in *Quartet*, an aunt who appears, significantly, only in a letter. She is introduced in a strange twist of syntactic ambiguity: "The day before Marya left the Hôtel de l'Univers she received a money order for five pounds from her aunt and namesake enclosed in a letter" (*Q*, 57). We are to presume that the money was enclosed, but syntactically, the aunt is herself enclosed in the letter, the Letter, in Logos. Like so many of Rhys's false mothers, she is trapped in the male code and cannot respond to Marya except through its discourse. Money and text both serve here as substitutes, displacements of the mother, in a system in which woman is a symbol of exchange. The aunt tells Marya that it is difficult for her to

---

[3]Teresa O'Connor also discusses the "false" mothers in Rhys, including Hester, but she does not set them in a linguistic context; she juxtaposes them primarily to black surrogates, emphasizing the racial split and Rhys's ambivalence toward black women substitutes, with whom she identifies her mother (33).

[4]At the time of Ford's involvement with Rhys, he was living with a painter named Stella Bowen; her impressions of Rhys are available in her *Drawn from Life: Reminiscences*.

offer any advice, to respond in any way "since you write so seldom and say so little when you do write" (57–58). She implies that there will be no help for Marya until she accepts the terms of signification and ends the letter by asking about Marya's husband: "You don't mention him" (58). We can see Rhys's attempt to reverse the andro-centric structure, to make the male unspeakable, unmentionable, but as is true for most of Rhys's women, the project is futile, leaving her alienated from both men and the women who occupy or vacate space as directed.

In *Voyage in the Dark*, Rhys's preoccupation with mother sub-stitutes intensifies both thematically and linguistically. It is important to remember that this book, published six years after *Quartet*, was written before it but suppressed. The text that most actively absents the mother has pushed aside the text that engages her and reactivates the phallic/preoedipal struggle at the center of much of the conflict in women's writing.

The novel initially conjures the absent mother through a series of flashbacks to Anna Morgan's island childhood. The text opens with her memory of a loss, of leaving her homeland, a geographical locus evocative of the author's native Dominica and a psychological space frequently associated by Rhys (as Greece is by H.D.) with her mater-nal heritage, a sensuous medium of smells and rhythms and chants which works its way into both body and language.

It was as if a curtain had fallen, hiding everything I had ever known. It was almost like being born again. The colours were different, the smells different, the feeling things gave you right down inside yourself was different. . . . I didn't like England at first. I couldn't get used to the cold. Sometimes I would shut my eyes and pretend that the heat of the fire, or the bedclothes drawn up round me, was sun-heat; or I would pretend I was standing outside the house at home. . . . When there was a breeze the sea was millions of spangles; and on still days it was purple as Tyre and Sidon. Market Street smelt of the wind, but the narrow street smelt of niggers and wood-smoke and salt fishcakes fried in lard. . . . It was funny, but that was what I thought about more than anything else—the smell of the streets and the smells of frangipanni and lime juice and cinnamon and cloves, and sweets made of ginger and syrup, and incense after funerals or Corpus Christi processions . . . and the smell of the sea-breeze and the different smell of the land-breeze. [*VD*, 7–8]

Being "born again" in this context has no religious connotations; it
suggests rather the loss of origins and of the "original" mother
followed by a rebirth that transmutes the child/woman Anna into a
kind of changeling, stolen and bestowed upon a "false" mother, an
English stepmother named Hester Morgan. Hester lives rather un-
graciously in the islands until the death of Anna's father, at which
point she takes his daughter to England, enrolling her in school in an
attempt to "civilize" her. When the money to keep her there runs
out, however, Anna begins to make a life as a chorus girl touring the
provinces, and she effectively dissociates herself from the cold,
northern substitute for her Creole mother.

Despite her geographical and emotional distance, Hester becomes
a central nexus where Rhys works through some of the questions of
articulation, loss, and maternal absence. Hester's voice, more than
her physical presence, intrudes into the novel as a representative of a
repressive cultural and linguistic structure: "She had . . . an English
lady's voice with a sharp, cutting edge to it. Now that I've spoken
you can hear that I'm a lady. I have spoken and I suppose you now
realize that I'm an English gentlewoman. I have my doubts about
you. Speak up and I will place you at once. Speak up, for I fear the
worst. That sort of voice" (57). It is Hester's language that severs her
from any kind of relationship with Anna. She talks in "that voice as if
she were talking to herself" (70), and much like the men in the novel,
in whose systems she willingly participates, she negates Anna's
attempts to express what she thinks or feels. When Anna responds to
one of her stories with, "My goodness," Hester answers, "Don't say
my goodness. . . . My badness, that's what you ought to say" (69).
The way she censors Anna's language is very like the way she
censors Anna's mother; she cuts off contact with her surviving family
and talks of her elliptically as a vague, pernicious entity, refusing to
speak her name.

In contrast to Hester Morgan, Rhys offers another kind of mother
substitute in *Voyage in the Dark*, Francine, the black servant girl.
Francine, like the nurse Christophine in *Wide Sargasso Sea*, operates
in a matriarchal rather than a patriarchal sphere; Hester and Francine, then, juxtaposed, embody the split between the acceptable
place of woman in white male language and culture and the rather

lush, forbidden power of island women, a split that replicates the two conflicting faces of the missing Creole mother.

Anna identifies strongly with Francine, but she fears that Francine dislikes her because she is white. "I would never be able to explain to her that I hated being white," she says. "Being white and getting like Hester" (*VD*, 72). Francine's blackness is important because it immediately associates her in a visible, physical, primitive way with Anna's "real" mother who was rumored to have been colored. "I wanted to be black, I always wanted to be black," Anna says. "Being black is warm and gay, being white is cold and sad" (31). Whereas Hester is associated with whiteness, England, culture, and convention, the images surrounding Francine are sensual. Anna remembers Francine's nursing her back from fever, cooling her head, fanning her with a palm leaf, singing. Just as Antoinette in *Wide Sargasso Sea* longs for the smell of Christophine, Anna lies in bed remembering the acrid sweetness of Francine.

Throughout the text, Francine is specifically associated with the maternal body. Anna says, "The thing about Francine was that when I was with her I was happy," and then describes watching her eat mangoes: "Her teeth would bite into the mango and her lips fasten on either side of it, and while she sucked you saw that she was perfectly happy" (67–68). Here Rhys conjures a moment of preoedipal bliss, associating Francine with access to the mother's breast— sucking, perfect happiness, the "warm centre of the world." Anna also perceives in Francine a certain voraciousness and ferocity, "biting" and "fastening," which further distance her from Hester's austerity and propriety and release the complexity of instinctual drives associated with the mother and the semiotic.

Francine represents not just infantile pleasure but other functions of the maternal body; she tutors Anna when she is "unwell for the first time":

> It was she who explained to me, so that it seemed quite all right and I thought it was all in the day's work like eating or drinking. But then she went off and told Hester, and Hester came and jawed away at me, her eyes wandering all over the place. . . . I began to feel awfully miserable, as if everything were shutting up around me and I couldn't breathe. I wanted to die. [68]

When Francine explains menstruation, it is "all right," natural; as the representative of the "true," primitive mother, she validates Anna's body. Hester, on the other hand, the false mother, suffocates Anna, turning her body into something connected in the daughter's mind not with life but with death, just as her language works through euphemisms that, by definition, substitute what is acceptable for what is taboo.

Just as Hester infects Anna's perception of herself and her body, she in turn feels infected by Anna's island. She can't "bear the scent" of the big flowers that grow where Anna's mother has her roots; they make her feel faint, lose boundaries, lose control. Similarly, she hates Francine, seeing her relationship with Anna as "dangerous." Hester focuses in particular on her corruption of Anna's language.

> I tried to teach you to talk like a lady and behave like a lady and not like a nigger and of course I couldn't do it. Impossible to get you away from the servants. That awful sing-song voice you had! Exactly like a nigger you talked—and still do. Exactly like that dreadful girl Francine. When you were jabbering away together in the pantry I never could tell which of you was speaking. [65]

Francine's jabbering recalls the mumblings of the maternal death-bed in *After Leaving Mr. Mackenzie* and the language of lying-in in the birthing scene in *Good Morning, Midnight*. Much of Rhys's work is punctuated with similar moments when women's language breaks down into snorting, song, ellipsis, and patois—all intimately connected with the maternal sphere, a dissonance in language, linguistic obeah, totally frightening and incomprehensible to the inheritors and perpetuators of the symbolic.

It is interesting to consider why these qualities of "nigger-talk" threaten Hester. First, this rhythmic, intonational, "sing-song" language does not repeat a superstructure of form and absence but solicits presence, bodily functions. It pulsates, contracts, beats, throbs, pumps, explodes in a kind of *jouissance* that gives Hester "the creeps" (83). It is both sexually and maternally connoted, and this conflation, as evidenced in Hester's inability to explain menstruation, is foreign to her language. Second, it is jabbering, or "rapid, indistinct, or nonsensical talk; gibberish." As such, it is an assault upon the priv-

ileging of the signifier in androcentric discourse, a threatening rep-
lica within language of linguistic, cultural, and psychological subversion. Third, Francine's patois decenters the speaking (female) "I"—
"I could never tell which of you was speaking"—implying a subject
like Kristeva's "subject-in-process," who no longer directs and com-
mands in a constituted unity but rather relinquishes the desire to
control for another desire, access to the mother. Francine's language,
then, becomes a maternally connoted site of pleasure, a kind of
luxurious, sensuous medium into which the subject is glad to release
itself. It threatens Hester because it invites a contact with the body, a
loss of control, and a release from unified meaning. Its importance
for Anna is that it allows her access to a primordial expression that
imitates and echoes the maternal body and voice.

One last quality of Francine's language, equally significant, escapes Hester's notice. Anna says, "When she wasn't working Francine would sit on the doorstep and I liked sitting there with her.
Sometimes she told me stories, and at the start of the story she had to
say 'Timm, timm,' and I had to answer 'Bois sèche' " (71).[5] Francine is
not, then, just a gibbering servant girl vaguely connected to the
rhythms of the maternal body; as Scharfman has noted about the
nurse in *Wide Sargasso Sea*, she is also "the figure for song, storytelling, and sorcery" (101). Like the semiotic, Francine's rhythmic jabbering operates both within the framework of narrative and text and
beyond it in a ritualistic realm; her stories are invoked, quite literally,
called into being with mysterious syllables and island patois. What
Francine offers, then, is not a radical reinvention of language but the
insertion into the system of another register, a space of "indetermi-
nate articulation," replete with sound, voice, and music, a *chora*, an
incantation that reaches back toward the lost mother. Through Francine, Rhys suggests that there are ways of soliciting maternal presence even in the face of maternal loss. Rather than accept a series of
false mothers who repress both emotional bonding and the speaking
self, the daughters in Rhys's work begin to find access to avatars of
the mother who are associated with the body and with an augmented
language as well, "mothers" who empower the writing daughter,

[5]Rhys reports that she later discovered "Bois sèche" to be the name of an obeah god
(*SP*, 31).

ironically, through the subversion of the very structure out of which the daughter must write.

This movement reflects Rhys's search for not only a physical but a textualized mother, a mother encoded both structurally and syntactically. The shape of *Voyage in the Dark*, which operates around a dead mother, a "false" surrogate, a "true" surrogate, and a maternalized subtext, reflects Rhys's linguistic dependence on this maternal inscription.

Up to a certain point in the novel, all the passages dealing with the maternal heritage of Anna Morgan's island begin with contrived transitions such as "I thought about home," "I tried to remember," "like that time at home." The syntax of almost all these sections is regular, effectively identical to that of the rest of the book except for occasional ellipsis or italics. When Anna describes her entry into England at the beginning of the novel, "A curtain fell and then I was here," she also accurately identifies the strategy of presentation of the islands, which appear like scenes in a play, controlled, kept within a neat proscenium.

Similarly, language does not initially serve to translate the primal element, although Anna attempts in early parts of *Voyage in the Dark* to explain about the islands. When one her lovers, Walter Jeffries, takes her on an excursion to Savernake Forest, he dares her to compare her island with the beech trees and the little English flowers:

> Walter said, "Have you got flowers like these in your island? These little bright things are rather sweet, don't you think?"
> I said, "Not quite like these." But when I began to talk about the flowers out there I got that feeling of . . . two things that I couldn't fit together, and it was as if I were making up the names. Stephanotis, hibiscus, yellow-bell, jasmine, frangipanni, corolita. . . .
> "I like it here," I said, "I didn't know England could be so beautiful."
> But something had happened to it. It was as if the wildness had gone out of it. [77–78]

The sensuousness of Anna's island, the flowers that make one faint, are transformed in England to little things that are "rather sweet." Like translated flowers, transplanted women are reduced from their sensuality and lushness, taught to conform to the geographical and cultural climate, where they die "sickening for the sun" (*ALMM*,

105). More important for my discussion here is that attempting to participate in the father's (or lover's) system affects Anna's language. Her attempt to describe the maternal sphere in male terms disorients her, strips her memories and language of "wildness," and dissociates signifiers from what they signified. The two things she can't "fit together" are in fact the semiotic and the symbolic, the smell and rhythm of the island and Walter Jeffries's language.

There is, however, a moment in the text after which the language begins to change. Walter Jeffries breaks off with Anna, and she begs him to meet her one last time; during their conversation in a hotel restaurant she imagines herself saying, very calmly, "The thing is that you don't understand. You think I want more than I do. I only want to see you sometimes, but if I never see you again I'll die. I'm dying now really, and I'm too young to die" (97). Following this scene, in which Anna can only "imagine" what to say, the text opens into a memory of her mother's death: "The candles crying wax tears and the smell of the stephanotis and I had to go to the funeral in a white dress and white gloves and a wreath round my head and the wreath in my hands made my gloves wet—they said so young to die" (97). Here Rhys both associates Anna with her mother—"too [so] young to die"—and underlines the mother's vacancy, inscribing her as an elliptical absence. The mother's death, then, becomes a kind of trope for textlessness (as opposed to the male system in which the dead mother is a trope for text), reflected in both her daughter's and her own inability to operate or appear within language.

Anna's memory of this death introduces a disturbance in the text which begins to break syntactical norms. From this pivotal moment on, the island passages begin to wash in and out of the text like tides—fever, patois, menstruation, virgin forests, scent, sea-breeze, sounds, dreamlike images of carnival and masquerade, obeah, zombies, *soucriants*. A disembodied voice begins to punctuate the text, opening into long sections of a highly charged hallucinatory past. Syntax separates. Dashes, ellipses, fragments, and participles begin to dominate.

Morne Anglais Morne Collé Anglais Morne Trois Pitons Morne Rest—
. . . and Morne Diablotin its top always covered . . . its top always veiled

and Anne Chewett used to say that it's haunted and obeah . . . (obeah-women who dig up dead people and cut their fingers off . . .—it's hands that are obeah). . . .

Obeah zombis soucriants—lying in the dark frightened of the dark frightened of soucriants that fly in through the window and suck your blood—they fan you to sleep with their wings and then they suck your blood—you know them in the day-time—they look like people but their eyes are red and staring and they're soucriants at night—looking in the glass and thinking sometimes my eyes look like a soucriant's eyes . . . [163]

These textual ruptures—confusion of tense, blurring of the bound-aries of subject, loss of punctuation, predication, chronology—occur simultaneously with the memory of the mother's loss but also with the appearance of obeah women who "dig up dead people," dig up, I suggest, the mother. This textual subversion also coincides with a second pivotal moment, when Anna first suspects that she is preg-nant. Her nausea permeates the novel, "everything heaving up and down" (162) in a swirl and rhythm that the text itself begins to imitate. Anna's refrain as she counts back days and dates becomes a kind of chant: "It can't be that, it can't be that. . . . Pull yourself together; it can't be that" (162).

The rhythm of her "illness," the heaving bed, imprints itself even in her dreams, where she imagines herself on a ship with an expand-ing deck, a ship from which "somebody had fallen overboard" (164). Besides reflecting Anna's pregnancy and prefiguring her abortion in part 4, Rhys encodes here her contemplation of suicide, her fear that the child will be deformed, and her anticipation of society's disap-probation in images of someone drowned, a sailor carrying a child's coffin, and a dwarf wearing a priest's robes, whose ring she must kiss (165). The conflation here of death, deformity, a certain sexuality, "an island, which was home except that the trees were all wrong" (164) ends with Anna trying to get ashore: "I took huge, climbing, flying strides among confused figures. I was powerless and very tired, but I had to go on. And the dream rose into a climax of mean-inglessness, fatigue and powerlessness, and the deck was heaving up and down, and when I woke up everything was still heaving up and down" (165).

The hallucination and syntactical rupture reach their climax during the actual abortion and the delirium brought on by its complications. As Anna lies in bed, hemorrhaging, the text turns to italics, unpunctuated except for dashes, and the dream begins to come "true" for her as she passes back across the cold sea to her childhood during the three days of Masquerade. Much of part 4 becomes ambiguous, flooded with phrases that appear to exist both in hallucination and in the "reality" of Anna's room. Anna's giddiness, for example, emerges out of her pain and loss of blood and simultaneously out of her "dancing" through the streets of the carnival, translated here into a register of prelinguistic images and sensations: masks, musicians, color, dancing, children beating tins, a "triangle-man," his foot tapping, a horse who sways and lilts in motion like a rocking horse, whirling, concertina music, the smell of a woman cooking fishcakes, the smell of a black man's sweat. The boundaries of language begin to break down, a disorder that is reflected in the structure of the text.

> I'm awfully giddy—but we went on dancing forwards and backwards backwards and forwards whirling round and round
> The concertina-man was very black—he sat sweating and the concertina went forwards and backwards backwards and forwards one two three one two three pourquoi ne pas aimer bonheur supreme—the triangle-man kept time on his triangle and with his foot tapping and the little man who played the chak-chak smiled with his eyes fixed [186]

At the moments of most intimate confrontation with the maternal form—the mother's death, the daughter's abortion—the text almost abandons the surrounding thetic structure. As the novel progresses in the "present," syntax and chronology are increasingly ruptured by the maternal subtext, mother as both memory and rhythm breaking through the surface of English life and language.

Ultimately, however, all maternal contact within the novel is denied or deformed. The women who parade through the streets, including Anna's old nurse, wear "close-meshed wire covering the whole face and tied at the back of the head" (185); they are silenced, able only to stick out their tongues through little slits in their masks. It is the triangle man (Lacan's "third element," the father, which breaks the mother-child dyad) who provides the structure in the surrounding chora, the triangle man who keeps time.

In similar fashion, Rhys was herself silenced, forced by her publishers to mask the text and change the original ending in which Anna died. The original version ends with the sentence "And the concertina-music stopped and it was so still, so still and lovely quiet very quiet like just before you go to sleep and it stopped and there was the ray of light along the floor like the last thrust of remembering before everything is blotted out and blackness comes . . . "[6] In the revision, the cynical doctor who comes to Anna's room and remarks sarcastically that she'll be "ready to start all over again in no time, I've no doubt," (187) "saves" her, "allowing" her the final, uncharacteristic reverie: "The ray of light came in again under the door like the last thrust of remembering before everything is blotted out. I lay and watched it and thought about starting all over again. And about being new and fresh. And about mornings, and misty days, when anything might happen. And about starting all over again, all over again. . . . (187–88).

The most interesting aspect of the new ending—besides the fact that it sounds nothing like Jean Rhys—is the totality of the revision; when Rhys fills in the ellipsis and disallows the "blackness" (associated, through Francine, with what she wants and wants to be), she also restructures the entire fourth section; there is no textual necessity for this, but there is, apparently, a psychological one. It is what happens to the whole when a single event is censored that becomes important, and it is the omissions that become far more significant than the new material, which serves as a screen to the subtext.

In *The Interpretation of Dreams* Freud writes, "If the first account given to me by a patient of a dream is too hard to follow I ask him to repeat it. In doing so he rarely uses the same words. But the parts of the dream which he describes in different terms are by that fact revealed to me as the weak spot in the dream's disguise. . . . In this way he draws my attention to the expression which he has dropped out" (553–54). Freud's observation that "that is the point at which the

[6]Jean Rhys, original ending to *Voyage in the Dark*, TS, Department of Rare Books and Special Collections, McFarlin Library, University of Tulsa, 20. I am grateful to Caroline Seydell Swinson, former Curator of Manuscripts, Department of Rare Books and Special Collections at McFarlin Library and to Francis Wyndham and the estate of Jean Rhys for access to Rhys's unpublished manuscripts and permission to publish passages from the original version of *Voyage in the Dark*.

interpretation of the dream can be started" is useful in thinking about what has happened to *Voyage in the Dark* during the "retelling," for in changing the ending, Rhys also "dropped out" five pages of the original manuscript. The first draft of part 4 begins not in the English boardinghouse but in the islands, where the child Anna is having her picture taken: "SMILE PLEASE THE MAN SAID not quite so serious" (*VD*, TS, 1). The photographer, however, is not quite successful in seducing the child into compliance. He turns to the mother for aid: "You tell her to madam" (*VD*, TS, 1). Anna tries to smile as her mother bids, but she is unable to please either her or the photographer:

> Now keep quite still Mother said
> I tried but my hand shot up of its own accord
> Oh what a pity she moved   now it'll have to be done all over again
> I began to cry
> Now now now the man said
> A big girl like you I'm ashamed of you Mother said   just one second
> and you are ten years older. Meta was fanning her with a palm leaf fan to keep the flies away and she was too young to die Meta said with tears running down her face but I was only thinking of my new white dress and the wreath I would carry. [*VD*, TS, 1–3]

The significance of this passage we know not only from Freud's suggestion but from the fact that this scene, slightly revised, turns up some forty years after its initial deletion as the opening page in Rhys's autobiography. It is clear, then, that there is something about this suppressed memory so important that Rhys returns to it both to open and to name (*Smile Please*) the story of her life.

In this passage we see, first, the loss that surfaces throughout Rhys's canon, not only the mother's death but her failure and the ways in which the child takes that failure upon herself. Despite the mother's distance and austerity, her unsympathetic demands, it is the act of incurring her anger, failing *her*, that leads textually—and psychologically—to her absence; the child displeases her and in "just one second" the figure of the mother becomes a corpse being fanned for flies, a corpse whom the child can no longer mourn.

Immediately following this scene of the mother's death, Rhys continues without transition but as if there were some connection:

The song went
>   Ma belle ka di maman li
>   Petit ké vini gros

I can play that tune on the piano
She can   she picks out all the nigger tunes by herself
But this one's very melancholy Hester said and the words don't seem to
me to make any sense
I said it means My beautiful girl is singing to her mother . . . [VD, TS, 3]

What occurs in this typographical and psychological space between
the corpse and the song? It is the space in Rhys, the censored space,
in which the mother fails the daughter, in which Rhys turns from the
mother to the maternal, in which the body is transmuted from flesh
to voice, in which the mother's absence is finally inscribed. Just as the
child cannot keep still, her body shooting off of its own accord,
refusing to be framed, Rhys releases the mother from form into
rhythm, a process that is played out in the language, the interplay of
language, in the text.

Rhys's work is censored to avoid the death of the daughter, but
what results is the concurrent censoring of the mother. When wom-
en give *in* to androcentric language, they also give *up,* and what they
give up to fit *in* is access to the mother, for as we have seen, the
system of representation is structured on loss; since it is a system of
oedipal, castrating repression, what is lost is, by definition, the maternal body. Thus when the doctor, a kind of patriarchal deus ex
machina, comes at the end to "save" Anna, he is destined to fail just
as the man who tries to photograph her must fail, for in Rhys's world
men do not save or represent women. They imprison them in catechism, in pregnancy, and in the attics of ancestral mansions. The irony
of *Voyage in the Dark* is that Rhys was ultimately kept from the textual
voyage she set out on, denied the darkness of her vision. Having
developed in her work the dead mother as a trope for textlessness, a
way of registering the loss in narrative, she is ultimately refused her
(dark) matrilineage in which the daughter would replay the mother's
death in her own.[7] Rhys always regretted changing the ending,

[7]Scharfman discusses *Wide Sargasso Sea* in terms of Antoinette's need to reproduce
both her mother's madness and her death in her own, set in "the dysfunctioning of a
system which inhibits Rhys' heroine from distinguishing whether she is telling her
own story or her mother's" (88).

referring to it at various points in her correspondence for at least thirty years afterward. She was initially paralyzed by the request to alter her work. "I minded more than I would have believed possible. . . . I really began to feel as if I were crazy or wrong headed or something," she writes, acknowledging that she doesn't know what to do: "I suppose I shall have to give in and cut the book and I'm afraid it will make it meaningless. The worst is that it is precisely the last part which I am most certain of that will have to be mutilated" (*Letters*, 25).

Critical evaluation of Rhys is often clouded by a refusal to accept her psychological and moral terrain. When the death in these novels is stripped of the sense of victimization and read instead as narrative strategy, it becomes clear that Rhys is in control of these texts in a way that the women in the novels are not in control of their lives.[8] Ironically, the male literary establishment's insistence upon Anna's affirmation at the end of the novel is a way not of saving her but of killing her textually. Rhys's encoding of Anna's death would have been a more significant way of talking about her position as daughter, mother, and speaking subject than is giving her the voice to repeat the doctor's prescription for her life. *Voyage in the Dark* remains, finally, a masquerade of loss which registers a woman's inability either to locate the sustaining interval of maternal contact or to find a place within the sexual, cultural, and linguistic code of the Father.

[8]Judith Kegan Gardiner has made a similar observation in "On Female Identity and Writing by Women": "Jean Rhys' heroes . . . repel many readers by their passivity," she writes, yet we readers are "reassured because we know that the author is herself a survivor, in control of her prose and of her heroes' destinies as none of them are" (358). Elizabeth Abel has also taken up this issue from a different perspective in "Women and Schizophrenia," asking, "Does Rhys's unremitting pessimism become an artistic failure that drives us to dismiss her vision despite her insight and control?" (156).

5

Words That Are Not Words

In *Good Morning, Midnight* (1939), Jean Rhys positions near the beginning of the novel a dream I would like to juxtapose to Midget's fantasy of matricide in H.D.'s "Paint It To-Day."

I am in the passage of a tube station in London. . . . Everywhere there are placards printed in red letters: This Way to the Exhibition, This Way to the Exhibition. But I don't want the way to the exhibition—I want the way out. There are passages to the right and passages to the left, but no exit sign. . . . I touch the shoulder of the man walking in front of me. I say: "I want the way out." But he points to the placards and his hand is made of steel. . . .

Now a little man, bearded, with a snub nose, dressed in a long white night-shirt, is talking earnestly to me. "I am your father," he says. "Remember that I am your father." But blood is streaming from a wound in his forehead. "Murder," he shouts, "murder, murder." Helplessly I watch the blood streaming. At last my voice tears itself loose from my chest. I too shout: "Murder, murder, help, help," and the sound fills the room. I wake up and a man in the street outside is singing the waltz from *Les Saltimbanques*. [13]

This scene once again takes up a central motif—the relationship of father, daughter, and language. Elsewhere, we remember, Sasha Jansen runs through passageways looking for the "kise" and finds herself surrounded by signs that confuse and entrap her. She looks for the way out, but there is no sign for exit, no sign that does not point to the "exhibition." To the dreamer there is no sign for escape but for the reader there is: the murdered father. This is perhaps, then, Iphigenia's dream, the sacrifice revised: she is not dragged to the "exhibition" by men of steel but instead watches *their* blood pour. Unable to escape through a sign, she escapes through their wounds. And when Sasha wakes up, what she hears is a kind of pierced discourse, a different exhibition, the dead father translated into a man singing in her mother's native tongue.[1]

One of the ways this novel sustains this transformed language is through a variant of return to the maternal body—the childbed—and through the relationship of this liminal scene to the writing daughter's identity and language; woman, specifically, defines herself in part through what Kristeva has called "the strange form of split symbolization (threshold of language and instinctual drive, of the 'symbolic' and the 'semiotic') of which the act of giving birth consists" (*DL*, 240).

Good Morning, Midnight is structured as a tidal wash between Sasha's current life in Paris and the time she lived in London, married to a man called Enno. Rhys uses not "flashbacks" precisely but rising waves or whitecaps of memory that periodically break through the discourse. When she writes "the sound of the sea advances and retreats as if a door were being opened and shut" (93), she effectively describes the movement of the novel.

The memory focus of the novel is Sasha's pregnancy and the birth of her child. There is nothing thematically idealized or mythologized about this maternity: Sasha and Enno are poor; he periodically abandons her; her labor is difficult; her milk dries up; and the child soon dies, "lying so cold and still with a ticket round his wrist" (139). (Like H.D., Rhys lost her first child; she gave birth in 1919 to a son, William Owen, who died three weeks later). It is not, then, as I stated earlier, motherhood *per se* that interests me here but the "nature-culture" threshold where the mother-child dyad is created, for that moment, regardless of subsequent events, provides a trope in women's writ-

[1]Teresa O'Connor notes, "In much, perhaps all of Rhys's fiction, the introduction of . . . musical melodies or lyrics is a trigger to experiencing (often unexpected) feeling and internal revelation" (44), but O'Connor does not pursue this suggestive line of thought. There is some rich work to be done on music in Rhys, both textually and biographically. As we have seen in *Voyage in the Dark*, rhythms, chants, lyrics, and song fragments are important both thematically and syntactically and continue so throughout Rhys's work; some of this influence is the result of her island heritage and some undoubtedly emerges from the early years she spent touring the English provinces as a chorus girl.

ing which offers them a space they do not have in other scenes of language.

Margaret Homans writes brilliantly of the mother-infant relationship to language in *Bearing the Word*, beginning with the thesis that the female is identified with nature and the literal while the male is identified with the figurative, which (to the male) is more highly valued (5). The child, in Freudian terms, is a figure, a figure for the phallus. But as Homans reads Chodorow, she sees that "Chodorow's revision would remove the baby from the register of the figurative altogether. That baby is not . . . a replacement for the lost phallus and . . . the baby is not phallic, that is, not a symbol dependent on it" (26). The baby, when taken out of a Freudian or Lacanian framework that insists on lack and castration anxiety, embodies presence, not absence. "It would be impossible," Homans writes, "for the daughter to find the lost relation to the mother in any figure for it, since the preoedipal bond to the mother preceded the entry of the daughter into the world of figures, the symbolic, and thus the preoedipal bond could not be reimagined in symbolic terms. Quite possibly, a new child is just such a nonsymbolic figure" (25). In Rhys and H.D., however, the child often dies, and thus it is not the "literal" baby that becomes important but the language associated with it, a language not of the father but of process, of birth.

In *Good Morning, Midnight* Sasha gives birth in a house run by a *sage femme* in the Boulevard Magenta. All around women are having babies, calling out, "Mother, Mother," a call that echoes in various transmutations throughout Rhys's work and confirms Chodorow's theory that motherhood, in a sense, reproduces daughterhood through the reactivation of the preoedipal bond. Sasha describes the midwife:

> She comes and wipes my forehead. She speaks to me in a language that is no language. But I understand it.
> Back, back, back. . . . This has happened many times. . . .
> She darts from one room to another, encouraging, soothing, reproaching. "Now, you're not trying. Courage, courage." Speaking her old, old language of words that are not words. [58]

Rhys makes explicit connection between maternity and a kind of language that is not language, not the symbolic but rhythm, intonation, gesture, the sound of words detached from signification, words not words, old, old, back, back, thrusting into some primordial space; but it is this "language," as opposed to any other, that Sasha, *as* the maternal body, finally "understands." It is not the disoriented, hallucinatory wash of images of *Voyage in the Dark* but a *language*, reflecting Rhys's movement toward the interplay Kristeva emphasizes between oedipal and preoedipal spheres. Later in the novel, Sasha thinks back on the birth: "The sage femme has very white hands and clear, slanting eyes and when she looks at you the world stops rocking about. The clouds are clouds, trees are trees, people are people, and that's that. Don't mix them up again. No, I won't" (139). This is a striking passage, reminiscent of a letter Homans quotes from Elizabeth Gaskell, written as she sits outside watching her first baby, then about twenty months old. Homans comments on the pleasure Gaskell takes in the "literal generally, that is, in the immediacy of the mother's and especially of Baby's contact with flowers and animals" (*BW*, 34). It is a state of being and of language in which "the literal always takes precedence as a tangible good, on the basis of Baby's criteria of excellence" (35). Although Sasha has no baby to watch in the garden, the experience of birth itself has provided her with the same sense of primacy related to the language she finally understands: clouds are clouds, trees are trees, people are people. Even, perhaps, the mother is the mother in a system—old, old, language— in which the referent does not have to be absent to be represented, in which language is contingent on presence (as well as) loss.

Both Rhys and H.D. are extremely important in the understanding of what maternity, even aborted maternity, might mean to women's language and writing because they deal with the *inside* of both body and text, unlike the women described by Carol H. Poston in "Childbirth in Literature," who write birth scenes

seen from the outside, from the viewpoint of the attendants; those watching birth see a profusion of blood . . . and they hear screams that sound maniacal because they are not themselves involved in the birthing. . . . [S]ome women have adopted this outside perspective . . . this posture of watching, rather than giving, birth; and perhaps they have chosen the language they have because the genital area is a "secret" place, a place of darkness, uncertainty, sometimes of physical loathing and dread. They . . . are willing—even eager—to take another's word for it, and the "word" has been male. [23]

This "outside perspective" runs throughout *Good Morning, Midnight* as well, as the door opens and closes, only it is associated not with childbirth but with everything that surrounds it. The streets, rooms, and cafés of the everyday world are, for Rhys, dark, uncertain places, and the encounters are events full of dread, male words, and maniacal sounds. The novel is surely Rhys's most schizophrenic, associating Sasha's "understandable" language with madness as the "literalness" of her language punctures the figurative structure.

The novel is a disorienting book to read, a rather plotless masquerade, a whirl of masks and funhouse mirror reflections; it is grotesque, surreal, full of images and sensations just slightly off, so slightly as to be more terrifying than if they were totally fantastic. The first chapter, in fact, opens with a hotel room talking to Sasha. " 'Quite like old times,' the room says. 'Yes? No?' " (9). The streets are "powerful, magical"; one of them "walks in" to the *tabac* where Sasha sits drinking. " 'Oh, there you are,' it says, . . . 'there you are. Where have you been all this long time?' Nobody else knows me, but the street knows me" (107). The novel is full of scenes of waddling, pig-eyed waiters who make no sound when they speak, of bald old women trying on hats, of shop windows full of artificial limbs, all of which give *Good Morning, Midnight* its strange, severed quality.

Sections of broken syntax are not isolated as dream or hallucination but wash into the fabric of the text.

> They explain people . . . by saying that their minds are in water-tight compartments, but it never seemed so to me. It's all washing about, like the bilge in the hold of a ship, all washing around in the same hold. . . . Fairies, red roses, the sense of property—Of course they don't feel things like we do—Lilies in the moonlight—I believe in survival after death. I've had personal proof of it. And we'll find our dear, familiar bodies on the other side—Samuel has forgotten to buy his suppositoires—Pity would be out of place in this instance—I never take people like that to expensive restaurants. . . . Nevertheless, all the little birdies sing. . . . English judges never make a mistake—The piano is quite Egyptian in feeling . . . [168]

Elizabeth Abel suggests that "the basic style of the novel is paratactic: the short declarative sentences have few connective words to suggest relationships among the parts" (164). Just as Sasha is cut off from relationships, so too is the internal structure of her language. But more important in relation to what Homans has suggested about literal language is that "throughout *Good Morning, Midnight* phrases acquire an independent existence and recur in Sasha's mental world as autonomous entities which shape her thoughts as much as they are shaped by them" (Abel, 166). "At times," writes Abel, Rhys "constructs a verbal world of sounds detached from references" (164). While "not as disorganized as the 'word-salad' created by the schizophrenic's combination of words according to their personal associations, the tendency of her thoughts to develop through sounds as well as meanings recalls the 'klang association' . . . that is often noted in schizophrenic speech" (165). Abel gives examples of this linguistic word play in Rhys's text.

> Sasha's response to the word "sadness," for example, is a chain of associations evoked by the sound of the word in French: "Tristesse, what a nice word! Tristesse, lointaine, langsam, forlorn, forlorn . . . " (47). More dramatically, Sasha's response to being told that Mr. Blank wants to speak to her is a panicked flight of verbal play in various languages: "I at once make up my mind that he wants to find out if I can speak German. All the little German I know flies out of my head . . . Ja, ja, nein, nein, was kostet es, Wien ist eine sehr schone Stadt, Buda-Pest auch ist sehr schon, ist schon, mein Herr, ich habe meinen Blumen vergessen, aus meinen grossen Schmerzen, homo homini lupus, aus meinen grossen Schmerzen mach ich die kleinen Lieder, homo homini lupus (I've got that one, anyway), aus meinen grossen Schmerzen homo homini do re mi fah soh la ti doh . . . " [165]

This is more than verbal "play," however; the space in which Sasha loses context is the space of an important and recurrent subtext. Just as Jane Eyre "accordingly" sits and says nothing when Rochester bids her speak, Sasha forgets language when interrogated. But just as Jane's silence is a full one, textually, so is Sasha's. Her "response" is *not* a "chain of associations"; her linguistic descent is neither random nor without referent. She frames her nonsense within the polarized economy of Mr. Blank—"Yes, yes, no, no, what does it cost?" She then reproduces the geographical polarity of all of Rhys's novels, European capitals contrasted, elliptically, with her native land in a passage reminiscent of the scene in *Voyage in the Dark* where Anna Morgan tries unsuccessfully to recall the names of her island flowers. "I have forgotten my flowers," Sasha says, like Anna because of an intense "Schmerzen"—ache, grief. Then, out of this sorrow and loss appears a little song, associated through the layered meanings of *kleinen* with children—childhood songs—just as in the original version of *Voyage in the Dark* the pain of the mother's death is followed by "Ma belle ka di maman li / Petit ké vini gros," which means, we remember, "My beautiful girl is singing to her mother." Sasha's "flight," then, passing back through the male frame of Latin—Rome, the church, Romulus and Remus, in "homo homini lupus" (man is a wolf to man)—"disintegrates" into notes and scales, textually reenacting the "itinerary" of the semiotic, the return from discourse to song.

Before returning to the relationship between this language and madness which Abel posits, I would like to offer an almost identical scene from *HERmione*, a conversation between Hermione and a friend: " 'But *you* with that lovely place in the country—' 'Yes, *you* with that lovely place in the country—' '—can't feel the heat—' '—as we do.' Everything people say rhymes in *rhythms*, you do, do—you do re mi fa so la si do" (59).

Although Sasha's speech is clearly more schizophrenic than Hermione's in its derangement of syntax, loss of signification, and reliance on parataxis and "the concrete nature of words themselves" (Abel, 165), these are also features of the semiotic: a cadence and musicality of rhymes and rhythms. Kristeva writes in *Desire in Language* that psychotic and infantile language are connected by their nonreferentiality. The infant, however, unlike the psychotic, does not panic "at the loss of all reference" (139), existing as she does in a state anterior to the perception of loss. In psychosis "symbolic legality is wiped out in favor of arbitrariness of an instinctual drive without meaning and communication" (139). Sasha *does* panic, as in her encounter with Mr. Blank, but it is important that the very same language is for her a space of peace and understanding when it is associated with the mother's body instead of the need to know more languages. The schizophrenic "word play" that Abel describes, when read as Kristeva's *interplay* between semiotic and symbolic, is not a threatening void but a space of tides and rhythms and biological hieroglyphs that transform psychosis into primal song. The reason Sasha's discourse, though unstable, is not schizophrenic, the reason her last words can be a kind of Molly Bloomian affirmation of encounter—"Yes—yes—yes" (190)—even if the encounter is disturb-ing, is that she has not lost all reference; her language operates within the paradigm of the midwife and the mother's body.

In H.D. there are a number of birthing scenes that work through an evolution of relationship between the maternal body and language. In *HERmione*, for example, where H.D.'s ambivalence is raw, there is a meal that contrasts with the dinner table scene discussed in Chap-ter 1. Hermione and Eugenia, alone in the morning room, linger over breakfast. Outside, "heavy tropic waters" pour down the window: "Thunder reverberated across wet lawns . . . like some beast growl-ing under deep-sea water" (87). What begins as an actual meteoro-logical event is transformed into a corresponding internal state; Her-mione feels inundated. Then "tropic water receded ever so slightly, they were as it were lifted up from underwater to a high layer of water. They were still deep underwater but breath came more natu-rally, not gasp on self-conscious gasp" (87). The "odd shut-in feel-ing" of the text opens here into a strange zone; Eugenia and Her-mione rise from the depths of drowning, displaced to a space where they can breathe underwater and where Hermione (who borders on anorexia throughout the novel) can finally, for unexplained reasons, eat.

H.D. has moved here from the outskirts of Philadelphia on a summer afternoon to an ambiguously tropical or classical terrain where Carl Gart, dripping wet, is "like Proteus," with "little Pericles white goat beard" (91), where the maid looks "like Etruscan bronze dredged from the mid-Ionian" (88), and where Eugenia, no longer the "dark" mother, is associated with Demeter. We are in islands here, Hellas or Leuké, where H.D. opens the sea wall to the under-pinnings of her myth and language.

In this space, Hermione and Eugenia pass through a sea of pro-foundly amniotic images, a space of mother-daughter intimacy, nourishment, a space "past consciousness," simultaneously present in and released from time. "*Unless you are born of water . . . unless you are born of water. . . .* they were born of water, re-incarnated, all their past million-of-years-ago quarrel forgotten in the firelight" (89). Born again, born of water, baptized, immersed in maternal fluid yet *rein-carnated*, flesh and blood, blood and water, water and fire, enclosed in translucence, water, membrane, sac, "little live flame [in] the midst of water" (89), spark of life in utero, in text.

The text quickens; both Hermione and Eugenia "forget" themselves as Eugenia plunges into a narrative of Hermione's birth:

> "Your father was *afraid* (the flood the year before had cracked Bolton's bridge) that the doctor wouldn't help us." Eugenia was speaking from somewhere outside herself. . . . Eugenia had forgotten Hermione. "It was such a funny *time* to have a baby. I don't know why but it seemed a funny *time* to have a baby. It seems odd having a baby (I don't know why) by daylight. It seemed such a funny *time* to have a baby."
> "It was all over in a few hours . . . it was so funny. It was all over in a few hours. It was so odd. I had you in the morning." [89]

Eugenia slips here into an uncharacteristic cadenced speech, labor and childbirth serving as an entry into a different kind of language, marked less by sense than by rhythm, in which words are the fins of sea fish seen through tide wave, recognizable in form and shape but distanced, buffeted, kaleidoscopic, characterized not by meaning but by movement. To read aloud the last seven or eight lines of the passage is to hear clearly the pulsation of a register to language which exists concurrent with but independent of signification.

H.D. uses almost identical phrases to evoke both the birth and the surrounding storm that conjures it in Eugenia's memory: "It was so odd. I had you in the morning"; "I never remember such a storm at this time. I mean it's so uncanny happening at this time of the morning" (89). The suggestion is twofold: that birth is a kind of storm that lashes the window of language with "hectic vermillion leaf-flash" (89) and that the storm surrounding the birth narrative is itself a kind of birth, one that allows Hermione an affirmation of maternal power she could not recognize before: "Words of Eugenia had more power than textbooks, than geometry, than all of Carl Gart and brilliant 'Bertie Gart' as people called him. Bertrand wasn't brilliant, not like mama. Carl Gart wasn't brilliant like Eugenia" (89). Suddenly the mother, flung with Hermione into the heavy sweep of waves and prebirth, emerges out of the tropical, mythical terrain more brilliant than Carl and Bert, her words, for the first time (contrast the dinner table scene) full of power. Like the Hermione who aims to "disprove science and biological-mathematical definition" (76), Eugenia can now, in a new kind of maternally connoted brilliance, supersede text/books. This epiphany is interrupted (or sustained) by Eugenia's voice, continuing the story:

"Then the doctor came. But she was such a dear nurse, so much better than the doctor, she was *like a mother* to me. . . . "

Demeter (such a dear nurse) lifting the tired shoulders of a young Eugenia had driven the wind back, back. . . . the house was sitting on its haunches. The house took a deep breath settled down, decided to settle down for another re-incarnation. It was Eugenia who had saved it. [89–90, my emphasis]

H.D. conflates two kinds of contact here: as Hermione journeys back toward Eugenia, she offers her, as Rhys offers Sasha, her *own* mother, producing not a chain of desire or a chain of signifiers but a chain of contact. In both scenes, the midwife, or *sage femme*, becomes a pivotal figure, perceived through Hermione as Demeter, transforming the mother herself from Clytemnestra into the mother who redeems, who retrieves the daughter, calls her back, saving her, cryptically, "from the numbers" (90), opening the way for the daughter's intimacy and releasing her from ciphers into the flight of mythopoeic mind.

Within the context of *HERmione*, the epiphany is, on one level, lost. When the storm is over, Eugenia's powers seem to evaporate; she becomes quarrelsome and intrusive, unable to understand Hermione's inner life. The revelation, however, has not really involved the biographical mother, except for a brief rainstorm intimacy; rather, it involves a textualization of the mother, a discovery of the power of her words, language born of the maternal body, born of water, born of rhythm and translucence.

In 1915 H.D. gave birth to a stillborn daughter, whose death she attributed to the shocks she endured during the first World War. As H.D. solicits the maternal presence by textualizing not only her mother but her own maternity, this dead child appears over and over again in H.D.'s work, a silent little form around whom constellate significant moments of rupture. We find this child in "Asphodel" and *Bid Me to Live* and in "Murex," the second section of *Palimpsest*, where Raymonde Ransome gives birth to a dead baby.

Somewhere a nurse was saying, "she hasn't much grit.". . . There was another voice. "She has had a hard bout; too much—too much—" but what it was that was too much, remained, must forever remain one with this nebulous quality that she could never quite define. . . . A voice that said with an arrant hardness, a shrill hard-as-nails cruelty, "no grit"—

another voice far and far and far and far of an insuperable delicacy, and undercurrent of masculine sympathy, a sternness, an inviolable rectitude, a strength, the very timbre all somehow entangled in the not-pain that was her sudden release, her escape from herself and a dragging recurrent slashing that was not death . . . not once only but many recurrent, definite death-wounds. . . . There were two voices, "no grit" . . . and another—another—"too high strung. Making a good fight—" Another voice. God might have spoken with it. Another voice and annihilating blackness. [110]

This moment of birthing, like so much of women's experience in these texts, consists of some "nebulous quality" which escapes definition or articulation. As we begin to see here through Raymonde's "death-wounds" of labor, the significant aspect of the childbed is not that it involves a joyous contact; Raymonde's experience is horrifying, and the nurses, in response to the child's death, ask, "interested, had she been disappointed, it was a girl anyhow, as if it being 'a girl anyhow' (were they Chinese simply?) made up for all that" (111). What is important, however, is that at these liminal moments and in the preoedipal relationship (which, like birth, involves both a "warm centre" and rage) there emerges a language specific to mothers and their bodies, a language that goes back, back, back, or far and far and far in a state where the severance, discontinuity, and rupture of experience and flesh work their way into the fabric of the text and where the surrounding discourse is structured of dis-embodied voices. Be they shrill, arrant, or insuperably delicate, they bear no connection with the dark, elliptical rhythm of the womb.

In *Bid Me to Live* H.D. replays this stillbirth. Julia Ashton, like H.D., loses a child and is then emotionally abandoned and sexually betrayed by her husband, Rafe. Julia's link with her dead child is fierce. H.D. merges the two so passionately that the line death draws between them becomes indistinct: "Then 1915 and her death," writes H.D., "or rather the death of her child" (24). Later she says again, "Herself projected out in death, was that dead child actually" (141). The loss of the baby causes something to close in, "shuttering her in, something had died that was going to die. . . . they were just where they had been except for a gap in her consciousness, a sort of black hollow, a cave, a pit of blackness; black nebula was not yet concentrated out into clear thought" (12–13).

Bid Me to Live, constructed around this grotto, this gap, is a novel singularly preoccupied with writing, and particularly with women's writing. Begun in 1921 (the same year as "Paint It To-Day"), revised in 1949 (three years after *Trilogy*), and published in 1960 (the year before *Helen in Egypt*), it spans the psychological space of matricide and palinode and offers a vision split between maternal loss and a genderless "child consciousness" that H.D. calls the *gloire*. Emerging out of the war years in London, when H.D. had broken with Ezra Pound, married the poet Richard Aldington, and lost a child, the focus of this roman à clef is the time in 1917 that D. H. Lawrence (here called Rico) and his wife Frieda spent at the Aldingtons' flat in London. Through Julia Ashton, a poet, *Bid Me to Live* reflects many of H.D.'s concerns about her own poetry, particularly in the context of her relationship to Lawrence/Rico's genius.

As much as Julia believes that her true essence exists in her work— "I am tied up in the rough copy of the poems hidden behind the *Mercure de France* volumes. . . . that is me" (77)—Rico's censorship of the poems she sends him has the power to blight all of her production. He responds to her efforts in a letter: "I don't like the second half of the Orpheus sequence as well as the first. Stick to the woman speaking. How can you know what Orpheus feels? It's your part to be woman, the woman vibration. Eurydice should be enough. You can't deal with both" (51). On the one hand, he encourages her to seek out the "woman vibration," which in fact becomes central to H.D.'s work and to an understanding of the maternal register of discourse as well, but at the same time, he limits her, controlling her vision, setting her boundaries, flaunting his mastery. Eurydice, we remember, is the dead woman who cannot be looked at; she is at the threshold between life and death, *behind* Orpheus, invisible, forbidden. In this sense she reproduces the position of the preoedipal mother in language: we can "have" her only by not looking at her, by keeping her in the blind spot. Rico, however, operates under a double standard, entering the female sphere, defining it, naming it, appropriating it, and then granting it back to Julia as if he had some power over it: "If he could enter, so diabolically, into the feelings of women," she wonders, "why should she not enter into the feelings of men?" (62).

Torn between her own bursts of creativity and her anxiety of influence—"I am susceptible, would catch something, I would catch your mannerisms, your style of writing, your style of thinking, even" (176)—her doubts and self-deprecation, Julia's conflict about her writing and her life is conflated with her identity as a woman: "For women, any woman, there was a biological catch and taken at any angle, danger. You dried up and were an old maid, danger. You drifted into the affable *hausfrau*, danger. You let her rip and had operations in Paris . . . , danger" (136). The dialectic of desire and caution which H.D. confronts here resonates in the novel both sexually and artistically. Women like Julia (like H.D. and Rhys), trapped in unhappy marriages, trapped in self-doubt, trapped in "romantic thralldom,"[2] are unable to formulate or articulate an identity, female or poetic. There is, however, a "loophole": "one might be an artist" (136), but an artist redefined outside of Rico's cry of "man-is-man" and "woman-is-woman" (136), in a space where "the woman [is] man-woman, the man [is] woman-man" (136).

This suggestion of androgynous monism which follows H.D.'s admonitions against domesticity and motherhood initially seems to be the way "out" for Julia, as it is in much of H.D.'s earliest writing. As Julia/H.D. begins to explore her writing self, however, releasing it from Rico's control, she discovers that the text in which she might find voice operates *within* the "danger," within the space of confrontation between a poetic and maternal identity. The space of (aborted) maternity is the space in which the current of the mother rises, the space of an absent presence, which begins to work within the language of women who want to write. In H.D.'s earliest work, to be a woman who writes is to be Iphigenia, snatched away from her primal heritage by the patriarchal world of the fathers.[3] In *HERmione*, it means madness, the inability to reconcile her role as dutiful daughter, as dutiful wife, with the hieratic visions played across the inner screen. By the end of *Bid Me to Live*, H.D. no longer requires the appropriation of the male sphere, a claim on either Orestes or Orpheus, but attempts rather to find a space beyond or anterior to male-female polarity, a space that precedes gender (or at least gender-

[2]The term is from Rachel Blau DuPlessis, "Romantic Thralldom in H.D."; I will discuss it more fully in Chapter 7.

[3]For a discussion of H.D. as Iphigenia, see Janice Robinson, *H.D.: The Life and Work of an American Poet*.

consciousness)—"sexless, or all sex, it was child-consciousness" (62).[4]

Julia attempts throughout the novel to explain this *gloire* to Rico.

> Perhaps you would say I was trespassing, couldn't see both sides, as you said of my Orpheus. I could be Eurydice in character, you said, but woman-is-woman and I couldn't be both. The *gloire* is both.
>
> No, that spoils it; it is both and neither. It is simply myself sitting here, this time propped up in bed, scribbling in a notebook, with a candle at my elbow.
>
> The child is the *gloire* before it is born. The circle of the candle on my notebook is the *gloire*, the story isn't born yet.
>
> While I live in the unborn story, I am in the *gloire*.
>
> I must keep it alive, myself living with it. [176–77]

She associates the unborn text with the unborn child, both contained within the body of the mother, biological mother and mother-muse. "When I try to explain," Julia says to Rico, "I write the story. The story must write *me*, the story must create *me*. You are right about that great-mother" (181). In a kind of infinite, mystical regress, a layering or palimpsest of concentric images, a woman writing creates/ becomes a great mother who thrusts herself both around the story and into it: inside the mother is child/writer; within her is the unborn text, and within that story, herself again, both mother and daughter, parthenogenic, birthing the word, born of the word, born of the *gloire*.

This discovery comes partially out of the death of Julia's child, a loss that simultaneously severs her from maternity and makes a sense of the maternal available to her, born out of a hollow in consciousness and a dislocation of language which transcend the male-female tension and "sex-emotion" and challenge the structure of meaning, flooding it with an interiority, a woman's epiphany, a woman's metaphor: "She brooded over each word, as if to hatch it" (163). For the first time, Julia stops her self-effacement and becomes

---

[4]For a slightly different discussion of this aspect of the novel, see Rachel Blau DuPlessis ("Romantic Thralldom in H.D."), who reads the *gloire* primarily as a way to avoid a confrontation between male and female. DuPlessis alludes to the *gloire* as a mother-child nexus but focuses on the monistic implications of the release from sexual polarity.

both "arrogant" and "intrinsically humble" (163) in the face of the realization that "words themselves held inner words" (162). It is a moment much like the one when Rhys's Julia in *After Leaving Mr. Mackenzie* senses something "behind all the talking." Confronting her power to give birth to the Word with an awe of the process in which she participates, Julia/H.D. realizes that the rigid, arbitrary systems of signification, which can neither translate nor reveal the *gloire*, are not just a walled-in space but a walled-in space that contains a world.

H.D.'s sense of the space out of which she will be able to write and in which she will be able to take a poetic identity, then, is associated with the body, specifically the maternal body. "Anyone can translate the meaning of the word," she writes; she, however, wants "the share, the feel of it" (163). This "feel of it" comes to her in *Paint It To-Day* as a hot wave for which there are no words, felt at the moment she attempts to speak to the mother. It comes to her in *Palimpsest* as a sense of "authentic metre" discovered in the dead mother's presence. It comes to her in *HERmione* through the invocation of her own birth, through a scene in which she finds both Demeter and access to a maternal hieroglyph, the mother's cartouche. In *Bid Me to Live*, the novel she worked on sporadically for almost thirty years, H.D. engages most intensely (at least in her prose) the dialectic between the maternal and her own poetic identity as she explores the *gloire*, a working of language through a textualized mother who is at once teller and told, no longer the signature of silence and loss but flesh made word, a rhythm that both ruptures and cadences the language of the father's temple.

6

Fishing the Murex Up

Textualization becomes the key in both Rhys and H.D. for coming to terms with the figure of the mother. Each writer develops strategies for working through this encoding which are often intuitive rather than intellectual. One technique, used by H.D. in particular, is the palimpsest, the ancient parchment that has been written over several times, earlier versions having been imperfectly erased. It creates a strange, marginal writing, both intentional and accidental; like the lost mother, it must be excavated, sought after, at the very moment it is seeping through unbidden. Coincidentally and rather remarkably, the word is an anagram, a "text" containing/concealing another text; rearranged, the letters read "simple past." *Palimpsest*, then, actually enacts its own functioning, both erasing and engaging the "simple (preoedipal) past" which engenders it. This overwriting/underwriting suggests two contradictory impulses: it creates an augmented or extended text and a reduced or narrowed one; it accommodates multiplicity and yet, in the privacy of its intersections, creates a cryptic and distorted space as well.

In 1926 H.D., highly attuned to the resonances of this ancient form and its parallels to consciousness, published an important work called *Palimpsest*. Written contemporaneously with Rhys's *Voyage in the Dark*, this "rather loosely written long-short-story volume," as she called it (*TF*, 148), is difficult, disorienting, and often irritating. It is "un-even" and "badly punctuated," according to its author (*CF*, 28). "It is hallucinated," she writes, "and I must become hallucinated in order to cope with it." Nonetheless, years later H.D. found that it "held and astonished" her (*CF*, 29). It is extraordinarily compelling both as a text and in the place it occupies in the canon of her work, falling midway between 1919 and 1934 and thus serving as a kind of fulcrum for the psychic and literary period bounded by H.D.'s child-birth breakdown and by the termination of her analysis with Freud. It is in a sense her "masquerade," marked as it is by the distortions of a regressed and privileged discourse anterior to "mastery" and related through its gaze—it "holds and astonishes"—to the mother.

As various critics have observed, 1919 marked a turning point for H.D. "The previous years had been a period so filled with both achievement and anxiety, so critical and traumatic that she would spend the rest of her life mythologizing it: rehearsing it in verse, in prose, in direct autobiography and in historical and legendary per-sonae, again and again seeking to unriddle her destiny as woman and poet" (Gelpi, TS, 7). Indeed, after her break with Pound and Imagism, the loss of a child, the death of her brother and father, the dissolution of her marriage to Richard Aldington, the trauma (par-ticularly strong for H.D.) of world war, and her illness following the birth of her daughter, Perdita, H.D., at thirty-three, became under-standably preoccupied not only with unriddling her destiny but with making some sense of her past.[1]

During the fifteen artistically frustrating years which followed, novels and their sequels or "pre-quels" appeared rapidly, eclipsing the poetry.[2] The early autobiographical "fiction," as we have seen in *HERmione* and "Paint It To-Day" is marked by a feverish, hallucina-tory intensity alternating with an extraordinary detachment. One has the sense that H.D. never really comes to terms with any of the material and therefore must act it out—textually—over and over, revising, altering, intensifying, disclaiming, but never exhausting her obsession with the forces of her early life.

[1]For fuller discussion of the impact of these events on H.D.'s life and work, see Janice Robinson, *H.D.: The Life and Work of an American Poet*; Barbara Guest, *Herself Defined: The Poet H.D. and Her World*; and particularly, Susan Stanford Friedman, *Psyche Reborn: The Emergence of H.D.*.

[2]Only three novels of this period have been published: *Palimpsest* (1926); *Her* (1927) (published as *HERmione* in 1981); and *Hedylus* (1928). The others, including "Paint It To-Day" (1921) and "Asphodel" (dated 1921–22) remain in typescript at Beinecke, although four chapters from "Paint It To-Day" have recently appeared in *Contemporary Literature* 27 (Winter 1986).

Palimpsest surges with this psychological and textual confusion. It is a text superimposed as if "photographic negatives had been pasted together and rolled over swifter, swifter, swifter from some well controlled cinematograph. Her mind behind her mind turned the handle (so to speak) for a series of impressions that devastated her with their clarity, with their precision and with their variety" (*P*, 157). She has reentered the past and reengaged it, releasing herself into it as she eventually released herself into her work with Freud, until she understood that the spiritual, psychological, and textual transformation of the "simple past" into palimpsest would reflect and encompass all the significant aspects of her voice and vision: division of selves and consciousness, the layering or imbedding of language, the seepage of past into present, ambivalence about the mother, and revisions and palinodes as impulses.[3]

It is difficult to know where or how to enter this "devastating" text as *Palimpsest* rolls forward, subverting and concealing the generating units and frames on which it is nonetheless dependent, just as the semiotic is "heterogeneous to meaning but always in sight of it" (Kristeva, *DL*, 133). The text, like the consciousness which creates and is created by it, is a kind of hallucinated, layered cinema: a film frozen, a film melting with the heat of an incandescent brain, a film rewound, a film reversed, a film alternately speeded up and slowed in motion; to read the text is also somehow to view it.[4] There is, consequently, because of its structural convolutions and its reliance on image, no sense of determining syntax here, no familiar structure that consistently constructs the direction of the reading. The use of the image, then, in Lacan's sense of the formative nexus of the pre-oedipal imaginary, is what both maintains and deconstructs H.D.'s text.

[3]Understanding H.D.'s "voice and vision" is obviously a complicated undertaking. Susan Friedman's *Psyche Reborn* remains the definitive text; it opens into biography, psychoanalysis, sexuality, mysticism, and aesthetics. The work of Rachel DuPlessis is also focused with an unerring sense of H.D.'s psychic and artistic struggles. See, for example, "Family, Sexes, Psyche," *H.D.: The Career of That Struggle*, and "Romantic Thralldom in H.D." Many critics allude to the notion of palimpsest as metaphor in H.D.; for the most specific discussions, see Friedman, who relates the metaphor to H.D.'s personal history, traumas, and breakdowns (*Psyche*, 29–30), and Joseph Riddel, who discusses palimpsest in terms of the enactment of *Ur* patterns ("H.D. and the Poetics of 'Spiritual Realism'").

[4]For a discussion of film as "psychic medium" in H.D., see Adalaide Morris, "The Concept of Projection: H.D.'s Visionary Powers," 422–24.

Despite H.D.'s abandonment of conventional structure and syntax, however, it is possible to locate oneself within the textual topography. The text is divided into three distinct spaces. "Hipparchia: War Rome (circa 75 B.C.)" centers on a vanquished Greek living in Rome as a poet and courtesan. The "plot" is interior, the only external markings being Hipparchia's movement among villas. H.D.'s focus is Hipparchia's struggle to reclaim and renounce her mother, to embrace and repudiate several lovers, and to maintain the Hellenic spirit in the Roman mosaic. Part 2, "Murex: War and Postwar London (circa A.D. 1916–1926)," works around a split figure, Raymonde Ransome/Ray Bart, a poet whose task it is to utterly forget the trauma of her past. Through a teatime encounter with a jilted friend, her own history—loss of a lover, death of a child—is unearthed against her will, brought up from the depths of her subconscious despite all her linguistic and psychological defenses, until everything is "altered horribly" (117). "Secret Name: Excavator's Egypt (circa A.D. 1925)" centers on Helen Fairwood, a "high-class secretary" to a famous archaeologist who finds herself at liberty for several days in Luxor. Involved in a brief relationship with Rafton, a former captain on his way to Aswan, and in indulging an American parvenue and her daughter, Helen moves from temple to tomb, attempting to "keep her balance, suspended between two worlds" (176). The core of these three sections, once again, reenacts the triad offered by Rhys's exasperating child—the ambiguous mother figure, the lost child, and the stubborn male text.

Despite the differences in character, chronology, and plot, there are important connections among the sections. On the most basic level there is the shared juxtaposition of past and present, always the basic division in H.D.'s work. For H.D., in fact, there are always two pasts, her own and the historical past, antiquity. Just as her own past compelled her, the classical world had an intense and unabating attraction for H.D., for archetypal and mythological figures seemed to provide a clarity and order the war-torn twentieth century could not. I think it was important to H.D. that although antiquity itself was "split," the split was very clear. The essential division, as H.D. saw it, did not involve the schisms and rifts of world war or the gaps and chasms of madness; the split was between this world and another, a split which was irrevocable but somehow negotiable. The far past, for H.D., was more "helpful" than the present. It participated in psychic life; it offered signs, omens, auguries, visions, voices, which the poet could borrow or translate to close the gap. It is not difficult to understand H.D.'s intense connection to and affection for the classical and preclassical world or her association of her mother Helen with Hellas when we understand that her lifelong project was to cross the gulf, to learn the language of repair, to close the gap both within and between past and present: "I mend a gap in time" ("May 1943," CP, 492). This "gap," of course, might also be read, in Margaret Homans's terms, as "the gap between child and mother opened up by the simultaneous arousal and prohibition of incest" (BW, 7). And as Homans reiterates, it is *language* that "promises to cross, even while operating through dependence on, that gap" (7).

All other polarities are subsumed under this initial means of dividing experience: "Her mind was a glass that was set between this world, this present and the far past that was eternal. A glass, a lens, a living substance lies between ourselves and our final attainment. Antiquity." (163). In a rather remarkable passage H.D. sets a mirror between past and present, reproducing as the generating image of her text the mirror stage, in which identity is both constituted and shattered. The far past, which in H.D.'s work, through the classical/maternal associations, turns out to *be* the preoedipal past, is clearly a privileged and invested space; the present distorts and dilutes the immediacy of experience and vision:

> All of modernity . . . was as the jellified and sickly substance of a collection of old colourless photographic negatives through which gleamed the reality, the truth of the blue temples of Thebes, of the white colonnades of Samos. . . . Modernity was unfamiliar and semi-transparent and it obscured antiquity while it let a little show through, falsified by the nervous movement of its transparent surface. Falsified by the nervous erratic jerks of its deep-sea members modernity was the unfamiliar, always baffling substance. [158]

The old "truth"—Hellas, mother—has been falsified by an unfamiliar representation that obscures her. In *Palimpsest*, each section operates individually around the tension between these two spheres: Hipparchia is haunted by her own past and by ancient texts; Raymonde Ransome is consumed by the split between her present and her past and by some ancient past which informs her own; Helen

Fairwood searches for herself in an ancient mystery she invokes to clarify both modernity and herself.

At the same time, however, H.D. attempts to "close the gap" both within each section and in an intertextual project, which appears in early allusions to later textual spheres; she structures a triad that erects boundaries of time and space and then abandons them. In part 1, for example, the discourse becomes increasingly suffused with images of Egypt, anticipating part 3. Hipparchia, in a delirium that ruptures boundaries between reason and madness, perception and imagination, self and other, senses everywhere "Egypt in the shadow" (47) and feels herself suffocating under "some Egyptian coffin lid" (81). She merges Aphrodite and Isis (80), believes herself to *be* Isis, believes that Isis has come finally to recall her (92). She endows her lover, Verrus, with "late-Egyptian tendencies" (51), then merges him with a hallucinated vision of Osiris. Similarly, part 2 presages the excavations in part 3 as Raymonde Ransome identifies her visitor Ermy with "some unearthed Queen Nefertiti" (126) and listens to her story as to "some past Egyptian's odd and sorry history" (108). And just as Hipparchia feels the presence of ancient tombs, Raymonde thinks of her past as "far and far and far as far as a buried Egyptian's neatly painted coffin" (110), "that long pre-Egyptian past of 1917" (109). These are more than random images. They form the connective tissue of the text; they will be retrieved in the actual Egypt section and then wash backward to redetermine "Hipparchia" and "Murex," like a sea that is both eroding and increasing the shoreline. This is the function of the palimpsest, which simultaneously erases and glosses the earlier texts in the same rhythm of advance and retreat which forms *Good Morning, Midnight*.

Once H.D. has set this tide into motion, it works in both directions. Images initially engendered in "Hipparchia" resurface in "Murex" and "Secret Name." Raymonde Ransome, for example, is flushed with the "lightning of vivid thought that was her Athenian inheritance" (171). She imagines her ex-husband with hair "like a conqueror's helmet" (134). She, like Hipparchia, writes, knowing that the "Greek formula must not be forgotten" (155). Helen Fairwood, similarly, "[thinks] across towards Athens" (173). Scarabs make her imagine "some exquisite, incredibly slender Graeco-Egyptian, some incredibly carnal Roman" (179), and these images invoke Hipparchia and her lover Verrus as if Helen Fairwood were privy to their past as well as her own. Her own companion, Rafton, seems to her a conqueror, an "authentic, Roman, officer of one of the flashy and distinguished legions of the middle-ageing procrastinator, Caesar" (175). Captain Rafton has momentarily merged with Verrus, just as Verrus earlier became Osiris. Ancient Rome and Egypt, both modern and encrypted, wash together through time and space so that "the present and the actual past and the future were . . . one. All planes were going on, on, on together" (166).

Hipparchia, Raymonde Ransome, and Helen Fairwood, like many of H.D.'s protagonists (not coincidentally since this wash and interplay is determined by both experience and *language*) are also linked by being writers. All produce texts, and their relationships to these texts and to the surrounding discourse are central to an understanding of this work. On one level, language fails, becoming a system of checks and "counters" used only to parry, to keep others at a distance, to defend oneself against the rising of buried material, imitating the postoedipal symbolic, which resists what is buried—the mother—to constitute itself: "In their static and exact speech they questioned and they answered. Each knew the other perfectly versed in this common practice of speaking one way and of thinking other. . . . There was no arrière-pensée. Simply a simple knowledge that all she said was falsehood" (32). Raymonde Ransome, similarly, engages in conversation "holding to the letter of the talk, thinking, as was her manner, elsewhere. She had trained herself . . . to carry on her apparently eager and ecstatic conversation and to stand posed, apart, sustained in some other region" (102). And Helen Fairwood likewise carries on "a merely outer shell of conversation" (231). Reading through the lost mother, we see a possibility H.D. does not make explicit: women who are trained in the Letter might nonetheless simultaneously exist "elsewhere," sustained in the inner space the shell conceals.

Language for these women seems to be connected to obligation, a kind of social contract they fulfill but in which they do not really participate; as writers, translators, and transcribers, however, text compels them, and through this compulsion H.D. explores the struggle to form a relationship between psychic life and the written word, a relationship beyond Helen Fairwood's "heavy and weary research into Graeco-Roman texts for . . . tiresome facts, for authentic and tiresome information on lost fragments" (189).

Of the three women, Hipparchia's immersion in manuscripts is the
most consuming, the least like Helen Fairwood's and the nineteenth-
century women Margaret Homans describes, "who act as amanuen-
ses or as readers for others, usually men" (*BW*, 31). As poet and
translator, Hipparchia is involved in finishing a book begun by her
dead uncle, a scientific book on plants, which she is suddenly compelled to transform into "a fervid compilation of poetry, religion, and
ethics" (71). While Jane Eyre can hope only to read the books left by
her dead uncle, Hipparchia attempts to rewrite them. In her project
to work Greek poetry into Latin, she is torn between intense labor
with "odd untranslatable fragment[s]," which become "set, stubborn, unmalleable metal in her head" (77), and "the sudden appearance, from nowhere, of some magic turn of speech" (77) some
"authentic metre." Hipparchia discovers translation to be a "desecration," "the dark sputtering of an almost extinguished wick in an
earth bowl which before had shown rose in alabaster" (72). We have
here clearly the mark of modernism, the impulse that sets H.D. (and
other early twentieth-century women) apart from the women Homans reads, the rupture of the patrilinear text and the refusal to
adhere completely to the "female duties of selfless transmission, just
as, mythically, Mary facilitated the transmission of Word into flesh"
(*BW*, 31).

> The translation in the heavier tongue read faulty, repetitive. It was as if a
> light that had been burning in clear agate was set now in granite. What the
> Greek could manage with [its] honeyed delicacy of curious vowel syllable,
> the foreign tongue was forced to contrive by neat fitting of pallid mosaic.
> Here wit and shrewd planned phrase . . . must net the senses; . . . neat
> paraphrase must serve instead of true intoxication. [72]

This description resonates with the writing daughter's struggle: the
conflict between the "foreign" tongue—the name-of-the-father—
and the "mother tongue," in this case Hipparchia's native Greek.
The "mother" language works through curious syllables, intoxica-
tion, and light suffused into text; the "father" tongue is a mosaic that
must "fit," that repeats form and planned phrase. Hipparchia begins
to realize that if, instead of a translation, she creates a palimpsest, a
text that does not replace the original but allows and invites the
struggling of overwriting/underwriting, there is an entirely different
result. She finds that "the Greek words, inset in her manuscript,

would work terrific damage" (73). The Greek in this context—she is translating Sappho and Moero—is associated with antiquity, her own past, and her mother, while the Latin, for Hipparchia, is the present; thus her own manuscript echoes the larger one and H.D.'s belief that the past can be called upon to both disrupt and redeem the present. The struggle to displace the desecration, the layering she calls palimpsest, is essentially no different from Kristeva's conflation of semiotic and symbolic into "poetic language."

This same impulse reappears in Raymonde Ransome, who is linked to Hipparchia through avocation and language as she "grub[s] at odd manuscripts" (116) with "paper and pencil. Parchment and stylus" (151). The real connection between the two women, however, surpasses the lexical. Each exists in a kind of split self, Hipparchia as herself and as a replication (both solicited and repudiated) of her dead mother, Raymonde Ransome as her public self and as Ray Bart, her poetic alter ego. Both women have an ambivalent relationship to their work; they are riveted to it and repelled by it. At various points they burn with the intensity of it; at others they disclaim it and try (unsuccessfully) to extract themselves from it. The play here between sameness and difference reproduces the Iphigenia/Orestes conflict in the sense that one version of the writing daughter depends on alliance with the mother while the other requires another (male) self to house and produce the texts. Raymonde Ransome severs herself from the mother to write, but she does it through the transformation of gender. She "wins" as Midget cannot; she *does* become not Electra but Orestes. Nonetheless, she is not in control of her power. Writing often appears unbidden, replicating the unbidden presence of Hipparchia's dead mother: "Why was it . . . when she especially repudiated her genius, it so came to plague her?" (150).

Hipparchia's relationship to writing is more complicated through its closer association with her mother, who compels the writing daughter but who wandered off, renouncing her family, pleasure, beauty, and her body for the intellect. In a reversal of work where the conventional Victorian mother appears as a selfless wife cut off from art, *Palimpsest* explores the other side of the choice, the mother so involved in the life of the mind that she abandons the daughter. This is not the mother who betrays the jewel, the gift, the birthright through emotion but the mother who steals it and disappears. Hipparchia, an intense, icy courtesan, courts the sensuous as a way of separating herself from her mother. Unlike Midget, however, Hipparchia attempts to dissociate herself from her father as well, afraid that he will transform her as he did his wife: "Don't let my father get me. He wanted me to be like Hipparchia who put aside the diadem. I wear my crown" (80). Although Hipparchia sets up this opposition between an intellectual life and the sensuous life of physical beauty, maintaining that she will be true to the diadem (instead of the jewel) she is continually drawn back to poetry and language, never able to escape from her vulnerability to the mother, with whom she is in a kind of intellectual competition, fearing that her own writing will be "a mere feeble copy, a counterfeit" (78) of her dead mother's.

The text itself is constantly ruptured by the presence of the mother, who surfaces as a phantom throughout the text to "plague" her (78).[5] She also appears as a fragmented poem, a tribute written by the poet Antipater (anti-pater) on the occasion of her death. Here, in a kind of maternal palimpsest, the dead mother is inscribed not just into the text but into a text within the text, lines of poetry that wash through the current of the novel and through the daughter herself: "*I cast my lot with cynics, not* was running through her head. She had apprehended poetry physically as she had never apprehended loving—*with women seated at the distaff*. The metre beat and beat rhythmic and undeniable hypnotic refrain in her tired body" (34). Through the fragmented inscription of her ambivalence and the failure of her writing self, Hipparchia both condemns her mother for relinquishing her womanliness and yet is haunted by the disembodied voice which proclaims: "*My fame exceeds (as Wisdom's must / excell mere winners of hill-games) / Atalanta's of Mount Maenalus*" (15). The pulse of this work is between regaining the mother and finding one's own "authentic metre" to set one apart from her, something that will endure and stamp Hipparchia as one whose own fame must also excel.

At a certain point, Hipparchia thinks she has succeeded: "Hipparchia was dazed, drugged and drunk with phrases of poems,

---

[5]The issue of Hipparchia's relationship to her mother and to language originally appeared in slightly different form as part of my "Flesh Made Word: Maternal Inscription in H.D."

snatches that for days she had neglected and then found, as if the very air held static strips of authentic metre. . . . [S]he had found . . . an almost frightening satisfaction in the sudden appearance, from nowhere, of some magic turn of speech appearing vagrantly to astound her" (76–77). Her success, however, is followed immediately by a hallucination in which her mother torments her, telling her cryptically that "there is no help save in renunciation" (78). "Round and round and round. It went round and round and round" (78), H.D. writes, echoing the hallucinatory sensation in Rhys's *Voyage in the Dark*, until Hipparchia is plunged into a vertiginous, delirious state in which she keeps demanding parchment and stylus and is denied them. Within the swirl of her madness emerges the association between authentic meter and the mother's presence, connected, significantly, with her inability to write. In this state, Hipparchia finds comfort, union: "She was one being. Blue, blue, blue, blue Isis to recall her. . . . She had disclaimed a place with poetry" (86). The movement in this section is both maddening and radiant. The mother is inscribed variously as absence, as Isis, as artistic denial, as muse, as severance, as integration, all the conflicting states reflecting through and within the text. H.D. begins to allow here the multiplicity, the rush of contradiction which she refused in "Paint It To-Day." Instead of trying to order it, control it, slay it, she, like Francine in *Voyage in the Dark*, releases herself into it, finding on the other side of madness a mother who both inspires Hipparchia's poetry and releases her from it, transporting her to a space where "thought and creation" are "severed" (85).

H.D. uses a rather astonishing image to bind the projects of Hipparchia and Raymonde despite the differences in their strategies. When Raymonde feels the presence of her poet self overtake her, it appears as a very particular sensation: "With the very pencil she held poised, she tried to fend off her recurrent metres. . . . The icy glamour of the thing she knew was Ray Bart's helmet closed above her. Above Raymonde's forehead (where she would have worn some slight and fragrant but soon withering little crown of field flowers) Ray Bart's helmet rested" (147–48). Not only does the imagery here suggest the diadem and the Roman helmets that fill part 1, the sense of a head constricted as a prelude to creative release is an echo of Hipparchia's own sense of the "high-water mark of intellectual achieve-

ment": "The mind developed beyond normal, developed and tyr-
anized, must again flow back and back or else a string bound tight
around a frozen skull will, by just one minute hair-breadth of a
tightening, cut through; cut (she visualized it) a skull neatly like a
thread dividing a round cheese or ripened melon. Her head was
about to be split like some ripe fruit overweighted on its trellis" (35).
What H.D. creates here is a kind of double palimpsest. Within each
section the images are layered—Ray Bart overlaying Raymonde Ransome; Hipparchia the mother rising up through Hipparchia the
daughter—and then both sections are superimposed like negatives,
the images bleeding through time and space and other texts like the
pulsing mercury Hermione feels, which threatens to explode the
careful markings on glass.

H.D. works her palimpsest, however, not just through overlaid
images or impulses. It is also extraordinarily integrated into the
structure of the language itself. The narrative voice, for example, is
layered, a conflation or alternation of interior monologue and indi-
rect discourse and omniscient third person, moving through dialogue, turning back on itself, amending, confirming, repeating. In
each section, stories are told in layers of present conversation, private perception, retrieved memory, and hallucination coded in italics, interrupted clauses, and parentheses:

> He spoke, though she hardly heard his utterance, something far and far—
> "when all these Mithradatean blusterings are over—Capua—the villa—"
> something about Hipparchia being set, as any gem more suitably, some-
> thing from far and far and far about some suave and golden Eros—"a
> child sometime"—and feel sleeping—down and down into some ap-
> prehended beauty, some world of suave utterance and of chaste renewal.
> *Couches spread in the palace of Zeus.* So Hebe removing affectedly small
> dainty bracelets (she thought of Hebe with small bracelets) held close her
> giant lover. [36–37]

Hallucinated sections like this, like Rhys's, imitating the intrusions
and convolutions of consciousness, appear throughout *Palimpsest,* as
it ruptures itself, rises up from within itself, spills over, broken open
by images, desires, voices, other times and space.

The linguistic palimpsest operates out of imbedded refrains as well
as disturbed syntax. Some of them are intratextual, lines that once

engendered reappear over and over in a particular section. In "Hipparchia," for example, phrases and questions, such as "Greece dissociated from any central ruling" and "since when . . . has one been able to escape the dead?" become a cadence to the surrounding discourse, an insistent throbbing that beats like the metronome Ray Bart hears inside her head. Moreover, they are particularly maternally connoted, removed from the father's "central ruling" as the dead mother reappears, inescapable in the language her mourning and terrified daughter struggles to reinvent.

Initially these phrases are marked off from the surrounding text, but eventually italics and quotation marks disappear until whole sections (79), beating with an incredible, almost unbearable intensity, are formulated entirely of reconstituted refrains, until the present of the text is simultaneously its past. And like so many of the visual images, these auditory ones, which initially seem confined to their generating sections, cross textual boundaries resonating in other sections until we are hearing "from far and far and far and far," "feet—feet—feet—feet—feet," soldiers' feet, metrical feet, an endless process of synthesis and return not unlike Hipparchia's description of her own work: "Things formed and reformed and when finally discarded (it had so often happened) had a strange way of reappearing in third startling manifestation" (77).

A second kind of "refrain" takes the form of disembodied poems written or remembered or translated by the women whose discourse they interrupt. In a replication of the intensely complicated functioning of consciousness, they break through the text and then, having once appeared, split and reappear in fragments. "Murex" is interrupted, for example, by poetic texts in the form of Ray Bart's developing poem, the lines of which accumulate through additions and revisions as Raymonde Ransome/Ray Bart offers successive drafts of a poem centered on her confrontation with the woman who releases her own repressed past. H.D. accomplishes this development initially through repetitions; subsequently she recasts and splinters the verses, annotating them line by line (153) until finally the annotations themselves become refrains of earlier lines (164) no longer quoted but thoroughly integrated so that the text is constantly washing through both other texts and itself.

Hipparchia, similarly, offers "crude beginning" (40) of her own

poetry and then revises, correcting the original, replacing with subsequent versions the engendering poems. The text is also punctuated
by two poems by Antipater of Sidon, one on the fall of Corinth and
the other, as mentioned, on the death of Hipparchia's mother. H.D.
uses these poems in curious ways: she offers them in pieces; entire
verses are "forgotten" and then remembered later; they float in the
text and are then dissociated, like the Greek cities, from any central
ruling only to reappear as refrains. The text is further layered by
translations of Moero's grape song (71) and of verses of Euripides,
which Hipparchia then borrows into her own verse until she is
"dazed, drugged and drunk . . . with the new Alexandrians" (77).
Something really remarkable is going on here as Hipparchia "borrows" not only her own verse but H.D.'s as well, incorporating
Sapphic fragments and Euripidean choros, the very verses, some of
them, which H.D. was herself writing and translating several years
earlier in *Hymen* (1921) and *Heliodora* (1924). The text, then, is marked
by first drafts, evolving into revisions, which then begin to merge
into a true palimpsest, not poems set off typographically but fragments "imperfectly erased," which appear throughout the larger
text. At the height of her delirium, the lines of poetry couple with
each other and with Hipparchia's (and H.D.'s) own story until there
are no more boundaries between her own work, her translations, her
revisions and palinodes, and her subconscious: "Which was actual
communion, . . . which was poetry? Metres, memories formed and
reformed" (76). This question anticipates by a good fifty years Julia
Kristeva's questioning of "poetic language," the "cracking [of] the
socio-symbolic order, splitting it open, changing vocabulary, syntax,
the word itself and releasing from beneath them the drives borne by
vocalic or kinetic differences" (*RPL*, 79–80). H.D.'s memory/meter
split augurs Kristeva's juxtaposition of "sacrifice and art"—"the prohibition of jouissance [incest] by language and the introduction of
jouissance into and through language" (*RPL*, 80). What H.D. begins
to entertain is the idea that perhaps art does not have to entail
sacrifice for the writing daughter; perhaps she can create a new myth
in which she is neither Iphigenia nor Orestes, in which memory
might be retrieved through meter and meter retrieved through (preoedipal) memory.

H.D., decades prior to her analysis with Freud, was intensely taken with this "ineffable quality of merging" and the experience of levels of consciousness, levels to which she gains access if she will "let go perception, let go arrow-vibrant thought" (95). She finds an "inner world," "a scroll that unwinds before shut eyes" (82), a kind of Freudian subconscious, which "was shifted, was opened up as if a layer of hardened, protective sand and lava had been sifted. Behind that layer, the things that had been (really because of that layer) blighted were, by the same token, now fresh" (145).

It is clearly very difficult to talk about consciousness in H.D., a poet dependent on the enmeshing of "arrow vibrant thought," "frozen intensity," hallucination, dream, visitation, "lotus vision," and "actual image," in some incredibly complicated palimpsest of insight and despair. An interesting point of departure, however, which spans in some way the contradictions and convolutions is "bicamerality" in the sense that Julian Jaynes uses it in *The Origin of Consciousness in the Breakdown of the Bicameral Mind*. Bicamerality refers, by definition, to two-chamberedness; in Jaynes's terms it refers to a mind with no "analog I," which operates nonetheless as self and other with no "consciousness" of either and no ability to narratize. He offers a flawed but compelling model for reflecting on a number of modernist texts, particularly H.D.'s, for her concept of the function and locus of poetic consciousness is very close to Jaynes's notion of bicamerality, which refers in more mythic and neurological terms to what poststructuralist critics are attempting to accommodate within their "vertiginous" discourse. Jaynes suggests somewhat more simply (and somewhat more naïvely) that ancient people, up to a certain point of linguistic inscription, operated through a mind one hemisphere of which responded to the instruction or admonition of the other through the mediation of hallucinated voices—the muses, gods, and goddesses of ancient texts. This "otherness," really "other chamberedness," is perceived as external and divine (although how human beings without the ability to create analogues, to recognize otherness, or to narratize could conceive of the "divine" Jaynes leaves unclear).

Jaynes attributes the "appearance" of bicamerality to the acquisition of language—speech—and the disappearance of bicamerality (the emergence of consciousness) to the development of language into written text, which localized and therefore disempowered the auditory hallucinations as well as author(iz)ed the analogue self. His work does not make gender distinctions, but I suggest that what he is specifically telling is the story of the lost mother, present in the rhythms and intonations and musicality of the oral tradition but disempowered and sacrificed in text to the signifying "I."

To H.D., however—and this is crucial to an understanding of every word she wrote—the sign is the mark not of absence but of presence. For this reason, she grapples to textualize "the story," working her experiences and relationships through verse and prose, obsessively. In the word she finds not the sign of the gap but the way to close the gap.[6]

Jaynes's model, while it seems to concur that the sign is the mark of absence, that once there is the written sign, the ability (the need) to represent, there is by definition a loss, a gap, a split between the "I" and the narratizable "me," between self and other, between signified and signifier, nonetheless offers a way of understanding H.D.'s sense of presence. Whether what he says is "true" is irrelevant here; what is important is that H.D.'s work functions "as if" it emerged out of or returned to bicamerality, a state in which language does not represent loss but rather speaks its presence. That this "presence," according to Jaynes, is a neurological phenomenon in no way dilutes the intensity of the experience; it is "as if" there were a space which gave voice to poetry, which offered a gift and was the gift and was the giving. Jaynes, in fact, suggests that poetry, by nature, is a a memory, a nostalgia (374) for that "space," for those voices, that poetic creation is, almost by definition, bicameral (373). Although Jaynes cautions against a topography of consciousness, he nonetheless creates one, a split "world" bridged by voices. H.D. had some instinctive sense of this strange psychic "space" that "spoke" to some other "space"; the one difference between what Jaynes describes and what H.D. experiences is that H.D.'s split world is colored by the consciousness of it. In Jaynes's view, bicamerality disappears with consciousness and written text, but one of the ways, perhaps, of understanding H.D.'s vision is to imagine her in possession of both,

---

[6]Norman Holland also discusses H.D.'s search "to close the gap with signs," although his emphasis is on her need to "concretize" rather than "textualize." See "H.D. and the 'Blameless Physician.'"

existing always, writing always with the conscious sense of a pre-
conscious (preoedipal) experience. This sense of conflicting spheres
into which one abandons oneself and yet which one somehow mediates is central to her work and her attempts to comprehend and
codify what links varying "states of manifestations" and to close the
gap between them. The bicameral mind is another version of what
she calls palimpsest.

All these convolutions of engendering and retrieval and layering of
text and consciousness can be seen within the boundaries of *Palimpsest*, but I would now like to move outside the text to explore how this
form functions as a paradigm of a kind of intertextuality throughout
H.D.'s canon as her earliest struggles with language and consciousness, her earliest attempts to translate early psychic life into text,
appear and reappear.

Tribute to Freud, H.D.'s account of her analytic sessions in 1933 and
1934,[7] is itself a kind of palimpsest, composed as it is of "Writing on
the Wall" and "Advent," two separate records of her relationship
with Freud, the first, oddly, written ten years after analysis (1944)
without the aid of the journal (1933) on which the text of the "adden-
dum" (actually composed in 1949) is based. It is in keeping with the
convolutions of the form that "Advent" appears after "Writing on
the Wall," the generating forms always surfacing last in H.D. as the
symptoms give way to the underlying events and images that engendered them.

The title "Writing on the Wall" refers to the visions H.D. saw
projected on a hotel wall in 1920 during her trip to the Greek islands
with Bryher. Much of her "tribute" to Freud is devoted to a description of these images, which surfaced in her consciousness and which
resurface in the text as hieroglyphs, ancient writing psychically excavated. H.D. herself recognized the palimpsestic quality of her attachment to these images: "But there I am seated on the old-fashioned
Victorian sofa in the Greek island hotel bedroom, and here I am
reclining on the couch in the Professor's room, telling him this, and
here again am I, ten years later, seated at my desk in my own room in

[7] I am looking at a very limited portion of a very rich document. For broader
discussions of this work, see Friedman, *Psyche Reborn*; DuPlessis and Friedman,
"'Woman Is Perfect': H.D.'s Debate with Freud"; Norman Holland; and Joseph N.
Riddel, "H.D.'s Scene of Writing—Poetry as (and) Analysis."

London. But there is no clock-time, though we are fastidiously concerned with time and with a formal handling of a subject which
has . . . no time-barriers" (*TF*, 47).

H.D. connects here 1920, 1933, and 1944; the connection she does
not make is to 1926, although she echoes Raymonde Ransome's
experience of "over-consciousness" to explain her own "symptoms"
as "over-thought" (*TF*, 51) and borrows the topography of *Palimpsest*
to locate her Corfu vision: "But symptom or inspiration, the writing continues to write itself or be written. It is admittedly picture-
writing, though its symbols can be translated in terms of today; it is
Greek in spirit, rather than Egyptian" (*TF*, 51). Its form, then, is
Egyptian, its spirit Hellenic, its translation modern.

The reason H.D. instinctively reaches into the 1926 text to articulate the 1944 one is, I think, that both texts are concerned with the
Greek experience. As Susan Gubar has pointed out, the first section
of *Palimpsest* alludes to H.D.'s trip with Bryher: like H.D., Hipparchia
is ill and exhausted; like H.D., she is "rescued" by a younger woman
who woos her back to health with the promise of a "regenerative
voyage" to Greece (53). I would go further, however, and suggest
that decades before they are deliberately inscribed in "Writing on the
Wall," the "picture-writing" images are acted out through Hipparchia, Raymonde Ransome, and Helen Fairwood, all of whom are
prone to "constant aberrations, these psycho-hysterical visionary
sensations" (*P*, 187).[8] There is this strange double convolution, then,
for the initial writing (on the wall) preceded *Palimpsest*, seeped into it,
and then was "erased" so that by the time H.D. finally transcribes
the vision for the "first" time it is really a second draft; *Palimpsest*
thus reveals itself to be an engendering text of *Tribute to Freud*.[9]

[8]Several critics have alluded to H.D.'s reprocessing of hallucinated material in her
1920s novels. Adalaide Morris focuses primarily on another vision, the apparition of
"Peter Van Eck" (Peter Rodeck) on the deck of the *Borodino* on the trip to Greece,
suggesting that H.D. "struggled to tell the story" for more than twenty years. ("Projection," 420). Janice Robinson writes that "a particularly vivid re-creation of the
central images associated with the Corfu vision appears in *Hedylus*" (251), but after
identifying Helios in the 1928 novel, she does not pursue this suggestive train of
thought.

[9]Adalaide Morris makes a fascinating observation that adds yet another layer to the
palimpsest: she traces the images of the Corfu vision to an earlier text, the poem
"Helios and Athene," written during the trip to Greece just after H.D. and Bryher
were denied access to Delphi and just before their arrival in Corfu. According to

To understand how this intertextual palimpsest functions, we must look at the images themselves. The first projection H.D. sees in Corfu is the head of a visored soldier or airman, "a silhouette cut of light" (*TF*, 45). Before she can assess it carefully, it gives way to "the conventional outline of a goblet or cup," which suggests "the mystic chalice" (45). Almost immediately the third image draws itself—"a three-legged lamp stand," a familiar object that H.D. associates with the tripod of Delphi. H.D. calls these first three projections "cards" (48), alluding to tarot figures, but the "reading" is suddenly broken "as if there were a slight question as to the conclusion or direction of the symbols" (46). During the pause, H.D. fears that her "mind may not be equal to the occasion" (47); she describes the experience to Bryher, who is standing near her, and asks her whether she should go on. While H.D. hesitates "there is a sort of pictorial buzzing" emanating from "small creatures . . . in black . . . [like] very small half-winged insects" (48), which then seem "tiny people," but Bryher encourages her to continue, and the buzzing ceases. As the first three pictures remain "static," dots of light appear. They form lines that constellate excruciatingly slowly into a ladder, "Jacob's ladder if you will" (54). The intense concentration required seems almost unbearable, but fortunately, the last figure forms quickly, H.D. reports, manifesting itself as an angel, "Niké. Victory" (54), who floats up the ladder past a series of half-S patterns, a kind of scrollwork. She moves toward "a series of tent-like triangles" (55) at which point H.D. "shut [s] off, 'cut[s] out' before the final picture" (56). She is disturbed at the premonition of war but assured by Victory, H.D.'s "own especial sign" (56). H.D. is exhausted; she has had "maybe just a little too much" (56). Bryher, however, takes over and "reads" the final image, "a circle like the sun-disk and a figure within the disk; a man, she thought, was reaching out to draw the image of a woman (. . . Niké) into the sun beside him" (56).[10]

Morris, "the Corfu vision is structured like a hermetic re-creation of the Delphic session" (162), which, denied in one space, H.D. first imagines into text and then projects into vision. See "Reading H.D.'s 'Helios and Athene.'"

[10]Various critics have discussed these images. Morris reads them in tems of a pervasive "projective process" in H.D. ("Projection," 411-13). Holland looks at H.D.'s vision in terms of "mother fixation," megalomania, and castration complex and as a symbolic intermediary "to close the gap with signs" (492); Riddel reads the Corfu

Freud considered these images to be H.D.'s "most dangerous" (*TF*, 41) symptom; I find this judgment fascinating, for in a sense the vision at Corfu marks rather her release from symptoms in an intermediate moment, a moment in which H.D. projects "visionary sensation" and conflates it with text. What she sees is different from her other reported "visions" precisely because it is "written." H.D. suggests that we can read the writing, even "the fact that there was writing" (51) in several ways. In Freud's view, she reports, it suggests "megalomania," a "suppressed desire for forbidden 'signs'" (51). When we remember that Freud "translated" the pictures on the wall as H.D.'s "desire for union with [her] mother" (*TF*, 44) what is *really* forbidden becomes clear—not the sign but the referent, the mother. What also disturbed Freud, one supposes, is that unlike the poetic visions she "created," the Corfu vision appeared to her readymade. Moreover, she interpreted it, in part, as belonging to "a tradition of warnings or messages from another world or another state of being" (*TF*, 50). When H.D. thinks through Freud, she sees the experience as "freakish" and "dangerous," thought "that had got out of hand, gone too far" (51). Her own inclination, however, is to read the writing on the wall as "an extension of the artist's mind . . . projected from within (though apparently from outside), really a high-powered *idea*, simply over-stressed, *over-thought*, you might say" (51). Julian Jaynes's idea that "bicameral men did not imagine; they experienced" (371) is also helpful in trying to understand what was happening to H.D. as she stared at the hotel room wall. She did not "imagine" or "create" the signs at Corfu but *experienced* them as if they had been given to her; rather than a pathological moment, it was an imaginary, or bicameral, one.

There is a fine line, however, as Jaynes continually intimates, between pathology and bicamerality: in the modern world we are expected to function consciously; severe or prolonged aberrations move us from art to madness. What salvages the Corfu experience, what saves H.D., continually, is projection into text. She textualizes

---

experience as a "dream" centered on "the question of the sign" ("H.D.'s Scene," 56). Robinson discusses them as an "omen of apocalyptic catastrophe" (303), and Friedman suggests that Corfu represented H.D.'s confirmation of "an artistic destiny in which she would unite prophecy, art, and healing into a message of resurrection for the modern 'city of ruin'" (*PR*, 186).

both to register and to repair the rifts, the gaps, the losses, the aberrations: "My thought / would cover deplorable gaps / . . . reveal the regrettable chasm, / bridge that before-and-after schism, / . . . in an endeavour to make ready, / as it were, the patient for the Healer" (*Walls Do Not Fall*, 54). Textualization is the way that H.D. heals herself and the world: writing in images, like the "literal language" Homans describes in *Bearing the Word*, replaces the symptom, because what that symptom, like the sign, "stands in" for reappears, obviating the necessity to distort and re-present it.

One of the important aspects of *Palimpsest* is that it is the space in which she explores this process and begins to close the gap opened at Corfu. Reading H.D.'s account in "Writing on the Wall," one is struck not only by the intensity of her experience or the nature of the images but by the realization that the same "vision" washes through the 1926 novel.

The first image, the visored soldier, is reflected in the helmeted men who appear throughout *Palimpsest*, the former captains and World War I airmen and the Roman soldiers who surround Hipparchia. The chalice is central to Hipparchia's imaging of her head as a "chaste goblet" filled with a "subtly dangerous" "bubbling fire," "bubbling wine" (35), and also in her distorted reflection in a "chased pure metal goblet" (69) that, like "an enchanter's crystal," also offers images of the dead. The motif of triangles appears in references to Egyptian pyramids and Roman tents; the black flies appear insistently as Hipparchia's sense of "small insinuating black-winged monsters" (43) and "her just realized fearful suspicion of an inimical dark world buzzing beneath her amethyst water-clear indifference" (43). Niké is recuperated both in the phantom Niké birth house Helen Fairwood hallucinates in the desert and in Hipparchia's sense of herself as "Delphic priestess" (41) reaching out toward "a just-invisible and just not-embodied Helios," impossible to dissociate in his various manifestations in *Palimpsest* (all three women are preoccupied with him) from the last image in Corfu, "invisible" to H.D. until "seen" through Bryher.

Moreover, in "Writing on the Wall" H.D. describes the entire experience in a passage remarkably similar to passages in *Palimpsest*, a passage worked in images reappropriated from the earlier text as if the experience were somehow the same, as if securing the vision in

Corfu were related to Helen Fairwood's need "to dive deep, deep, courageously into some unexploited region of the consciousness, into some common deep sea of unrecorded knowledge and bring, triumphant, to the surface some treasure buried, lost, forgotten" (179). In *Tribute to Freud* H.D. writes: "I have the feeling of holding my breath under water. As if I were searching under water for some priceless treasure, and if I bobbed up to the surface the clue to its whereabouts would be lost forever. . . . [I] am in . . . another element, and as I seem now so near to getting the answer or finding the treasure, I feel that my whole life, my whole being, will be blighted forever if I miss this chance" (*TF*, 53). And Raymonde Ransome, faced with the "writing on the wall," the inevitability that her own past will bleed through "faces, people, London. People, faces, Greece . . . people, faces, Egypt" (157), plunges underwater in the same search. "On, on, on, on, and out of it like some deep-sea jewel pulled up in a net squirming with an enormous catch of varigated [sic] squirming tentacled and tendrilled memories, just this, this— *who fished the murex up?*" (157).

What is it, then, the women in *Palimpsest* are looking for? What is it H.D. finds in Corfu: "just this, this." The appositive line from Robert Browning's "Popularity" becomes one of the most important refrains washing through the text; from it H.D. takes the title of the second section, and it becomes an emblem of the palimpsest. Beyond the "sense" of Browning's tribute to Keats, which explores the psychic and material price of the writing life, there is the central image of the murex, the mollusk that yielded the Greeks their coveted purple dye. Drawn up from antiquity, drawn up from the sea, drawn up from another poet's poem, it is a living link between present and past, the "liquor filtered by degrees," which H.D. draws on "to paint the future from the past" (Browning, 217). The nature of the murex, encoding as it does the poles she worked around in the poetry—air and crystal, sea and jewel, form and essence—undoubtedly appealed to H.D. A shell enclosing mysterious substance, a substance that had to be distilled and refined almost alchemically, is a sign for H.D. of the pulse she felt so intensely, the pulse between the tightening helmet and the diadem, between arrow vibrance and release. Like the jewel in *The Flowering of the Rod*, which opens into infinity and releases for Kaspar "the whole secret of the mystery" (152), the shell, which releases a suffusion of purple, provides the way of closing the gap, for the murex is the sign of the inner spaces of both consciousness and language: "Verses, verses, verses. *Who fished the murex up?* Verses were the murex. They dyed all existence with their color" (160). This treasure, then, "buried, lost, forgotten" is both memory and meter, repressed biographical material and the poet's language itself. It is also, I would stress, the mother's body. In a similar way, the vision on Corfu is also the murex, and "herself sunk down, down to some unexplored region of the consciousness" (221) is the murex, as vision, verses, identity merge into one so that "she herself is the writing," is the shattered poem, is the voices, is the writing on a hotel wall.

This forgotten treasure becomes, then, both what is sought and the means of seeking it(self). In H.D.'s palimpsest of language and desire, she excavates earlier texts, the "texts" of the mother's body, to release the writing that will initiate/has initiated the excavation. The extraordinary importance of *Palimpsest* is that it both generates and recuperates the mode central to H.D.'s aesthetics and psychology. It is a hermetic text, which nonetheless spills out of itself freely. It opens into the future and into the past and then conflates both impulses in the present. This vastly underestimated modernist murex explores the relationship between language and consciousness through images and strategies that connect three minds as if we were in the presence of one layered consciousness, a textual consciousness which is the reflection of H.D.'s lifelong literary and personal struggle to "[merge] and [make] one of all the selves, the self of the slave locked into the silver barred and shimmering intellect, the slave more languorous . . . the other, the slave that held, a solid link, her everyday self, enslaved to both these others" (*P*, 212).

7

Bitter Jewel

As a writer often cast within a male tradition through her association with a constellation of artistic and intellectual luminaries—Ezra
Pound, D. H. Lawrence, Richard Aldington, Cecil Gray, and Sigmund Freud—H.D., as protégée, muse, wife, lover and analysand,
continually strove within this male context to find her own voice and
vision, a voice that evolved out of a matriarchal mythos culled, as we
have seen, at no small price, from dream, imagination, memory,
desire, and ancient text, transmuting spiritual, psychological, and
physical ruin into "true rune." How is it, we might ask, that H.D.
finally managed to create a mother amid so many jealous, appropriating, demanding "fathers" to whom she was so tightly bound for
the better part of seventy-six years? Part of the answer to this question lies in her *Trilogy*, a poem that reformulates her relationships to
the significant male and female figures in her life and advances a
sexual poetics evolving from the tension between the symbolic and
the semiotic, and between heterosexual and lesbian desire.

As many critics have observed, H.D.'s feelings about the men who
surrounded and filled her life, who influenced, absorbed, censored,
or inspired her work were intense and complicated. Even at the end
of her life she was incredibly susceptible to both their praise and their
condemnation; shortly before she died she sent Pound a copy of her
poem "Winter Love" enclosing a note: "It might be a little divertisse-
ment to you to slash it to pieces & return—or not."[1] As Susan

[1]Quoted in Friedman and DuPlessis, " 'I Had Two Loves Separate': The Sexualities
of H.D.'s *Her*."

Friedman and Rachel Blau DuPlessis suggest, "It is hard even to believe that we are dealing with a 75-year old major poet who had just completed several major works" (21). Alicia Ostriker, in *Writing Like a Woman*, reads H.D.'s relationship with Pound as paradigmatic of her relationships with other men: "He defines her. By the same token he can destroy her. He, not she, is strong, authoritative. 'He' is any man [H.D.] is attracted to, physically, emotionally, intellectually" (15).

H.D., unlike Rhys, is not merely a victim of the men in her life; she solicits, in a sense, the very relationships that undermine her work. Rachel DuPlessis has used the term "romantic thralldom" to discuss this damaging, "culturally mandated and seductive pattern to male-female relations" to which H.D. constantly returned, relationships in which a "sense of completion or transformation" is bought at "the high price of obliteration and paralysis" (RT, 178, 179). DuPlessis suggests that part of the reason H.D. buys into this "psychocultural script" is that, ironically, it invigorates her work; "the pain of thralldom seemed to fire H.D.'s creativity even as it undercut the conditions necessary for her fullest, uncensored flowering" (186).[2] In psychological rather than linguistic terms what DuPlessis refers to is really a replication of the interplay between the semiotic and the symbolic: to enter the androcentric system of representation requires always a certain censoring (of the mother's body) and yet to refuse entry is to defeat oneself as speaking self, especially if what one wants to speak is the mother.

What sets H.D. apart from many women writers is her attempt, despite profound and painful ambivalence, to revise the "script," both the plot of the family and cultural romance and its inscription. Sometimes, particularly in her early work, this attempt at transformation involves an androgynous persona always in the context of a "fundamental premise of hermetic tradition: the existence of an androgynous Divine One transcending all dualism" (Friedman, "I Go," 238). Sometimes, as Friedman and DuPlessis observe, H.D.'s struggle is to "invent and to encourage a companionate visionary male"

[2]DuPlessis has done important seminal work on H.D.'s relationship to male figures. "Romantic Thralldom" reads through H.D.'s major published prose and poetry, examining how the poet attempted to revise the script of thralldom. For related work, see also "Family, Sexes, Psyche" and *H.D.: The Career of That Struggle*.

(23), transforming "the actual male suitor, whose love had been experienced as an attack, into a spirit twin to her own soul with whom she transcends the patriarchal divisions of male and female, victim and victimizer" (Friedman, "I Go," 241). By twinning herself with a male, she calls upon the early incestuous dyad on which she relied before the appearance of the sister motif in her work; through this heterosexual incest, which is later replaced by homoeroticism, she attempts thematically to rupture the tenets of discourse, based on the incest taboo, and to find a more comfortable entry into the space of language. As we have seen before, however, the oedipal configuration, in its asymmetries, does not prohibit father-daughter incest in the same way as it prohibits incest with the mother. Thus, H.D.'s initial attempts at androgyny as an alternative to access are not sufficiently disruptive to the structure of discourse.

Clearly, however, H.D. senses a need to reinvent the male myth that underlies her work.[3] Even more important, perhaps, than the *nature* of these companions, twins, or lovers is the *function* they come to serve for the poet. It is not until *Tribute to Freud* that it becomes possible to fully understand how the male figure functions textually for H.D.; it is perhaps not until her sessions with Freud in 1933 and 1934 that she begins to understand that process consciously herself, to understand not how she is influenced by men (or male culture) but how she might revise and replace them in her work.

H.D.'s evolving relationship with Freud reflects the evolving relationships with other male figures in her life. Several critics have explored the succession of roles Freud took in the transference.[4] Ostriker, for example, notes Freud as "a father-figure, brother-figure, semi-lover, and Muse" (29). For Norman Holland, "Freud has come

[3]For a discussion of how H.D. attempts to define the nature of male figures, see particularly Ostriker, "The Poet as Heroine: Learning to Read H.D.," in *Writing like a Woman*.

[4]Various interpretations of H.D.'s relationship with Freud can be found in Friedman, *Psyche Reborn*; DuPlessis and Friedman, "'Woman is Perfect'"; Norman Holland; and Joseph N. Riddel. One of the most interesting works is Adalaide Morris's "Concept of Projection: H.D.'s Visionary Powers." It is worth noting for its insights into the dreams, magical acts, alchemy, and transmutations of *Trilogy* and into H.D.'s relationship with Freud, particularly her complicated transference, which in one way "enabled H.D. to affirm herself" (427) but in its "murkier" aspect "was a condition not of cure but of compulsion" (428). See also H.D.'s own *Tribute to Freud*.

to stand for the whole ambiguous network of wishes and relationships associated with the oedipal wishes of a little girl: that she could
become a mother with her brother as father; that she could, by
marrying her father, become her brother's mother; that she could, by
marrying her brother, become her father's mother" (483–84). What
Holland, like Lacan, leaps over here is the significance of *preoedipal*
wishes, on which, as it turns out, H.D.'s psychology turns. It was the
figure of the *mother* that emerged as the center of H.D.'s analysis, the
focus of her sessions with Freud, who diagnosed H.D., we remember, as having a "mother-fixation." H.D. reports, "The professor
said I had not made the conventional transference from mother to
father" (*TF*, 136).

Holland acknowledges that Freud finally became the mother in the
transference, but like Freud himself, who told H.D. frankly (and
rather crankily), "I do not like to be the mother in transference—it
always surprises and shocks me a little. I feel so very masculine" (*TF*,
146–47), Holland seems a bit uncomfortable. What does one do with
a middle-aged woman "fixated" on her mother? Holland "allows"
H.D. two variants of relationship: Freud can take the role of the
"oedipal mother," the mother one relinquishes, or, "most important, the cosmic, oral mother of earliest infancy" (501), the mother
with whom one fuses, the mother who has not yet appeared as other.
Holland, in effect, issues a psychocultural mandate for women:
abandon the mother or merge back into her until there is no sense of
either you or her as self. What neither Freud nor Holland allows,
what in fact the patriarchal world in which H.D. operates does not
allow, is *adult* relation with the mother, because, in strict Freudian
terms, for a woman to become "adult" means, by definition, to give
up the mother.

Even more dangerous than relation, however, is desire. What if a
woman were to desire the mother? What if there were an erotic
component to the bond as, in fact, there was for H.D., not in terms of
Helen Doolittle, perhaps, but in terms of the Helen/Thetis/Mary
figures who begin, after analysis, to fill her work?

Although many critics (and Freud himself) want to read H.D.'s
relationship with the mother as pathological, it is this "fixation" that
begins to free H.D.'s work. Heretofore willing to keep the central
women in her life confined to unpublished prose, H.D., through her

awakening understanding of the significance of those forces, both readjusts her relationship with Freud and opens a matrilineage in her poetry.[5] The fixation, then, which Freud wanted to cure, becomes to H.D. a kind of liberating center to be cultivated, much like the *chora* Kristeva describes, opening a gap in language.

At this point in the H.D. tapestry, we need to pick up earlier threads, threads held behind the warp. Concurrent with H.D.'s complicated involvements with men is a series of complicated relationships with women. As Friedman and DuPlessis have described, "H.D. anchored her fiction in a life that contained the culturally forbidden love of woman for woman. . . . The persona, always a mask for H.D. herself, experiences a fusion of erotic and spiritual passion for another woman, a bond associated with H.D.'s centered identity as both woman and artist" (8). Friedman and DuPlessis, however, read these relationships with women in "the context of H.D.'s equally intense, but even more ambivalent emotional and sexual entanglements with a series of men."[6] The reverse is perhaps (also) true: H.D.'s involvement with the women in her life is more profoundly ambivalent than is her involvement with men.

Besides her mother, Helen Wolle Doolittle, two women figured strongly in H.D.'s early (and later) life. One was Frances Josepha Gregg, a young woman H.D. met in Philadelphia about the time she was being courted by Pound. Although the intensity of their relationship was relatively short-lived, it was for several years the locus of H.D.'s awakening bisexuality. Gregg, the prototype for Fayne Rabb in *HERmione*, figures prominently in H.D.'s early autobiographical prose as the force that agitates both her homosexuality and her relationship with her mother.[7] The second important woman in H.D.'s life was Bryher, who served alternately/simultaneously as companion, muse, protector, antagonist, and lover in an intense and

[5]The most substantive work on matrilineage in H.D. has been done by Friedman; see *Psyche Reborn*, particularly chap. 5, pp. 131–54, and chap. 8, "Born of One Mother." Also useful in this regard are Friedman and DuPlessis, " 'I Had Two Loves Separate.' "

[6]This passage, however, is not entirely representative of their subsequent work, which increasingly acknowledges the complications of H.D.'s relationships with women.

[7]See in particular *HERmione* and "Asphodel."

uneven relationship that nonetheless often provided the center for
H.D.'s emotional and creative existence.

Freud apparently tried to convince H.D. that her attraction to both
Gregg and Bryher "had been unconsciously motivated by her desire
for union with her mother," according to Friedman and Duplessis
(18); thus H.D.'s relationship to women is complicated by both a
"maternal fixation" and a lesbian eroticism, whose conflation is even
more culturally taboo than love of woman for woman. The love of
daughter for mother, mother for daughter—incest—is the nexus of
mother and Eros that many critics avoid,[8] although the trend of
H.D.'s imagination and mythmaking and desire reveals itself to be,
discovers itself to be, matrilinear, not only in the sense of poetic
revisionism but in an insistent, maternally connoted homoeroticism.
Friedman and (particularly) DuPlessis have made the most powerful
contributions in this area, although in their early work they talk
about H.D.'s autobiographical prose in terms of what they jointly call
"two binary sets: the parental and the erotic" (13). They recognize,
however, an important pattern: "While H.D.'s probable transformation of the lesbian sister of *Her* into the goddess figures of her later
work represents a turning away from the direct affirmation of a
lesbian eros, it is important to recognize the common origins of these
different representations of love between women. When we understand the connection both Freud and H.D. made between her love
for Gregg and Bryher and her search for the powerful mother, we can
decipher the sister-love that is deeply encoded in H.D.'s later works"
(19).

Before turning to the forays into incest of *Trilogy,* I would like to
look at Hermione's relationship with Fayne Rabb, who is clearly a
sexual presence in *HERmione*.[9] As sister surrogate, mother substi-

[8]Ostriker alludes to a kind of incestuous passion in rather hurried subordinate
clauses: "If in ['Demeter'] H.D. hints that the ultimately 'passionate' eroticism is
between mother and daughter, 'Thetis' hints that it is between mother and son" (24).
Friedman writes that H.D. "accepted, without any moral hesitation, the incestuous
base of erotic passion implicit in Freud's theory of adult sexual love," but she reads this
only in terms of heterosexual incest (*Psyche Reborn*, 143). Rachel DuPlessis examines
this issue most fully in *H.D.: The Career of That Struggle.*

[9]My reading of *HERmione* here is informed by the important work of Friedman and
DuPlessis in "'I Had Two Loves Separate.'" This essay establishes the conflicting
plots of lesbian and heterosexual desire and betrayal in the novel and examines H.D.'s

tute, and object of desire, she conjures a displaced maternal language as well as lesbianism and incest, thus providing, as DuPlessis has written of H.D.'s *Hedylus*, "a wiry subtext of persistent matrisexuality" (*H.D.*, 44).

One of the important aspects of *HERmione* for my purposes is Hermione's desire for a sister to replace the failed sister-in-law we remember from the Garts' dinner table.

> "Minnie is my sister" had been enjoined on her by [her mother] who said, "In our family my mother never referred to Nell or Carnia as daughters-in-law." Minnie, Her's sister-in-law, therefore, . . . became by some illogical reasoning "my sister." A sister was a creature of ebony strung with wild poppies or an image of ivory whose lithe hips made parallel and gave reflection of like parallel in a fountain basin. . . . A sister would have companion hound. . . . A sister who owned such a hound . . . was supplanted by Minnie. [10–11]

Part of the conflict for Hermione centers on the fact that Minnie has married her brother, Bertrand, one of the "things she would never get into words" (17). "She did not know why and how she loved her brother. He did not know how and why he loved Hermione. . . . Hermione had not been able to predict . . . 'cerebral-erotic affinities'" (17). Minnie remains on the outside of Hermione and Bertrand's relationship, although it is clear that the intensity of the "affinity" is rather one-sided. Hermione finds it impossible to explain "family matters" because, "in order to explain to Minnie, Hermione would have to explain to herself things that had no palpable explanation" (21); these include her mother's "still days," which Her attributes to Eugenia's loss of a baby. Hermione thinks, "It was impossible to explain to Minnie that the baby was one between herself and Bertrand, a girl, stillborn" (21). The suggestion here is not only of birth order but of incest, a baby between brother and sister. This passing reference is actually a pivotal moment in the text, for it both establishes and ruptures the brother-sister dyad; it couples them but simultaneously introduces the stillborn sister.

bisexuality within the context of her analysis with Freud. Friedman and DuPlessis also undertake a preliminary reading of the Hermione-Eugenia relationship and sketch the development of the mother figure in H.D., particularly the movement toward maternal "revelation" in H.D.'s later poetry.

Just as Minnie severs Hermione from the brother, she also severs Hermione, through her father, from her "real sister": "To hear Minnie say 'father' was a two-edged theft. It stole from Her a presence that left her (no one else had) alone and that again stole from her a presence: the thing that would have had that other hound, twin hounds, . . . the half of herself that was forever missing. If her father was also the father to . . . this thing, then the half of her, that twin-self sister would be forever blighted" (16). As Minnie, the sister *in Law*, steals from Hermione the possibility of "reflection of like parallel," Her slips between one identity and another—"She was not Gart, she was not Hermione, she was not any more Her Gart, what was she?" (4)—grappling for some "pool or mirror that would refract image. She was nothing. She must have an image" (5).

Fayne Rabb, initially, provides just that; she appears at the very moment when the unstable Hermione seems about to vanish. Hermione realizes "her head—the bit here, the bit there, the way it fitted bit to bit—was two convex mirrors placed back to back. The two convex mirrors placed back to back became one mirror . . . as Fayne Rabb entered" (138). Fayne becomes associated with a series of refrains from Swinburne which cadence the text—"*O sister my sister O singing swallow, the world's division divideth us*" (179)—refrains that open into sections of lesbian eroticism represented, as Friedman and DuPlessis have observed, as this " 'sister-love,' the narcissistic passion of twin souls for themselves in each other" (18).

Initially Fayne functions to shift Hermione from the brother and from the "Law" into the sister's story, which, as we continue to see, is a necessary detour for the writing daughter. It is not surprising, then, that it is also through Fayne that H.D. gives Hermione access to the mother which she cannot have in "real" life. She creates, in fact, a scene that parallels the summer storm, a scene in which the imagery of pregnancy and birth has been conflated with a lesbian sexuality.

Her Gart saw rings and circles, the rings and circles that were the eyes of Fayne Rabb. Rings and circles made concentric curve toward a ceiling that was, as it were, the bottom of a deep pool. Her and Fayne Rabb were flung into a concentric intimacy, rings on rings that made a geometric circle toward a ceiling, that curved over them like ripples on a pond surface. Her and Fayne were flung . . . to the bottom of some strange element and looming up . . . there were rings on rings of circles as if they had fallen

into a deep well and were looking up . . . "long since half kissed away."
[164]

Like Hermione and Eugenia, Her and Fayne have been plunged here
(and in similar passages) below the surface into an erotic and linguistic space pulsing with "long throats" and "small hands" (145), "a
hard dynamic forceful vibrant hand" (145), kissing, rippling, fling-
ing, falling, tightness, swift, heavy thrusting, "the hand of Fayne
Rabb," "the throat of Her Gart" (145).

There is a commingling here of both bodies and identity, Hermione saying, "I will not have her hurt I will not have Her hurt. She
is Her. I am Her. Her is Fayne. Fayne is Her. I will not let them hurt
HER" (181). This confusion of selves runs throughout the Fayne
section of the novel, splitting and doubling: "She is some amplifica-
tion of myself like amoeba giving birth, by breaking off, to amoeba. I
am a sort of mother, a sort of sister to Her" (158). In one sense Fayne
is her sister, twin, daughter; in another she is a version of the mother.
The sexual nature of her relationship with Hermione underlines
Hermione's ambivalence, suggesting both a turning from the mother's body in favor of Fayne's and a refusal of men to return instead to
the female (maternal) form.

The other phase of Fayne's influence is linguistic. She takes the
language within which she and Hermione are forced to operate and
begins to manipulate it, reinvent it, disturb it, replacing conventions
of syntax and representation. As Shari Benstock has observed, Fayne
attempts to teach Hermione that her lesbian desire puts her "under
penalty of linguistic law," that it not only culturally displaces her but
is reflected in "the sense of displacement she feels *in language*" (339).
In Fayne's first conversation with Hermione she challenges Hermione's intellectual discipleship to George Lowndes. Fayne, the in-
quisitor who reveals Hermione's indecisiveness and dependence,
forces Her to take stock of herself, persistently unearthing Her's
hesitancy and imprecision.

Hermione becomes progressively aware of Fayne's oddness and
difference, feeling as though she has entered an unfamiliar zone
where words are played for different stakes: "There was a zone she
had not explored. She could use the same counter, the same sort of
password that she used with all these people, but she had passed . . .

into another forest. This forest was reality. There, the very speaking of the words, conjured up proper answering sigil" (61). Suddenly the closed system of George Lowndes and Carl Gart opens up, and Hermione finds herself on the threshold of a space where words are a kind of talisman, transporting the initiate into other planes where Her feels a rhythmic communion, a vibration or register to discourse, participating in some incantation or evocation: "Words with Fayne in a room, in any room became projections of things beyond one. Things beyond Her beat, beat to get through Her, to get through to Fayne. So prophetess faced prophetess over tea plates scattered and two teacups making delphic pattern on a worn carpet" (146). Just as two signs of ordinary life, plates and cups, become transformed into Delphic patterns, ambiguous and oracular, so too does the language the two women share transcend the arbitrary sign. As in the first section of *Trilogy*, where H.D. writes of "the meaning that words hide; / they are anagrams, cryptograms, / little boxes, conditioned / to hatch butterflies" (53), language in *HERmione* becomes hieroglyphs, images which do not immediately, arbitrarily confer "meaning" or stand in as substitutes; they must be consulted, returned to, interpreted through their presence.

As in the breakfast room scene with Eugenia, Hermione begins, through Fayne, to sense her ability to "supercede [*sic*] a scheme of mathematical-biological definition":

Now I will reveal myself in words. . . . Words may be my heritage and with words I will prove conic sections a falsity and the very stars that wheel and frame concentric pattern as mere very-stars, gems put there, a gift, a diadem, a crown, a chair, a cart or a mere lady. A lady will be set back in the sky. It will be no longer Arcturus and Vega but stray star-spume, star sprinkling from a wild river, and it will be myth; mythopoeic mind (mine) will disprove science and . . . definition. [76]

H.D. anticipates here a way of relating to words which will release her from the confines of patriarchal definition and naming, from the symbolic, will merge jewel and diadem (the key images in "Paint It To-Day" and "Hipparchia") and link them, finally, with the mother, a lady set back in the sky.

But Fayne, despite her association with this linguistic alchemy, is an enigmatic and duplicitous creature who not only opens paths for

Hermione but lies in wait for her in the surrounding forest. She becomes increasingly cunning and faithless, alternately validating and negating Her, reviving and abusing her, promising her the freedom of Delphic vision and then telling her, "You can't *see* what I see," to which Hermione intones, "No, Fayne. I don't pretend to" (161). Fayne attacks the very thing she has opened to Her—her writing—calling it "unreal." It is Fayne who first allows Hermione a vision beyond "superimposed standards" but then denies her the affirmation of her separate truth.

Fayne becomes at the end of the novel more constricting, more repressive, more damaging than the mother from whom she initially helps Hermione escape. (Fayne, significantly, is involved throughout the novel in an incestuous relationship with her own mother, from whom she cannot extricate herself.)[10] Having severed Hermione from Eugenia and won Her, spiritually, aesthetically, and sexually, Fayne enters into a relationship with George Lowndes, whom she has made such show to despise. This final betrayal, buried elliptically in the text, is largely what catapults Hermione into the madness of the last section, a madness she has anticipated from the first pages—"I am certifiable or soon will be" (6).

Although her dementia is occasioned by loss—alienation from Eugenia, betrayal by both Fayne and George—it is also a space where the current of the subtext rises, where the discourse of madness, its stray star-spume, is intricately related to birth language, the language of the summer storm, the language of lying-in. This madness, like maternity, like sexuality, dissolves the boundaries of self and other, inside and outside, in a vertiginous moment in which language unlatches. Unintentionally, Fayne gives Hermione the very language she held back from her by denying it to her, by betraying her, by causing her to go "mad." Thus, although Fayne is in one sense a false prophet, she is also the force that redeems the mother textually, filling the text with body and sexual rhythm and delirium—all aspects associated with maternal, semiotic discourse.

It is not surprising, then, that in her delirium Hermione finds not only her voice but her mother: "I will say wakening, perhaps

---

[10]The incestuous mother-daughter relationship is explored most fully and most explicitly in "Asphodel."

tomorrow, where is Eugenia? I have been delirious. I will take Eugenia's hand, forget, remembering . . . I will . . . say 'Mama' " (215).
Through the novel Hermione has called Eugenia "Eugenia," unable
to say "Mother": here in her madness, occasioned by Fayne, both
catalyst and obstacle, Hermione relates to Eugenia precisely as
daughter.

The state that has allowed this maternal contact opens into a new
kind of language integrally related to Hermione's body and total
being, not just her intellect. As she starts to recover, she has the
lingering sense that "everything has been erased, would be written
on presently" (221–22). She participates on the other side of madness
in a kind of writing in which "her feet were pencils tracing a path
through a forest. The world had been razed, had been made clear for
this thing. . . . Now the creator was Her's feet, narrow black crayon
across the winter whiteness. . . . She trailed feet across a space of
immaculate clarity, leaving her wavering hieroglyph as upon white
parchment" (223–24). Her writing has become a writing through the
body, a "visible language" (213), much like that Hélène Cixous describes in "The Laugh of the Medusa": "She physically materializes
what she's thinking; she signifies it with her body. In a certain way
she *inscribes* what she's saying, because she doesn't deny her drives
the intractable and impassioned part they have in speaking" (251).
Through her ambivalence and desire, Hermione comes to read both
the biological mother (Eugenia) and the displaced mother (Fayne) as
cryptograms, boxes of containment which nonetheless might be interpreted for a subtext, a wild river, an explosion of birds or butterflies. This reading she translates into the discourse that surrounds
her, emerging in a linguistic space where she formulates the mother
as "mama" and discovers another kind of language born of the
approach to both "mothers"—hieroglyphs severed finally from the
formula of Bertrand and Carl Gart.

The issues of sexuality, incest and language emerge again in a later
text, *Trilogy*, in which it is possible to perceive H.D.'s ambivalence
toward the primary female figures in her life, the uses she makes of
the male figures, and the resultant sexual poetics of her work. Primarily, I suggest, she uses the male mystical and literary figure not so
much to represent her artistic "thralldom" as to displace her sexuality. Against Susan Friedman, who writes that "the poet invokes
the protection of the Goddess to fortify herself as she makes her

forays into the dangerous territory of heterosexuality" ("I Go," 241),
I argue that H.D. invokes in this work the mediation of gods and *male*
patrons to anchor and fortify herself as she makes her forays into the
dangerous territory of lesbianism and incest.

The first section of the trilogy, *The Walls Do Not Fall* (1944) begins as
an antiwar poem set amid destruction, schism, chasms, powerlessness, in a palimpsest of ancient and modern ruin. Moving into images of resurrection and healing—the phoenix, the tree of life, the
caduceus—H.D. conjures voyagers and initiates in a quest to recover
lost secrets, lost islands, havens, integration, unity. This journey
passes through war-torn cities and through writing itself; it is a
journey of regeneration associated, above all, with "protection for
the Scribe" (*T*, 15). We might, I think, read it through Kristeva's
"disintegrating voyage toward the mother" (*DL*, 27), the compelling
journey fraught with danger where a new language offers itself at the
risk of reabsorbing the subject altogether, where the "I" does not
survive the collision of the symbolic and semiotic.

H.D. sets this first section concerning both her artistic destiny
and her personal safety in relation to the "world-father," the "All-
father," Ra, Osiris, Amen. Although she is mindful of the difficulty
of disentangling the Christos image "from its art-craft junk-shop /
paint-and-plaster medieval jumble / of pain-worship and death-
symbol" (27), although she alludes to the usefulness of entreating
"the original great-mother" (47), in the initial phase of the poem the
poet clearly sets herself and her myth within a male context, confronting the split encountered by all women writers faced with the
initial realization that the privileging of symbol erases and replaces
(maternal) origins.

Hesitant particularly in a movement toward incestuous sexuality,
H.D. invokes a male patron, Hermes Trismegistus, to begin the
second section, *Tribute to the Angels* (1945). Instead of falling prey to
"thralldom," however, she solicits his complicity to oversee a trans-
mutation of language.

> Now polish the crucible
> and in the bowl distill
>
> a word most bitter, *marah,*
> a word bitterer still, *mar,*
>
> sea, brine, breaker, seducer,
> giver of life, giver of tears;

> Now polish the crucible
> and set the jet of flame
>
> under, till *marah-mar*
> are melted, fuse and join
>
> and change and alter,
> mer, mere, mère, mater, Maia, Mary,
>
> Star of the Sea,
> Mother. [71]

What is important here is the sudden central presence of a transmuted maternal figure who dominates, in various incarnations, the remaining portion of the poem. *Trilogy* is significant as the space in which H.D. begins to work through the intense ambivalence of her early work, taking early conflicting aspects of the mother and attempting to fuse them, change them, alter them, passing through maternity and bitterness and illusion and divinity until the *word*—Mother—lies in the crucible. To extract her requires this transmogrification through *language*, a textualization, alchemy worked not upon the lost maternal form itself but on the words that both contain and release her. This passage is reminiscent of another in "The Gift," written during 1941–1943, which seems in a sense to open the way for this textualization, this insistence that the mother appear within discourse: "Mary, Maia, Miriam, Mut, Madre, Mere, Mother, pray for us. . . . This is Gaia, this is the beginning. This is the end. Under every shrine to Zeus, to Jupiter, to Zeus-pater or Theus-pater or God-the-father . . . there is an earlier altar. There is, beneath the carved superstructure of every temple to God-the-father, the dark cave or grotto or inner hall or cellar to Mary, Mere, Mut, mutter, pray for us" (chap. 4, p. 10). Deleted from the published version, this articulation of the mother, like the mother herself, is suppressed in women's writing; the passage replicates both thematically and linguistically the place of the mother in androcentric discourse. First, it invokes a universal and archaic mother, positioning her as does the Rhys passage in relation to God-the-father and as does Lacan in terms of the name-of-the-father, caught within the "carved superstructure" of catechism and language. And yet, says H.D., beneath every temple to the father (the symbolic) there is a dark cave or inner hall where one might invoke the mother's voice and rhythm, a grotto in language (the semiotic), which is the mother's space. It is the space of the "mutter" in both its senses: the "mother" and the "mutter"—low utterances, rumblings, murmurings.

It is only after the mother has been worked through the mediation of text that the poet dares address her: "Bitter, bitter jewel / in the heart of the bowl, / . . . what do you offer / to us who rebel?" (72). In this rather astonishing passage the jewel of "Paint It To-Day," the gift the mother would betray, now becomes the mother herself. The daughter takes a great risk here and also makes a great demand, entertaining the possibility that the mother might be contacted as a source of power and expression that would fill the void created by the restrictive discourse that excludes her. H.D. reemerges here as the rebellious daughter, the daughter who left home to follow Ezra Pound to Europe, the daughter who remained abroad, despite a broken engagement, to find her place as poet. Thirty-five years later she reinvokes the (dead) mother to examine what relationship they still might have, a complex question contingent on the poet's understanding of an even deeper question: What is this unsatisfied duality / which you can not satisfy?" (72).

This duality involves, on one level, H.D.'s conflict about herself as poet and daughter, the other side of Margaret Homans's reading of "nineteenth-century woman's attempt to write as a subject in the symbolic order and at the same time as a mother" (BW, 33). To be poet/*daughter*, it seems to H.D., she must protect herself by denying the maternal, by resisting association with the self-effacing Victorian mother who alternately smothers and turns from her. Part of the danger is the mother's inability to recognize the daughter's "gift,"[11] her artistic identity; this is the mother of HERmione who knits compulsively because, as she tells her daughter, "I can knit in the dark. I can't sew in the dark. Your father likes the light concentrated in a corner. He can work better if I'm sitting in the dark" (HER, 79). The other part of the danger is the ambivalent or dual sexual territory staked by (versions of) the mother, who alternately encourages the daughter's heterosexuality and clings to her incestuously.

In HERmione H.D.'s ambivalence toward the mother, before her

[11]For H.D.'s sense of "the gift" and its connection to her matrilineage, see "The Gift" TS, Collection of American Literature, Beinecke Rare Book and Manuscript Library, Yale University, New Haven, Conn.

passage through textualization, shifts without warning between rejection and desire:

> Watching hands. Hands in the darkness, hands in the darkness . . . you have no midwife power, you can't lift me out of this thing. Oh, hands in the dim light, for Gart wanted one heady downstream just there, on just his papers, . . . light concentrated on just his microscope or on just his little dish of sizzling acids. Light must be concentrated under a green cone, a cornucopia, like you hang on the Christmas tree, cornucopia, horn of plenty, she had told them, Demeter hand hanging little horns of plenty on the tree and always enough horns of plenty to go round. It was right. Oh, she's so horribly right. Then what is wrong with everything? [HER, 80]

What is wrong with everything is that Demeter sits not in the living room but in the "inner hall" beneath the superstructure of the scientist father, a space to which neither Hermione nor H.D. has immediate access. H.D. recognizes the hierarchy and interplay between the mother and father: "Carl Gart . . . and Eugenia moving through it powerless, all powerful. One should sing hymns of worship to her, powerful, powerless, all-powerful" (81). If we substitute "symbolic" for Carl and "semiotic" for Eugenia, we get the same rhythm of loss and access which Kristeva describes as the functioning of "poetic language," "the jouissance on the border of primal repression, beyond, although always coexistent with, . . . full, mimetic, and true signs" (DL, 263), the "aimless wandering," introduced by presymbolic relationship to the mother, "within the identity of the speaker and the economy of its very discourse" (DL, 137).

Decades after her earliest expression of this interplay, which she at first experiences only as anguished ambivalence, H.D. begins the reexamination and reinscription of the figure of the mother begun at the end of HERmione. In Tribute to the Angels she conjures in the alchemist's bowl not only the maternal aspect of the mother as Mary but her sexual nature as Venus. "O swiftly, re-light the flame," she says, "before the substance cool" (74), attempting to right the "impious wrong" done to Venus, "for venery stands for impurity / and Venus as desire / is venerous, lascivious" (74). Just as she works "marah" into "Mary," she transmutes "venery" into "venerate, / venerator" (75), reconciling the unsatisfied duality and claiming the mother as both muse and desire.

Hermes tries to make her name what she has done, but the poet resists: "I do not know what it gives, / a vibration that we can not name / for there is no name for it" (76). This is the space of the *chora*, "this archaic disposition of primary narcissism that a poet brings to light in order to challenge the closure of meaning" (*DL*, 281) and to avoid the symbolic function of language, which "constitutes itself at the cost of repressing instinctual drive and continuous relation to the mother" (*DL*, 136). What H.D. wants is protection for the scribe while she distills the mother out of history and myth and frees her from a linguistic and cultural system, the language of which denies her.[12]

In this section of the poem, where the imagery returns to the womb, to the sound of maternal pulse and heart, and the poet grows smaller and smaller, drawn into the jewel, H.D. works toward the discovery of a language that might *retain* continuous relation to the mother. In this context, the jewel opens into another space, a dream in which "the Lady" knocks in the outer hall. At this moment, H.D. begins to reclaim the mother as inspiration, as muse, but in order to do so, she must temporarily defer and displace her exploration of the mother's sexuality and of her own desire for her.

The lady who comes to the poet appears in a vaporized form, rather like the mother who appears by moonlight to Jane Eyre or the lady Hermione imagines set back in the sky. She is an asexual being: none of her traditional images "suggest her as I saw her" (96) writes H.D.; "she bore / none of her usual attributes; / the Child was not with her" (97). Instead, this lady carries a book and appears in order to confirm the poet/daughter, not to judge or deter her: "she must have been pleased / with the straggling company of the brush and quill / who did not deny their birthright" (100).

Unlike the biographical mother, the lady validates writing; as muse, the lady "is not shut up in a cave / like a Sibyl; she is not / imprisoned in leaden bars / in a coloured window; / she is Psyche" (103); transmuted and freed from cave and nave, she releases both herself and her daughter/poet's word, carrying not the child but "the

[12]See in this regard Rachel Blau DuPlessis, *H.D.: The Career of That Struggle*, in which she discusses at length the "muted stories" struggling within "androcentric statements [which] tend to read out, disparage or marginalise the meaning of female figures" (26).

unwritten volume of the new" (103). The relationship here between the mother's release and H.D.'s poetry is complex; by creating a lady who is no longer "shut up," no longer either confined or silenced, H.D. seems to find a corresponding release in her own work. While the daughter's revision frees the mother, it is simultaneously the revised mother who frees the daughter. Thus H.D. establishes an intricate pattern of mutual revision and reconciliation, creating a new kind of mother who comes without the "Lamb," "either as Bridegroom or Child" (104).

What this means to H.D., writing with a biographical resonance we cannot ignore, is that the lady's "attention is undivided" (she no longer favors the father or the eldest son, as H.D. felt her mother did) and that "we are her bridegroom and lamb" (104). This "we" is a central nexus in the poem, a move from singular to plural in which H.D. suddenly allies herself with "nameless initiates, / born of one mother" (21), creating a company of Eleusinian pilgrims come to celebrate and participate in the mystery of Koré and Demeter, of a daughter stolen and redeemed, of a mother (whose lamb we still might be) who carries with her "our book." It does not matter, says the poet, whether the book is written or unwritten; it will reveal itself in both known and unknown ways as a text stripped of mytho-cultural, androcentric references and responses, a space of revision and redemption which values the daughter as much as the son and, more important, constitutes itself through the mother, not at her expense.

Moreover, there is that strange, elliptical moment when H.D. imagines herself as the lady's (mother's) lamb and as her bridegroom. It is here that H.D. touches on the poetic strategy she develops more clearly in the next book of the poem, where she casts herself as the male not to distance herself from the mother but to explore a forbidden access to her.

In part three, *The Flowering of the Rod* (1946), H.D. revises the Gospel to incarnate the mother as the two Marys, the Magdalene and the Virgin. These two women, who seem throughout the poem to be conflicting aspects of the same woman, operate in relation to the central figure, Kaspar, with whom H.D. associates herself as poet. He is the keeper of the legend with an "innate capacity / for transcribing and translating / the difficult secret symbols" (165). There is no mere appropriation of the symbolic here; H.D.'s poetry as crypto-gram, hieroglyph, is like Kaspar's jar of incense, on which the seal remains unbroken (the thetic) but through which the scent of myrrh (the semiotic) nonetheless manages to escape, simultaneously re-leased and contained. Through Kaspar's relationship to the two Marys, H.D. confronts the doubleness of language and also the two conflicting aspects of the mother—the erotic and the maternal.

H.D.'s identification with Kaspar, then, involves not so much a way to "insure against deficiency"[13] as a way of allowing herself relationship with Mary. The prototype for this strategy goes back to H.D.'s childhood identification with her brother, a figure formulated before her need to align herself with Orestes. The usefulness of this beloved and resented companion recurs as a significant motif throughout H.D.'s life, a motif she recovers in analysis. The heart of her relationship with Gilbert Doolittle centers, not surprisingly, around the mother: "It is *she* who matters. . . . About *her*, there is no question. The trouble is, she knows so many people and they come and interrupt. And besides that, she likes my brother better. If I stay with my brother, become part almost of my brother, perhaps I can get nearer to *her*" (TF, 33). Critics working out of a system founded on the mother's absence don't want to believe this. Norman Hol-land, for example, although he accurately paraphrases H.D., imme-diately abandons what she tells us for his own gloss: "Possibly to become one with her brother meant to acquire the special powers that men seemed to have . . . to understand the mysterious symbols her astronomer-father used or her brother's larger vocabulary" (482). This astonishing reading enacts the process at work in androcentric writing, which substitutes for the mother men's special "powers": symbols and signifiers. Holland literally removes the mother from H.D.'s text and replaces her with the name-of-the-father. The use H.D. makes of the male figure in *Trilogy* is *not* concerned with "larger vocabulary," nor does she want to "become one" with her brother; she wants, she says, to become "part almost." Her carefully chosen words, immediately transformed by Holland, emphasize

[13]Holland writes, "Fusion with a man meant both fusion with and escape from the mother. . . . Fusion with a man insures against deficiency: thus H.D. found it easy to project into and identify with Freud" (493).

"part" and "almost," a kind of "in-between." This is a space of doubleness, of shifting, of rhythm, of a subject-in-process, a space to which critics like Holland are blind. H.D. needs the brother as intermediary, not as self. He is a way of gaining access to the mother.

In *Trilogy* there is this same need, this same desire, with a somewhat more explicit erotic component. H.D. needs Kaspar not as intermediary to the mother as muse (the lady comes unbidden and unmediated) but as intermediary to the Magdalene, the "unmaidenly woman," whom she does not dare entreat without a symbol of difference (the magus) to mark the boundaries she fears to cross.

The sections concerning Mary Magdalene, while they deal on one level with a mystical and linguistic "entry," are also highly charged sexually. Midway through the poem, Kaspar experiences an epiphany in which a fleck of light on Mary's hair transports him back through the memory of "another head uncovered and two crowned, / one with a plain circlet, one with a circlet of gems / which even he could not name" (149). This passage opens into a zone of the "unnameable" associated, through the gem, with the jewel in the crucible—mother. In this suggestively maternal space there is a "point or shadow" that reveals "the whole secret of the mystery" (152) as the fleck begins to unfold:

> and the circle went on widening
>
> and would go on opening
> he knew, to infinity;
>
> but before he was lost,
> out-of-time completely,
>
> . . . . .
>
> he saw the circles and circles of islands
> about the lost centre-island, Atlantis;
>
> he saw what the sacrosanct legend
> said still existed,
>
> he saw the lands of the blest,
> the promised lands, lost [153–54]

H.D. allows Kaspar to take this journey for her, back into legend, before the fall, back where there is "a sound as of many waters"

(155). But through him she also takes another journey into an erotic space conjured by Mary, a sensuous fall through an ever-widening circle that opens like a flower, petal by petal, a tiny seed aroused into "the lost centre-island." The movement of this return through circles and circles pulses with sexual imagery reminiscent of H.D.'s more explicit lesbian eroticism: "there is purple flower / between her marble, her birch-tree white / thighs, / or there is a red flower, / there is a rose flower, / parted wide, / as her limbs fling wide in dance / ecstatic / Aphrodite, / there is a frail lavender flower / hidden in grass" ("The Master," *CP*, 456).[14]

Invoked as it is by the gem, the jewel, this lesbian sexuality is also incestuous, directed toward the mother in a passage resonant with both erotic and maternal imagery—prenatal harmony, timelessness, aqueous sensuality. H.D. needs no intermediary to the amniotic aspect; she needs Kaspar in relation to the erotic space, where she is in clear danger of getting "lost," moving toward some "force of attraction," some "dynamic centre" (153). She attempts here, despite the ambivalence of her evasion and displacement, to reappropriate the mother as object of desire, not only as a source of nurturance, not only as muse, but as Eros as well. And finally, desire, as embodied by Mary Magdalene, no longer seems an obstacle to integration, no longer seems a barrier between the self and mother, but becomes a way of entry.

This access for H.D. is textual as well as physical. It is access to an unfamiliar eroticized and maternal *language*, which Kaspar hears as "the echo / of an echo in a shell":

> words neither sung nor chanted
> but stressed rhythmically;
>
> the echoed syllables of this spell
> conformed to the sound
>
> of no word he had ever heard spoken,
>
> . . . . .
>
> it translated itself
> as it transmuted its message

[14]For an analysis of the significance of this eroticism, particularly in the context of H.D.'s work with Freud, see DuPlessis and Friedman, "'Woman Is Perfect.'"

> through spiral upon spiral of the shell
> of memory that yet connects us

with the drowned cities of pre-history. [156]

These rhythmically stressed words are very like what Kristeva describes as the result of the "consummated incest" with the "maternal mirage": "Know the mother, first take her place, thoroughly investigate her jouissance and, without releasing her, go beyond her. The language that serves as a witness to this course is iridescent with a sexuality of which it does not 'speak'; it turns it into rhythm—it is rhythm" (*DL*, 191).

The shell through which this unaccustomed sound translates itself is a conflation of genital and maternal images, associated with both female sexuality and the enclosure of the mother's body and also with the transmission of a prelapsarian matriarchal genealogy:

> *Lilith born before Eve*
> *and one born before Lilith,*
> *and Eve; we three are forgiven,*
> *we are three of the seven*
> *daemons cast out of her.* [157]

This cryptic message, Susan Gubar observes in "The Echoing Spell of H.D.'s *Trilogy*," suggests Eve's redemption through her "mothers" and promises "a submerged but now recoverable time of female strength, female speech, and female sexuality, all of which have mysteriously managed to survive, although in radically subdued ways, incarnate in the body of Mary Magdala" (213). Through a return to prebiblical time, prior to the Word, H.D. releases the articulation of preference from its moral and theological/patriarchal strictures and removes female sexuality from the realm of the father.

The poem is largely constructed around a series of similar backward movements, which, projecting the mother further and further into prehistory, redeem her in the present.[15] In a curious reversal at

[15]DuPlessis makes a similar observation about the structure of *Helen in Egypt*: "Because H.D. wanted to evoke the amount of 'backward' integration necessary to move the soul forward, she has Theseus tell Helen the butterfly to reenter the cocoon. . . . This corresponds to the mingling of backward-moving memory and forward-moving quest in the structure of the poem" (RT, 198).

the end of the poem, H.D. returns with Kaspar to the moment he first conferred the gift of myrrh on the other Mary, mother of Christ. Gubar reads this last section of the poem as H.D.'s validation of the whore through the virgin: "When Kaspar thinks in the ox-stall that 'there were always two jars' . . . and that *'someday [he] will bring the other,'* . . . we know that his prophecy *has been or will be fulfilled;* as he gives the myrrh to Mary mother, we know that he is destined to give the other jar to Mary Magdala, thereby authenticating . . . his knowledge that the whore is the mother" (213).

While Gubar's final evaluation accurately reflects H.D.'s reconciliation, the actual process is perhaps the opposite of what Gubar suggests: it is not through the virgin that H.D. redeems the whore but through the whore that H.D. finally claims the mother. That is: if the pivotal Mary figure can first be accepted erotically, be entered as a kind of sensuous, linguistic medium, then she can finally, in H.D.'s vision, be allowed maternity and be worthy of the "gift," both poetry and child. Joseph Riddel has suggested that the title of the poem, *The Flowering of the Rod,* evokes the "rod of power," authority, "the phallus of identity and the stylus of the old scribes" (SW, 465). He is partly right, but Riddel, like Holland, refuses the doubleness of H.D.'s language, extracting the rod/phallus as Holland extracted the father and ignoring both the mother and the sexual implications of the flowering. In H.D.'s version it is power/identity/language split by female sexuality, "rose flower / parted wide." Through this image H.D. joins the mother, lesbian eroticism, and writing, partially extricating herself from her identification with Kaspar, blurring boundaries, releasing him as well as herself from the confines of language and gender.

In the last poem, Kaspar finally confers the myrrh, Mary remarking on its beautiful fragrance; "But Kaspar knew the seal of the jar was unbroken. / He did not know whether she knew / the fragrance came from the bundle of myrrh / she held in her arms" (172). Besides the earlier association of myrrh with the semiotic subtext of language, struggling against but dependent on the "jar" of discourse, and the new identification of the myrrh with the child, we remember here an earlier image that broke through the text in a disembodied voice: *"I am Mary, the incense-flower of the incense-tree, myself worshipping, weeping, shall be changed to myrrh* (138). Thus the mother comes no longer to steal the myrrh but rather to give birth to it; she herself is myrrh, and all is contained within a palimpsest of birth, resurrection, and desire in which the mother is textualized, eroticized, and redeemed.

In *Trilogy* H.D. both inscribes and transmutes the feelings and ambivalence about her mother recovered during analysis. A key memory that comes to H.D. in her sessions with Freud becomes, I think, a turning point in her reinvention of the male and female figures in her subsequent work. She remembers being on a shopping trip or a visit; as they return, her brother defies his mother, plunking himself on the curb, refusing to go home. "He has told her that he is going away to live by himself, and he has moreover told her that his sister is coming with him" (*TF*, 28). Like the mentors and critics who try to remove H.D. psychologically, physically, sexually, and textually from the mother, the brother embodies and perpetuates here the oedipal and artistic dilemma. H.D. makes of this scene, sitting with her brother on the curbstone, "a little group, design, an image at the crossroads. It appears variously in Greek tragedies . . . and it can be found in your original Grimm's tales or in your nursery translation, called Little-Brother, Little-Sister" (*TF*, 29). Although she is never completely successful in her attempts to recast her relationships, in this scene she finds the seed of all her subsequent revisionism, a way of turning the tables on tragedies, myths, tales, and translations: "And their mother has walked away. *He* knows that she will come back because he is older and is admittedly his mother's favorite. But *she* does not know this. But though her brain is in a turmoil of anxiety and pride and terror, it has not even occurred to her that she might throw her small weight into the balance of conventional behavior by following her mother and leaving her brother to his fate" (*TF*, 29). In *Trilogy*, H.D. begins to throw her rather considerable weight as daughter and poet as she leaves behind the conventional script, abandons Orestes, and takes off after the mother.

8

The Syntax of Stained Glass

Wide Sargasso Sea (1966) is Jean Rhys's last novel, published after the decades of silence following *Good Morning, Midnight*.[1] The four early novels follow a common "itinerary," Dennis Porter has written, which is "nowhere completely written-up in a single novel" but which "exists as a kind of structural model that can be abstracted from the novels taken together and that reflects revealingly on any given novel" (551). From this itinerary, Porter suggests, "until *Wide Sargasso Sea*, the earliest and the final movements are largely missing" (551). When Rhys does finally write again, the terms have changed: instead of intruding into the frame of England and the

[1]In *No Man's Land*, Gilbert and Gubar announce Rhys as one of the markers in twentieth-century women's fiction, one of the writers who "have played variations on the themes of their foremothers in order to strengthen themselves by restoring and revising the past while restructuring the future." They note that "Jean Rhys's *Wide Sargasso Sea* . . . both celebrates and interrogates Charlotte Brontë's *Jane Eyre* by retelling the tale from the silenced perspective of Bertha Mason Rochester" (208). Although Gilbert and Gubar confess that the scope of their undertaking requires them to be "brief," it is disappointing that they read Rhys in such "celebratory" terms. A more useful contribution to reading this particular novel, and to reading H.D. as well, is their reference to the beginning of Ezra Pound's "Portrait d'une Femme": "Your mind and you are our Sargasso Sea" (16). The voice in this poem resonates with all the male voices in Rhys and reminds us of the man who slashed Hilda Doolittle's early work and "assigned" her the signet "H.D., Imagiste." "Great minds have sought you— lacking someone else," Pound writes (17). "You are a person of some interest, one comes to you / And takes strange gain away: / Trophies fished up; some curious suggestion; / Fact that leads nowhere; and a tale or two" (17). In the final analysis, claims H.D.'s mentor, (the) woman is a sea of flotsam and jetsam: "In the whole and all, / Nothing that's quite your own. / Yet this is you" (*SP*, 17).

Continent, the islands are the space of origin, the place where, finally, the mother's story begins to be told.

In speaking the mother, Rhys chooses, as we have seen, to speak through another text, a "mother" text, *Jane Eyre*, inventing a history for Bertha Mason, who appears early in the narrative as the child called Antoinette. The first section of the novel centers on Antoinette's early life in Jamaica, a space with which she associates her mother, Annette. The sounds and cadences of both island and body provide a subtext to the discourse of her English stepfather. But as much as the mother embodies the island's rhythm and freedom— "there was no need for music when she danced" (30)—she is a prisoner in it, bound and framed by her husband much as the portrait of "a lovely English girl with brown curls and blue eyes and a dress slipping off her shoulders" (36) is kept in a frame over Mason's dining room table. Mason is a man "so sure of himself, so without a doubt English," and Annette is "so without a doubt not English" (36); as this juxtaposition indicates, she is perceived not for what she is but for what she is *not* (the castration configuration). She is caught within a colonial system that identifies her in relation to an opposite pole that underlines (and underlies) her "lack."

Besides being controlled by her husband and constrained by propriety, she is also contained by her obsession for her boy-child, Pierre, who cannot speak distinctly and staggers when he walks. Annette constantly turns from her daughter in favor of her deficient son; many times in the novel Antoinette reaches for her mother, "but she pushed me away, not roughly but calmly, coldly, without a word, as if she had decided once and for all that I was useless to her" (20). When Pierre dies in the fire that destroys Coulibri Estate, Annette, already unstable and distracted, breaks down completely, trying finally to kill her husband. Unable to control his "mad" wife, Mason exiles her to the care of an abusive black couple, and Antoinette, ill and exhausted, is taken in by an aunt.

Antoinette is eventually allowed to visit her mother, but she does not really expect to find her: "She was a part of Coulibri, that had gone, so she had gone, I was certain of it" (48); her fears are confirmed when she arrives at the country house where Annette is kept. "I put my arms round her and kissed her. She held me so tightly that I couldn't breathe and I thought, 'It's not her.' Then, 'It must be her.'

She looked at the door, then at me, then at the door again. I could not say, 'He is dead,' so I shook my head. 'But I am here, I am here,' I said, and she said, 'No,' quietly. Then 'No no no' very loudly and flung me from her" (49).

But "all this was long ago," says Antoinette dismissively, "when I was still babyish and sure that everything was alive, not only the river or the rain, but chairs, looking-glasses, cups, saucers, every-thing" (38). Her memories of loss are inextricably bound with "the taste of milk and bread and the sound of the grandfather clock ticking slowly and the first time I had my hair tied with string . . . [and licking] raindrops from the Jasmine leaves after a shower" (132). The essence of the island is song, sense, scent, touch, images, rhythm, jeopardized by the lost mother but sustained and overseen by Chris-tophine, who smells "so warm and comforting" (109). These pas-sages echo Sasha Jansen's memory of the midwife's language, in which "clouds are clouds, trees are trees," and plunge us back into the same presymbolic, literal, "babyish" sphere where things are not dead substitutes but "live" objects.

One memory of Christophine in particular explores the mode of the island: "I can remember every second of that morning, if I shut my eyes I can see the deep blue colour of the sky and the mango leaves, the pink and red hibiscus, the yellow handkerchief she wore round her head, tied in the Martinique fashion with the sharp points in front, but now I see everything still, fixed for ever like the colours in a stained-glass window" (118). Here again we are privy to visual rather than narrative memory; Antoinette compares her way of see-ing and remembering to a stained-glass window, an image that serves as an alternative to text. The intensity of windows such as those at Chartres serve another pleasure, desire *consummated* in a sense, a merger with "story" in an immediacy of contact which the eye absorbs as a whole; there is no syntax in stained glass. Thus the name-of-the-father might be seen to bear the same relation to the semiotic of the island as the bible has traditionally borne to colored glass images: the one is the Word; the other is image fused with gaze and light.

Part 2 of the novel opens with Antoinette and her new husband, Rochester, leaving Jamaica for the Windward Islands and Granbois, another small estate that belonged to her mother. "I love it more than anywhere in the world," says Antoinette. "As if it were a person. More than a person" (89). Intensely associated with the mother, it is yet more than a mother, abstracted, released from the confines of biographical ambivalence or failure. A signature of loss, Granbois is also a site of inscription, a place onto which and into which Antoinette/Rhys projects her mother.

On the way, Antoinette and Rochester land in a small village called Massacre. "And who was massacred here?" Rochester asks. "Slaves?" Antoinette seems shocked: "Not slaves. Something must have happened a long time ago. Nobody remembers now" (66). This exchange is a kind of refrain in the novel until the very end when the daughter *does* remember, in a sense. It is a novel constructed around a series of hidden spaces, holes, gaps, like the crypt under the altar in the chapel of Antoinette's convent school containing the skeleton, according to legend, of a fourteen-year-old girl (54). How did she get there, the child Antoinette asks herself over and over: "We do not know her story, she is not in the book" (54).

This image of the young woman "not in the book" reflects not only the mother but Antoinette herself as her husband begins to "erase" her. During an argument, for example, Rochester alters Antoinette's name, and Christophine confronts him for it:

"She tell me in the middle of all this you start calling her names. Marionette. Some word so."
"Yes, I remember, I did."
(*Marionette, Antoinette, Marionetta, Antoinetta*)
"That word mean doll, eh? Because she don't speak." [154–55]

Just as men have silenced women in all Rhys's novels, Rochester encloses his wife in a word associated with puppets, dolls with painted mouths, resonant of the women in *Voyage in the Dark* who can only stick their tongues out through little slits in their masks; as Hermione knows in H.D.'s novel, "You call your doll or your toy dog by a name and it becomes *your* dog, your toy doll" (*HER*, 200). But "marionette" carries other suggestions as well. In it, for example, we hear "Marian"—"pertaining to the Virgin Mary" or, as a noun, "a person who has a particular devotion to the Virgin." Since Rochester's rage has been precipitated by rumors of Antoinette's sexuality, this attempt to rename her through the virgin is particularly significant and ironic, for as he attempts to silence and purify her, he encounters again the inescapable conflation of mother, child, and desire. "Marionette" subverts his intent in another way, through the name of Antoinette's mother, the woman who has gone mad mourning the loss of her son and her home and whose "madness," Rochester fears, will be or has been inherited by the daughter. By calling his wife Marionette, or "Marry-Annette," he simultaneously incants his own oedipal fear/desire and weds the daughter to the mother. This is a relationship, of course, already encoded in their names, "Antoinette . . . being a combination of Annette and 'toi': a hidden built-in bond between mother and daughter" (Scharfman, 103). Finally, Rochester changes Antoinette's name entirely, arbitrarily calling her Bertha, a name having nothing to do with who she is, which severs her from her past and from her mother. When she questions him about it, he answers, "It is a name I'm particularly fond of. I think of you as Bertha" (135). In fact, what he thinks of is less important than what he doesn't *want* to think of, and that is Antoinette's relationship to Annette.

Rhys has begun here the shifting through which the intersections with Brontë's text will emerge, a shifting which, like H.D.'s palimpsests, works in two directions—forward to prepare for Thornfield and backward to redetermine the events at Coulibri. The novel relentlessly recounts the story of a woman's struggle to regain her mother, herself, and her story as Antoinette begins to realize Rochester's intentions: "Bertha is not my name. You are trying to make me into someone else, calling me by another name. I know, that's obeah too" (148). Being called by an inauthentic name is a kind of "spell," which temporarily renders her unable to speak or be spoken. "Names matter," she says, "like when he wouldn't call me Antoinette, and I saw Antoinette drifting out of the window with her scents, her pretty clothes and her looking-glass" (180). This dissociation from both herself and her mother is the etiology of what Rochester calls her madness; in Rhys's version, however, Bertha is not a disturbed woman thrust upon an unsuspecting, victimized Rochester but rather a woman "sold off" and *driven* "mad" (although we may end up redefining the term) through denial of her language, her name, and her matrilineage.

Despite Rochester's attempts at control and his insistence at Granbois that Antoinette's mother's house legally belongs to him now, he clearly feels his powers diminishing in this maternal space where "the feeling of something unknown and hostile was very strong" (130). "I feel very much a stranger here," he says to Antoinette. "I feel that this place is my enemy and on your side" (130). Throughout the novel Rochester is haunted by a premonitory sensation of malice. He finds the island's beauty malignant, hostile, menacing, just as Antoinette imagines London as a "cold dark dream" (80). Rochester has the feeling that "all this" is a nightmare, tempered only by the "faint consoling hope that [he] might wake up" (120).

All these natural elements of the island, so foreign to him, make him "giddy" (83), overloading his senses: "Everything is too much, I felt as I rode wearily after her. Too much blue, too much purple, too much green. The flowers too red, the mountains too high, the hills too near. And the woman is a stranger" (70). Everything in this passage is visual, sensual, spatial; there is no linearity, no time. In this and the surrounding passage Rochester participates in the rhythm of the horse, the whistling of mountain birds whose names he does not know, the height and depth of mountains and sea, the weariness of the body, the intensity of color, sudden changes in temperature, the taste of mountain water drunk from a folded leaf. To enter the mother's terrain, as Antoinette knows, is to return to an ebb and flow of sensation; Rochester, however, like most men in Rhys's novels, fights to retain dominion over this other, this stranger. In part 2, in fact, his opening words are "So it was all over, the advance and retreat" (65), the very words Sasha uses in *Good Morning, Midnight*, to articulate the mother's rhythm. It is *not* over for Rochester, but he cannot accept the fact that the women speak a language that will not function by his rules, nor can he accept an environment that requires a relinquishing of control as the price of entry. The island terrifies him: for Antoinette it is a space of privileged contact with the maternal; for Rochester it is a zone of loss and impotence.

There is, as this scene and many others suggest, a relation between language and this maternally connoted space that privileges the literal. It is a space which makes Rochester extremely uncomfortable, a place where, like Hester in *Voyage in the Dark*, he is disturbed by the patois and where he finds in his one "refuge," a dressing room with a "small writing-desk with paper, pens, and ink" (74), that the books on the "crude bookshelf" are being "eaten away" (75). It is a space full of secrets and obeah and philters, which reduce him to "a child spelling out the letters of a word which he cannot read, and which if he could would have no meaning or context" (138).[2]

The island, then, seems to strip him of his powers, both sexually and physically; it infects and emasculates him, leaving him prey to fever and fears of cuckoldry. More significant, it also affects his language; although he calls the island dialect "debased" (67), Christophine's dark voice hypnotizes him. Antoinette and Christophine use this language of gesticulation and rhythm between them just as Francine and Anna do in *Voyage in the Dark*, and Christophine uses it to lull Antoinette with words her husband does not understand. She sings in fact the same song Rhys transcribes in *Voyage*. "Ma belle ka di maman li," emphasizing that the sounds of patois are connected to the maternal voice.[3]

Christophine as the embodiment of the island's power also serves a more explicit liguistic function: she allows Antoinette to gain the speaking voice in a novel that alternates between her telling of the tale and Rochester's. Of the three sections of *Wide Sargasso Sea*, the first deals with Antoinette's childhood, the second with her marriage to Rochester, and the third with her imprisonment in Thornfield as the mad wife. Antoinette narrates the first and third sections, Rochester the longer middle one. An interesting aspect of this flux in narrative voice is that Antoinette seems able to articulate only those portions of her life which deal with her mother; she can narrate her

[2]Teresa O'Connor also discusses Rochester's "conversion" at Granbois as he is "thrust into the role of neophyte and dependent" (148); she does not associate this dependency primarily with childhood but emphasizes that "Rochester at Granbois experiences what it is like to be a woman" (164).

[3]O'Connor reads Cristophine's power not in linguistic terms but rather in terms of her marginal status as "outsider," linked through her blackness "to an older and purer African past" (209). O'Connor insists on Antoinette's "attraction to and terror of the black woman's . . . Obeah" (209) and writes, "Antoinette, like many white Creoles, knows that beneath the Christianized surface lies another culture, another religion, the memory of another continent, one that is cloaked in mystery and power. It is this same mystery and power that Rochester himself recognizes and which he seeks to control and conquer, much like the earlier white colonizers and missionaries themselves" (209–10). This reading focuses on O'Connor's interest in "race and betrayal" and "the dialogue between good and evil"; my argument relies more heavily on the maternal and psychosexual associations of Christophine.

childhood (which centers on her mother's madness) and the period of time she spends imprisoned (like the mother) preparing to reenact and retell her tale. She cannot, however, speak about her marriage; its telling is left to the man who defines its boundaries, Rochester, who attempts "to extricate himself from her regression, to reassert his masculine authority, to reestablish the symbolic order" (Scharfman, 103).

In the middle of the novel, during Rochester's narrative section, Antoinette slips off to visit Christophine, begging her to give her a philter that will either poison or seduce her husband. Rhys at this moment leaves her intent rather ambiguous. What is more important is that at the moment of contact with Christophine, what Antoinette came for recedes into the immediacy of the moment; she buries herself in Christophine's smells and plays with her silver bangle as an infant might do, deep in the folds of the mother as we are deep in the folds of the text. It is in this space that Antoinette breaks out of the frame of Rochester's discourse and regains the narrative "I," a fact that critics, describing the alternating narrative in the novel, curiously overlook.[4] Rochester, who believes that whatever Christophine and Antoinette sing or say is "dangerous" and that he must "protect" himself from it, is temporarily stripped of his ability to signify; immediately after Antoinette leaves Christophine, however, Rochester's voice again picks up the story.

Despite the malice and sense of loss he feels, there is something about the island which attracts him. He lies in bed at night, listening to the rain, "a light capricious shower, dancing playful rain, or hushed, muted, growing louder, more persistent, more powerful, an inexorable sound." But, he continues, it was "always music, a music I had never heard before" (90). Rochester comes close to contacting the seductive center of the island: "I shall never understand why, suddenly, bewilderingly, I was certain that everything I had imagined to be truth was false. False. Only the magic and the dream are true—all the rest's a lie. Let it go. Here is the secret. Here" (168). His

---

[4]Francis Wyndham, in his introduction to *Wide Sargasso Sea* (12), observes the alternating narrative in the novel but overlooks the intrusion into the second section. Ronnie Scharfman talks briefly about Antoinette's loss of narrative control during the honeymoon episode. She does not, however, discuss the implications of Antoinette's *appropriation* of the "I" during the Christophine episode. O'Connor notes the shift to Antoinette's narration in part 2 but does not explore what that shift might mean.

certainty wavers. The truth about Antoinette's past, the truth about her mother, and the truth about the island all begin to blur and tilt until he is operating out of "mad, conflicting emotions."

One afternoon Rochester leaves the house and takes off into the forest, where he is disoriented geographically and psychologically, left with no sense of space or time. While he is wandering, he comes upon a little girl. "I met her eyes," he reports, "and to my astonishment she screamed loudly, threw up her arms and ran, a small frightened sound. Then she disappeared" (105).

This is a striking restaging of *Little Red Riding Hood*, a story Rhys uses in her autobiography as well. On her sixth birthday, Rhys recounts in *Smile Please*, her two brothers and older sister are to act out *Red Riding Hood*. All of a sudden, the brother who is playing the honest woodcutter—"if there is such a character" (*SP*, 23)—becomes bored and leaves the stage. The good-natured younger brother enters nonetheless, dressed as a wolf, determined to carry on. "However," Rhys writes, "Red Riding Hood was silent, confused by the woodcutter's abrupt exit and it was plain that the play couldn't go on" (23). Rhys is consoled with a birthday present from her *grandmother*, the character in the play who gets eaten. The present is "a large pale blue book": "When the play collapsed my mother picked the book up, opened it and put it on my lap. Perhaps she feared I was about to cry. I looked at a picture of a little girl in a pink dress. By her side was a huge spider and underneath meaningless print, for I couldn't read them, not even short words. That's all I remember" (24). We are back again in the space of children, texts, and images; when the visual or literal fails or is interrupted (or is eaten), it is substituted with text, a text sent, ironically, by the *dead* (grand)mother. But as consolation, the "pale blue" surface text, stripped of images, is useless because the child can't read, and even if she could, the words would *not* replace the play, the scene of presence, for they are a stand-in for what has been taken away.

Similarly, the landscape where Rochester finds himself is inhabited by girl-children carrying flowers, a space where he clearly does not belong. Rochester is an alien, certain of danger, and yet he is momentarily overwhelmed by the beauty and the calm of the place.

There had been a paved road through this forest. The track led to a large clear space. Here were the ruins of a stone house and round the ruins rose trees that had grown to an incredible height. At the back of the ruins a wild orange tree covered with fruit, the leaves a dark green. A beautiful place. And calm—so calm that it seemed foolish to think or plan. What had I to think about and how could I plan? Under the orange tree I noticed little bunches of flowers tied with grass. [104–5]

We are at a sanctuary here, ruins reminiscent of some lost temple as if we were in H.D.'s terrain instead of Rhys's, where little girls bring offerings in propitiation or love. Significantly, the priest who once lived here has been supplanted by an orange tree, which becomes a central figure (now we see the danger of the woodcutter). A number of women use the orange tree and its fruit, especially blood oranges, as an emblem for both female sexuality and "the need," according to Hélène Cixous, "to go further into the birth voice" (CD, 39), "to search for what is most secret in our being." Cixous explores this central image at length in *Vivre l'orange* in which the "nymph of the orange" appears to the "I": "She put the orange back into the deserted hands of my writing, and with her orange-colored accents she rubbed the eyes of my writing which were arid and covered with white films. And it was a childhood that came running back to pick up the live orange and immediately celebrate it. . . . There was originally an intimacy between the orange and the little girl, almost a kinship, the exchange of essential confidences" (15).

While the orange seems a somewhat arbitrary choice, Cixous makes an important conflation of an object, a secret, intimacy, a little girl, and writing. It is, moreover, a "live" orange, taking us back to Rhys's "babyish" sphere and Margaret Homans's reading of Elizabeth Gaskell and her baby. The imagery of this tree and fruit runs throughout Rhys's novels, always appearing at highly pitched moments of maternal contact. In *Good Morning, Midnight,* Sasha associates the *sage femme* with "the tisane of orange-flower water" (139) offered during labor. In *After Leaving Mr. Mackenzie,* the only coherent words that reach Julia out of her dying mother's delirium are "orange-trees" (99). In *Voyage in the Dark* the overture to Anna's realization that she is pregnant is "Connais-tu le pays où fleurit l'oranger?" (162). "Do you know the country? Of course, if you know the country it makes all the difference. The country where the orange-tree flowers?" (161). In the center of *Wide Sargasso Sea,* then, we are in the center of Rhys's mythology as well, the emblem of which—*l'oranger*—reverberates throughout the novels in scenes of childbirth, abortion, madness, and maternal death.[5]

It is clear to Rochester, even in his mania for mastery, that he is dealing here with forces outside his control. He cannot, however, accept the fundamentally different nature of Granbois, nor will he allow it to resist him: "It was a beautiful place—wild, untouched, above all untouched, with an alien, disturbing, secret loveliness. And it kept its secret. I'd find myself thinking, 'What I see is nothing—I want what it *hides*—that is not nothing'" (87). Rhys is manipulating here the androcentric sexual economy; this is the primal scene and the site (sight) of incest, the thesis I develop more fully in the next chapter. In preparation for that, however, I will use this passage to think about a "specificity" of female discourse. As I have said, the *chora* or the semiotic or the preoedipal dyad is, in the father's terms (Freud the father, the name-of-the-father), alien, disturbing, and via the oedipal "pavement," untouched and untouchable. This site at the center of the forest has overtaken the paved road, however, leaving only a track or "trace." It is a space prohibited to grown men but not to little girls, and yet Rochester, bartering with the incest taboo, *wants* what it *hides*. "What I see is nothing," he says, buying into the castration contract. But even he knows that there is something else there which, though unseen, is not missing, is not lack, is "not nothing." The mother's estate is to him "above all" untouched. That untouchability is the basis of the system within which, iron-

---

[5]In 1914, for example, Gertrude Stein played with the title "Orange In" (origin) in *Tender Buttons*. Curiously, H.D. uses this same image in much of her work. When H.D. describes Rafe Ashton (the Aldington figure) in *Bid Me to Live*, for example, she writes, "The words he said brought no scent of orange-blossom" (129). Even more remarkably, she ends *Tribute to Freud* with the Goethe poem, "Mignon I" (1795), which begins "Kennst du das Land." H.D., however, associates "das Land" not directly with the mother but with Freud and the journey she undertakes in psychoanalysis through "a strange land, a foreign land, a land of classic associations" (*TF*, 110). "Kennst du das Haus?"—the first line of Goethe's second stanza—suggests for H.D. Freud's apartment: "I want to go there with you, O my Guardian (O my Protector), *mit dir, o mein Beschützer, ziehn*" (110–11). She associates the *Berg*, or mountain, of the third stanza with her analysis and "our work together," toward which the weary "little donkey" plods. Rhys and H.D. use this poem in different ways, Rhys as an image of maternal topography, H.D. as metaphor for the analytic process that opened so many doors toward her mother. Although this poem was a well-known ballad in English at least as early as the mid-nineteenth century, that both Rhys and H.D. found it significant to their quests is a startling coincidence.

ically, he constitutes himself, and yet he becomes obsessed with the need or the desire to touch it, to rupture and violate finally the mother's domain, even knowing that for him it will never be available. He comes to hate the place because it will not yield to him, as infants learn the rage of the mirror: "I hated its beauty and its magic and the secret I would never know. . . . Above all I hated [Antoinette]. For she belonged to the magic and the loveliness. She had left me thirsty and all my life would be thirst and longing for what I had lost before I found it" (173). What he has lost, without being able to name it, is the mother.

Rochester's rage at the absent mother is then projected onto Antoinette. He cuts her off sexually. He betrays her with a servant girl. And as Antoinette in her despair begins to break down, Rochester writes it off to hereditary madness, recreating the mother in his wife, deciding to take her away to England and lock her up. "So we rode away and left it—" he relates, "the hidden place. Not for me and not for her. I'd look after that" (173). In a deliberate act of revenge, he sets out to alienate her from the wild, to destroy her maternal heritage just as Coulibri was destroyed in the early part of the novel.

On one level he is successful. "I loved this place," she says to him, "and you have made it into a place I hate. I used to think that if everything else went out of my life I would still have this, and now you have spoilt it" (148). Not only does he spoil the place for her, but he removes her from it physically as well, knowing that the most terrible punishment he can inflict on her is not abandonment or physical injury or death but rather exile from the land of the mother.

At the end of his narrative control Rochester says:

> Very soon she'll join all the others who know the secret and will not tell it. Or cannot. Or try and fail because they do not know enough. They can be recognized. White faces, dazed eyes, aimless gestures, high-pitched laughter. The way they walk and talk and scream or try to kill (themselves or you). . . . Yes, they've got to be watched. For the time comes when they try to kill, then disappear. But others are waiting to take their places, it's a long, long line. She's one of them. I too can wait—for the day when she is only a memory to be avoided, locked away, and like all memories a legend. Or a lie . . . [173]

This astonishing passage places Antoinette in the context of a larger whole, as one of "all the others" who have been denied access to their origin and to discourse. Rochester's description of his mad wife suggests a whole population of women who inhabit private homes and women's fiction—aimless, dazed, failed, unrecognized, inarticulate, but in possession of "the secret" they cannot tell. What they cannot tell is unspeakable because of the system in which they are confined, a system based on a memory to be avoided, locked away—the memory of the mother's body.

Wide Sargasso Sea, however, tells the secret and, moreover, tells it differently, tells it in ways Rochester cannot read. The narrative itself initially creates a kind of disturbing impasse in the sense that Antoinette seems to start a self-destructive journey in which she capitulates to Rochester's desire. She *does* begin to merge with her mad mother, as Rochester was warned and then predicted. On the boat to England, for example, she is confined in a cabin with a man and a woman who clean up after her when she smashes glasses and plates and attempts to seduce the man who brings her food. She is drugged and sleeps and believes "we lost our way to England" (181). In a sense Antoinette never *does* get to England. Where she "gets" on the ship is back inside another scene, a replay of a scene she observes as a child when she runs a second time, this time alone, to the house where Annette is kept. Peering in through the window, she hears her mother screaming and sees a fat black man pouring rum into her. Faithful, despite her mother's earlier rejection of her, she thinks, "I will kill anyone who is hurting my mother" (134). As she watches she sees her mother smashing a glass and the fat man laughing, hears her mother rambling in a hallucination of the past, and then sees the man pull Annette out of her chair and fasten his mouth onto hers. Antoinette flees. But she flees, ultimately, into her own captivity where *she* smashes glass and is drugged by a man who tells her to "sleep" as they tell Annette to "forget."

On one hand, this scene can be read as a treacherous undercurrent in the novel, through which Rhys not only releases the mother in ways I have discussed but encloses her. By choosing to tell the mother's story through Bertha Mason she has assured not only her madness but her death. And because of the convergence of mother and daughter, the intersection and replays in their lives, Antoinette emerges as a kind of Niobid, who herself pays the price for her mother's failure.

154 The Unspeakable Mother

Setting this story within the context of *Jane Eyre*, however, has other implications as well. If we read Bertha through Sandra Gilbert and Susan Gubar as Jane's "own secret self" (*Madwoman*, 360), which Jane keeps in control, part of Bertha's story involves her attempt to escape not just from the attic but from Jane Eyre's narrative; by inserting Antoinette/Bertha into Brontë's book, then, Rhys frames the tale of her search for a way out of Rochester's narrative with a tale of Bertha's search for a way out of Jane's.

Rhys begins to intertwine Antoinette with Jane in various ways.[6] When Antoinette anticipates her passage to England, for example, she thinks, "I know the house where I will be cold and not belonging, the bed I shall lie in has red curtains and I have slept there many times before long ago. How long ago? In that bed I will dream the end of my dream" (11–12). This rather cryptic passage recalls Jane Eyre's memory of the red room at Gateshead where she was kept and punished as a child; like the house of Antoinette's vision, it is a place of imprisonment but also, as I established earlier, the death chamber visited by the ghostly mother. Thus Rhys, while creating sets of mothers and daughters, begins to merge the daughters as well, all the little children—Jean and Jane and Bertha/Antoinette.

Antoinette also has two dreams that parallel two of Jane's dreams, reestablishing the connection made through the vision of the bed-chamber. Antoinette's dreams, however, are almost the inverse of Jane's. In the first, Jane finds herself on a road burdened with an "unknown little child." Rochester is on the road ahead of her, and though she makes repeated efforts to overtake him, to "utter" his name and to "entreat" him, her voice "die[s] away inarticulate" (*JE*, 247–48). In contrast to Jane's nightmare of a receding figure, Antoinette has a related dream centering on a menacing proximity. "I dreamed that I was walking in the forest. Not alone. Someone who hated me was with me, out of sight. I could hear heavy footsteps coming close and though I struggled and screamed I could not move" (27).

In both novels these dreams recur in more elaborate version. In *Jane Eyre* the locale shifts to a premonitory vision of Thornfield in

⁶For a more developed reading of this aspect of the novel, see Elizabeth Baer ("The Sisterhood of Jane Eyre and Antoinette Cosway"), who considers the two women doubles and reads (somewhat differently) the parallels between their dreams.

ruins through which Jane wanders and stumbles, still carrying the child, knowing "however much its weight impeded my progress, I must retain it." She hears a horse galloping away and is sure it is Rochester "departing for many years"; Jane scrambles to gain the summit, clinging to branches that give way, the child almost strangling her in fear. At the end of the dream, Rochester disappears, the child rolls from Jane's grasp, Jane herself falls and wakes (248–49).

Antoinette's second dream unfolds back in the forest of the earlier version; this time, however, she is following a man whose face she sees, "black with hatred" (60). They enter a garden enclosed by a stone wall. Although it is dark, Antoinette knows "there are steps leading upwards"; she is afraid her beautiful white dress will be "soiled" and thinks, "It will be when I go up these steps. At the top" (61). The ambiguous "it" suggests a rape. But Antoinette insists, "I follow him, sick with fear but I make no effort to save myself; if anyone were to try to save me, I would refuse. This must happen" (60). Rhys ends this dream with an image of Antoinette stumbling, clinging to a tree that sways and jerks as if to throw her off, finally stopping when a "strange voice" says, "Here, in here" (61).[7]

When she finally awakens she says, "I dreamed I was in Hell" (61). Later in the novel Rhys explicitly connects the "hell" of this dream and the hell of Thornfield. As Bertha wakes in the attic following her third dream, in which Thornfield burns, she realizes that the flight of steps she climbed in her second nightmare "leads to this room."

In thinking about the culminating scene of the novel (both novels) it is important to remember that Antoinette's mother has not really been dead but kept imprisoned. Late in the novel, Rochester, who has begun to disbelieve everything about his wife's past, demands to know whether Annette Mason is alive.

> "No, she is dead, she died."
> "When?"
> "Not long ago."

[7]Although there are clear parallels between Jane and Antoinette, O'Connor provides important information about Antoinette's second dream: "This particular dream apparently had tremendous significance for Rhys herself. It contains much of the unresolved problems of sexual initiation that Rhys experienced. . . . The dream, as it appears in *Wide Sargasso Sea*, is taken almost verbatim from a passage in the Black Exercise Book, which predates Rhys's last novel by about 30 years" (184).

"Then why did you tell me that she died when you were a child?"
"Because they told me to say so and because it is true. She did die when
I was a child. There are always two deaths, the real one and the one
people know about." [128]

The "real" death Antoinette refers to here is the moment at which
the mother turned away coldly and silently and forever after looked
past the child. Her death does not occur during the fire at Coulibri
(although that is the story told), when Annette, in fact, does not
actually appear on the roof. She is dragged along by Mason, "holding
back, struggling," attempting, as it turns out, to go after her parrot,
which has been trapped inside, a parrot who dislikes everyone but
Annette and whose wings Mason has had clipped. It is Coco who
appears on the glacis railing: "He made an effort to fly down, but his
clipped wings failed him and he fell screeching. He was all on fire"
(43). As Annette struggles to save the bird, save herself, her sister
Cora thinks she is trying to save her jewel case. Mason, enraged,
shouts back, "Jewel case? Nothing so sensible. . . . She wanted to go
back for her damned parrot. I won't allow it" (42). Annette, however,
does not want "sensible" jewels—currency, objects of exchange. She
wants the bird that asks the question "Qui est là? Qui est là?" and
then identifies himself, to himself: "Ché Coco. Ché Coco" (42),
"pos[ing] the question of identity . . . of place, of presence and
absence" (Scharfman, 105).

The parrot becomes a central figure in the last scene of the novel,
which has been interpreted as "the dysfunctioning of a system which
inhibits [Antoinette] from distinguishing whether she is telling her
own story or her mother's" (Scharfman, 88). In fact, however, the
last scene, in which she stands on the balcony of Thornfield like a
madwoman, is a *dream*, a dream not of what actually happened to her
mother but of what might have been the alternative. This is the
dream of what Mason would not allow, just as Rhys was denied her
original ending to *Voyage in the Dark*; here, however, she finally
allows herself the text the editors censored and the image the photographer—smile please—kept trying to revise.

Bertha is certain that all this is happening according to some plan:
"Now at last I know why I was brought here and what I have to do"
(190). But what *is* she to do? On the most obvious level, she seems to

prepare to act out the dream, but Rhys only *suggests* that Antoinette's fate will be the same as Bertha's as she takes off down the dark passage; I do not believe that "she can only grope helplessly towards creating a meaning for her dream by making it come true" (Scharfman, 104). What is more important, I think, is the reestablishment of visual, not premonitory, powers, the scopic field of the image. Bertha's dream, as Rhys tells it, actually retrieves Jane's portfolio, returning to a preverbal mode and resurrecting all the earlier images, which, like the mother, were shut away. It also reclaims the image of Antoinette "drifting out of the window" when she is stripped of her name and (thereby) severed from her mother.

The importance of reading this last dream as image rather than narrative is suggested by the drawing through which Rochester, under the sway of the island, plots Antoinette's confinement: "I drank some more rum and, drinking, I drew a house surrounded by trees. A large house. I divided the third floor into rooms and in one room I drew a standing woman—a child's scribble, a dot for a head, a larger one for the body, a triangle for a skirt, slanting lines for arms and feet. But it was an English house" (164). What Rhys is doing, I think, is reiterating through the image the central, subversive pre-oedipal power at work in the novel. In this passage, she has regressed Rochester to childhood so that what seems to be a premonition, like Bertha's dream, is perhaps also a memory. What woman would the male child draw? Not, surely, his wife but, more likely, his mother.[8] Through the preverbal image, Rochester once again encounters the intersection of the mother, sexuality (the "crime" for which Antoinette/the mother will be imprisoned) and the child.

In a sense, this scene reactivates the two drawings Julia Martin sketches in *After Leaving Mr. Mackenzie*, which we might now read as "after-leaving-the-father." In the first, the face of Mr. Mackenzie intrudes between her and the white page until she can only draw little flags of surrender and turn instead to a letter begging for money. At the end of the book, she sits in another café intending to write another letter; this time, however, after her attempts to write turn to

---

[8]O'Connor, on the other hand, writes, "There is little doubt that this non-woman, a figure that he has created (both in the drawing and in Antoinette), represents his wife, incarcerated on the third floor of Thornfield Hall" (169).

"meaningless strokes," she begins to draw faces, "the sort of faces a child would draw." Although, as we have seen, Julia does not ultimately succeed in extricating herself from the system of symbolic or economic exchange, she continually searches for an alternative that moves from the letter to the body. The significance of *Wide Sargasso Sea* is that Rhys attempts a new strategy in which she forces the son to experience her own psychological and linguistic space, positioning him where he can no longer confine the mother inside a repressed oedipal rage but must see her released through the daughter.

At the end of her dream, Antoinette sees another stained-glass "text" in the sky: "All my life was in it. I saw the grandfather clock and Aunt Cora's patchwork, all colours, I saw the orchids and the stephanotis and the tree of life" (189). She sees the chandelier and gold ferns and soft green velvet moss (189) and hears the parrot, becomes in fact the parrot as her hair "stream[s] out like wings" (190). She establishes herself as the voice that asks "Who am I? Who is there?"[9] We are back here to the cormorant, the wash of color, gold and green, the sea pool, the figure of a woman, veiled. Quite literally, Rhys has returned not to Coulibri but to Jane's drawings, reactivating the mode obscured by both Rochester's blindness and Freud's blind spot.

What Rhys creates, then, is not a double suicide but an alternative to the dead mother, at least an alternative to the death "people know about." We assume that Bertha will leap from the roof only because of a preexisting text. Part of what Rhys is doing, however, is distorting (the) text and its assumptions, inserting into it the trope of the "real" death, which is in fact what might save the daughter.

The flames at the end of *Wide Sargasso Sea* which make Bertha laugh, seeing "the lovely colour spreading so fast" (189), are flames that "protect" her, flames of both destruction and desire, which other women in Rhys's work experience: "She was a defiant flame shooting upwards" (*ALMM*, 131). They are also the same flames associated with language that H.D. discovers through the Presence in *The Walls Do Not Fall*, "rare as radium, as healing":

[9]Baer also discusses Antoinette's association with the parrot (143); Scharfman discusses the bird as "a metonym for the mother" (105).

my old self, wrapped round me,

was shroud (I speak of myself individually
but I was surrounded by companions

in this mystery);

                    . . . . .

peril, strangely encountered, strangely endured,
marks us;

we know each other
by secret symbols,

though, remote, speechless,
we pass each other on the pavement,

at the turn of the stair;
though no word pass between us,

there is subtle appraisement;
even if we snarl a brief greeting

or do not speak at all,
we know our Name,

we nameless initiates,
born of one mother,

companions
of the flame. [20–21]

9

She Herself Is the Riddling

In H.D.'s last major work, *Helen in Egypt*, the poet asks the central question, "What filled the eyes of the child, // with terrible fire— fire of battle? / fire of desire?" (285) and waits for the answer that "break[s] through the legend . . . like fire / through the broken pictures / on a marble floor" (259).

Helen in Egypt is a complicated and convoluted text, alternating between tercets and prose glosses, where the poet, working through a fifty-line fragment of Stesichorus's *Pallinode*, often seems at a loss "how [to] phrase or how frame the problem" (63). Stesichorus's revision retracts an earlier story of Helen of Troy; in the palinode, he maintains that Helen was never *in* Troy, that she was a phantom, an apparition, the real Helen having been spirited away to Egypt. Thus, *"the Greeks and the Trojans alike fought for an illusion"* (HE, 1). The "problem" of the text seems partly to emerge from H.D.'s source: how Helen could have been two places at once, how she has met with Achilles "among the shades," whether she was responsible for the war. The structuring of the poem into nonevents complicates all the conventional external markers.[1] Through the three major divisions of the poem—"Pallinode," "Leuké," and "Eidolon"—we discover that Helen shifts through time, space, and memory, appearing

---

[1]Susan Friedman has observed that "ordinary conventions of epic narrative are consistently violated. H.D. deliberately obscures for most of the epic the cornerstones of external reality and conventional narrative" (*Psyche Reborn*, 65). For a reading of important aspects of the poem outside the realm of my work here, see *Psyche Reborn*, particularly 59–67, 253–72, and 286–96.

in Troy, Egypt, and finally, on Thetis's "isle blanche." The poet tells
us that the Helen of the first sequence is *"translated to a transcendental
plane"*; the second Helen searches for answers *"near to her in time"*
through manifestations of former lovers, Paris and Theseus; and the
third Helen realizes *" 'all myth, the one reality,' is concerned with the
human content of the drama"* (255). Much of the poem leaves behind the
"source," then, and is informed by H.D.'s own preoccupations. It *is,*
as other critics have noted, about identity, consciousness, healing,
poetics, and revisionist mythmaking, but it is also about the fire of
desire and about breaking through legends; specifically, it is a poem
about incest as the unspoken and unspeakable force that ravages
Troy.

Early in the poem, Achilles attempts to strangle Helen, to silence
her. What has provoked Achilles' attack and set the cycle of the poem
in motion is a single word pronounced by Helen—Thetis, the name
of his mother. *"It may not seem a matter of great importance that in their
first encounter, [Helen] 'dared speak the name that made that of the goddess
fade,' but apparently, 'a whisper, a breath' of which Helen, it seems, was
unaware, had alarmed Achilles ('O child of Thetis'), provoked his attack and
projected the first of the series or circle of the ever-recurring 'eternal moments'"* (277). *Helen in Egypt* is an extraordinarily rich text, but a
singular reading emerges from this primal scene: this is the story
of the confrontation between the daughter's attempt to speak the
mother and the son's attempt to banish her. Achilles, H.D. tells us,
"could name Helena, / but the other [Thetis] he could not name; / she
was a lure, a light, / an intimate flame, a secret kept / even from his
slaves, the elect, / the innermost hierarchy" (*HE*, 251). She is a secret
kept *particularly* from the innermost hierarchy, for she is the gap, the
absence around which the elect maintain themselves. This is the
same secret Rochester encounters in *Wide Sargasso Sea*, "a memory to
be avoided, locked away, and like all memories a legend. Or a lie"
(173). *Helen in Egypt*, then, is constructed around the struggle between the surfacing of the mother and her repression: "teach me to
remember, / teach me not to remember" (186). Despite all the "pictures" and memories that break through the text, Helen finally realizes that "there is only one image, / one picture, though the swords
flash" (243). It is Thetis, the image Achilles, like Rochester, refuses to
see.

The initial "story," then, that I shall extract from this entangled narrative/poem, is the story of Achilles, "lying on [his] pallet, awake / . . . numb with a memory, a sort of ecstasy of desolation, / a desire to return to the old / thunder and roar of the sea" (256). Since Thetis is throughout the poem specifically formulated as "the sea-enchantment," we can understand Achilles' "desire" as desire for the ancient mother.

> It was only then,
> when the pictures had melted away,
> that I saw him stretched on his pallet,
>
> that I seemed to hear him say,
> she failed me, my Daemon, my Goddess;
> she had led him astray,
>
> prompting an Old Man to guide her son
> to a battered, unwieldly craft;
> true, the boat had a mast,
>
> but otherwise, it was a foreign
> unseemly thing, with awkward sails—
> where are the Thetis-wings?
>
> it was only, when I felt
> with him, lying there,
> the bitterness of his loss,
>
> that I knew he loved, that I knew
> the ecstasy of desire had smitten him,
> burnt him; touched with the Phoenix-fire,
>
> the invincible armour
> melted him quite away,
> till he knew his mother [260–61]

The Old Man is Chiron, the Centaur who, H.D. tells us, trained the young Greek heroes. Sent off by his mother so that he might "learn to rule a kingdom" (287), the child-apprentice Achilles lives in Chiron's cave with "his childhood's secret idol, the first Thetis-eidolon" (284); "he hid it in moss, in straw, / in a hole in the cave-wall / or in the tree by the cave-door, / and stone by fitted stone, / he built her an altar" (284). This eidolon, or little wooden doll, is the first layer of the underlying memory. The child Achilles builds his altar "far on the hill-crest / but the other was always near," the "other" being the

Centaur. It becomes clear how H.D. is dismantling the system, the code of the father; the "other" is not "woman" but the intruder between mother and son, the "other" who "did not help him, / nor try to find / what filled the eyes of the child / with terrible fire—fire of battle? / fire of desire?" (285). H.D. suggests that what goes unobserved or forbidden is not the terrible fire of myth but desire for another craft, not the "foreign / unseemly thing" but the original vessel: "I say there is one image, / . . . a picture, an image, an idol / or eidolon, not much more than a doll, old, old—for ship-rigging and beam / can be changed, a mast renewed, / a rudder re-set but never the hull; this is the same, this is my first ship, / this is my own, my belovèd" (244). The hull—the husk of a seed, the hollow portion of a vessel immersed in water—clearly suggests the mother's body and the prenatal experience of interior space. There is a curious regression from picture to image to idol to eidolon, culminating in an elliptical leap to the "first ship" where "this" loses its referent. The eidolon and the hull become indistinguishable from each other and from the mother.

The eidolon, however, is only a representation, the first transitional object midway between the beloved and the word. Achilles creates it to repair a loss and a failure: the wooden doll is a figure "that worked magic, always answering, / always granting his wish or whim" (284). Before he is released further back into incestuous memory through Helen's glance, the doll is a figure for desire: "He could thunder, entreat and command, / and she would obey—that was natural, / she was his mother" (284). But the doll is a cover for the real mother and her failure: "She had promised him immortality / but she had forgotten to dip the heel / of the infant Achilles / into the bitter water, / Styx, was it? / O careless, unspeakable mother, / O Thetis . . . / so she failed at last" (253–54). The perfect preoedipal mother, deathless, all-protecting, has turned out to be a wish, a dream; it is for her failure and for the child's desire despite the failure and for the loss of the time *before* she failed that she becomes "unspeakable." There is too much danger in this space of impossible return: "Was this his anger, / that something forgotten or lost, / . . . was taken from him, / and he only remembered it, / remembered and wanted it back, / when it was gone?" (283). It is this anger that both creates and results from the castration contract, for the mother's failure is also her "lack," much more threatening for the son than for the daughter. As revenge, he abandons her even though he creates increasingly elaborate eidolons to represent her: *"True, he forgot her and that is where her power lay"* (295).

Rachel Blau DuPlessis most clearly and forcefully understands that the "extremely peculiar and unsettling space/voice which this poem creates may begin to be comprehended in view of its . . . thematics of the maternal" (*H.D.*, 111) and that this space/voice in the poem is extended into a pervasive matrisexuality (114).[2]

> H.D.'s poetic history of consciousness traces the way Egypt—a symbol of the mother and therefore of fusion, incest, desire and death—has been tampered with and displaced from our understanding, replaced by the Graeco-Roman civilisation: the father, differentiation, violence (including rape and war), repression, The Command, and laws by which male power exercises itself to control death. To constitute itself, Western civilisation has made an "exodus from Egypt." H.D. wants to replace that bellicose father-civilisation with Hellas, the mother. [*H.D.* 113–14]

Helen tries to transform Achilles' relationship to Thetis because his relationship will ultimately determine her own. In a pivotal line of the poem, H.D. writes, *"The memory is really that of Achilles but [Helen] lives it with him"* (260), knowing that shifting the son's oedipal journey will shift the daughter's journey as well and that revising the script will have profound consequences not only for Orestes but for his sisters. Thus, Helen works to make Achilles confront the question at the heart of the semiotic: *" Was not his own mother more desirable than the 'wooden doll' he had made to represent her?"* (295). This is an astonishing question, really, one that perhaps only Helen—already "fallen," already reviled—dare ask, for it subverts the premise of both culture

---

[2]In *H.D.: The Career of That Struggle*, DuPlessis makes important contributions to an understanding of *Helen in Egypt* in the section titled " 'Desire Begets Love.' " Her work in this chapter is centered on a reading that maintains, "All kinds of contemptuous challenge and assault, all expressions of sexual hatred, desire to hurt women, H.D. shows are a shamed avoidance for an almost unspeakable depth of passionate attraction for the mother" (115). DuPlessis, however, although highly attuned to the "flickerings" of incest in the poem, works much more consistently within the framework of thralldom (established in her earlier work) and desire, always matching or balancing the "erotic/sensual, incestuous yearning for the mother" with "heterosexual passion" (115).

and representation and promises to explode discourse with an incestuous energy.

H.D.'s strategy has clearly developed from "Paint It To-Day,"
where, we remember, she aligns herself with the matricidal brother,
and from *Trilogy*, where she tries to use the male as *intermediary* to
gain access to the mother. *Helen in Egypt* is a radical text not because it
is an epic written *by* a woman *about* a woman but because in it, the
writing daughter, instead of attempting to escape from or to circum-
vent the code, tries to fundamentally reformulate the oedipal story,
forcing the son to confront the "too intense primary experience"
(162) of the mother.

Helen in Egypt does not take up a "new" problem, however; clearly,
the poem is to be a palimpsest. Figures from H.D.'s early life appear
disguised, altered, revised in a curious collapsing of family romance;
"roles" intersect, overlap, as H.D. reenters the configurations of her
earliest work. Helen is, we remember, Clytemnestra's sister. "*It is as
if,*" H.D. writes, "*Helen were re-living her own story and visualizing her
own fate in terms of that of her twin-sister*" (74). Moreover, "*she seems to
equate Orestes, her sister's son, with Achilles*" (91). This re-creation
involves an incredible role-shifting as the "mother" of "Paint It To-
Day" (Clytemnestra) becomes the betrayed sister, and the son/
brother (Orestes) becomes the son/lover (Achilles), who seeks to
reclaim, not slay, the mother. Moreover, Helen identifies herself
with her sister's daughter, Iphigenia (91) and, through her, with her
own daughter, Hermione. "*She would re-create the whole of the tragic
scene*" (91).

Helen's own daughter, eclipsed to large degree, appears in one
liminal memory late in the poem as her mother abandons her:

> my child
> prattling of a bird-nest,
>
> playing with my work-basket;
> the reels rolled to the floor
> and she did not stoop to pick up
>
> the scattered spools but stared
> with wide eyes in a white face,
> at a stranger—and stared at her mother,
>
> a stranger—that was all [228]

As Susan Friedman notes, H.D.'s craft and her ability to condense are evident in this powerful scene (*PR*, 63). We are back in the space of "immediacy" sketched by Margaret Homans; unlike the child Achilles, who creates a "token" for the mother, Hermione refuses to pick up the scattered spools, which recall Freud's *fort-da* paradigm of the child who replaces—with a spool, with an eidolon—the missing mother. The daughter here refuses this transitional signifier when the prattle of her preoedipal utterance is interrupted; instead, she stares, gazes. When we remember that *HERmione* is also the title of H.D.'s incestuous mother/daughter novel, we see that what also demands encounter with the disappearing mother is the daughter *text*.

The poem becomes, then, an extremely convoluted and parthenogenic event. Moreover, by the very layering of identity, the text replicates incest, where each relationship necessarily has two names; depending on the particular configuration, the mother is (also) her daughter's sister, the daughter is her sister's mother, the son is his brother's father, and so on. Once H.D. has returned to the archetypal patterns of the House of Thebes, we begin to understand the riddle of incest and identity in which she has been caught over and over again.[3] That many of her texts function through double or multiple names (like Rhys's Antoinette/Bertha)—Her/Hermione; Raymonde Ransome/Ray Bart; Amen-Zeus; Thetis/Isis/Aphrodite—suggests a kind of synchronic lineage at work in which the writing daughter's identity is contingent, finally, not on the model of desire but on the model of incest.

H.D. appropriates this model in her palinode, attempting to "restore sight." It is no accident that she chooses to detour through the work of Stesichorus, who *"was said to have been struck blind because of his invective against Helen, but later was restored to sight, when he reinstated her in his* Pallinode" (*HE*, 1). This blindness associated with reviling women's sexuality, particularly a sexuality associated with the mother, is operative in Rhys too, via Brontë; Rochester, remember, was stricken blind when he saw Bertha escape from the "story"

---

[3]For an extensive reading of the entanglements of Freud, Oedipus, incest, and the Sphinx, see Peter Rudnytsky, *Freud and Oedipus;* some of my thinking for this chapter is indirectly indebted to his work.

in which he had tried to confine her. Rhys's "palinode" of *Jane Eyre*, however, omits Rochester's blindness; she forces him to see the "unseeable," the mother. This coincidence between *Wide Sargasso Sea* and *Helen in Egypt* is perhaps no coincidence at all when we understand that the entire castration configuration is constructed around what is "not seen" and that the archetypal blindness in this regard is that of Oedipus, who, we know, put out his eyes when he realized that he had done the unspeakable: killed his father and committed incest with his mother. We begin to sense the heart of H.D.'s and Rhys's journey when we find them drawn to working through texts which defy the "blind spot," understanding, as Rochester senses reluctantly in the center of *Wide Sargasso Sea*, that what is not seen is "not nothing."

The impulse behind the daughter's story can perhaps best be understood at the end of *Helen in Egypt*, where H.D. writes, "The secret is no secret; / the simple path / refutes at last / the threat of the Labyrinth, / the Sphinx is seen, / the Beast is slain / and the Phoenix-nest / reveals the innermost / key or the clue to the rest / of the mystery" (303). The most telling line here is, I think, "the Sphinx is seen," not only in its continuing allusion to Sophocles but in its readjustment of "the story." Oedipus was set the task not of "seeing" the Sphinx but of answering her riddle. Like Rhys's little girl who refuses to answer the *nun's* "riddle," however, H.D. is less concerned with "right answers" than with vision, repairing the blind spot. When we shift positions and begin to interrogate the Sphinx, we see that through her conflation of identity—part woman, part beast—she herself is the riddling, two halves that do not "belong" together.

Claude Lévi-Strauss's interpretation of the Oedipus myth can take the significance of the Sphinx one step farther: "Between the solution of the riddle and incest, a relation exists. . . . Like the solved riddle, incest brings together terms meant to remain separate: The son is joined with the mother, the brother with the sister, *in the same way as the answer succeeds, against all expectations, in rejoining the question*" (23). If then, in a sense, riddling desires a "consummation" it simultaneously resists or forbids, the Sphinx, who embodies the riddle, becomes a figure for incest. But in H.D.'s version, the "threat" is "refuted"; the poet revises curses and prohibitions, refusing the snare. When we think through the Sphinx, in fact, H.D.'s entire text opens differently, and *Helen in Egypt* shows *itself* to be a riddle, a riddle not unlike that posed to Oedipus: what creature is it that can take three forms? H.D. knows the answer before the question is asked, has always known the answer—Helen. To write, H.D. needs not the right answer but the right question—"how phrase or how frame the problem?"—to accommodate the multiplicity of "Helen," which, we remember, was the name of H.D.'s mother. It is the riddling, finally, that permits the paradox, permits the conflation of sexuality and maternity and the text which inscribes them.

As riddle, *Helen in Egypt* is a poem to be read backward, inside out, for it is not until the end that we can read the beginning, or perhaps it is a poem that in its curious slippage can be read twice, differently, actually *becomes* a palinode, not the same once we have passed through the oedipal journey differently. If we, like Helen, enter a space where we suspend logic and physics, all preconception of what is mutually exclusive, all sense of regulated time and space, we find ourselves in the space necessary to experience the fullness of the poem; it is the space, we discover, of earliest relation—"no before and no after" (303)—to both the mother and the wor(l)d.

It is the space where Achilles' "glance" at Helen is no longer (just) a look born of desire but an encounter that is both textual and incestuous, the matrix H.D. has sought all along. Although H.D. borrows freely from myth in this poem, as Susan Friedman has noted, "the fatal glance that signals [Achilles'] absorption into the woman's world is entirely H.D.'s addition" (*PR*, 264). It is clearly significant to her, for she inscribes it twice, once in the small scene with Hermione, who watches her mother disappear at the top of the stairs, and again as Achilles watches Helen from the ramparts. The scene with the prattling child is a prototype of the gaze; Achilles' glance replicates, through his association of Helen with Thetis, this exchange with the mother: "all things would change but never / the glance she exchanged with me" (54). It is this glance that distracts him, causes his defeat, but the reason he is watching Helen in the first place adds an important dimension to the reading: "*He must have some direct guidance. Where will he get it? He seems for once, to be at odds with the Command 'Did the Command read backward?' He will consult a new oracle. . . . He will watch Helen, measure her paces, the direction she takes, how and where she looks. If she pauses here or there—yes. If she goes on there or here—no"* (53).

The significance of this scene is that Helen has become an inscription, a hieroglyph, just as the "indecipherable Amenscript" (21) opens for Helen only when she sees a bird swoop past: "I was not interested, / I was not instructed, / nor guessed the inner sense of the hieratic, / but when the bird swooped past, / that first evening, / I seemed to know the writing, / as if God made the picture / and matched it / with a living hieroglyph" (22–23). This is precisely Achilles' experience as he watches Helen's movements; his reading, however, proves fatal at the moment when this "writing" is disrupted by the gaze. It is this conflation of the mother, the lover, and the text which destroys the Command as we have seen over and over, starting with Brontë's gypsy in the library, who, we remember, talks, like a Sphinx, in riddles.

What H.D. seems to be providing here in this complicated and sometimes contradictory text is a way of access to the mother which allows a space for the daughter as well as the son and for an increase in language jarred free from the symbolic as Helen realizes "the script was a snare" (220). "*We were right,*" H.D. writes. "*Helen herself denies an actual intellectual knowledge of the temple-symbols. But she is nearer to them than the instructed scribe; for her, the secret of the stone-writing is repeated in natural or human symbols. She herself is the writing*" (22).

I offer this transfer from word to image, from symbol to body, from symbolic to semiotic, as the single most important contribution of Jean Rhys and H.D. It opens a way of thinking about the "specificity" of women's writing which does not rely on the "consensus" that "modern texts . . . rehearse a recurrent developmental saga: the successful or failed but in any event necessary passage from the Imaginary into the Symbolic, from the dangerous seductions of the mirror stage into the sobering realities of the law of the Father" (Schor, 217). Naomi Schor has claimed that "what remains unexplored are the specificities—if any—of the feminocentric examples of these genres" (217); perhaps, however, a "feminocentric" text, which might also turn out to be a "matricentric" text, would not *be* an example of the "genre" that relies on a "sobering reality." Perhaps a "matricentric" text relies on a riddle, relies on riddling in both its senses—posing puzzling questions and piercing holes, "impair[ing] [the symbolic] as if by puncturing"—so that the Command must look through the spaces.

Indeed, if we sketch the "action" of *Helen in Egypt* beyond the external markers, it is the movement not from seduction to "reality" but from "word" to "token" to "glance," as Hermione plunges back into a space just before the mirror, where she is interlocked with the vanishing mother through the gaze, and Achilles, gazing at Helen, is punctured, pierced.

What H.D. and Rhys teach us is that the passage from the semiotic to the symbolic is perhaps *not* necessary, at least not textually. Both *Wide Sargasso Sea* and *Helen in Egypt* are suggestively centered on women reviled for their sexuality, a sexuality linked specifically with the mother. Both Rhys and H.D., finally, reach inside male texts to create the daughter's story (although Rhys chose to work through *Jane Eyre*, what she was really retelling was not the narrator's story but the story initially told within the framework of the novel by Rochester and by Bertha's brother, Richard Mason), for they understand that without retelling the one, they cannot write the incestuous revision of the myths on which culture and language stand. *Helen in Egypt* suggests that a daughter's text might ultimately refuse or adjust the son's "saga," retelling not just the historical/mythological "plot" but the psychological narrative as well. Rhys never develops this strategy as fully as does H.D.; she leaves the daughter balancing on the "battlements" of Thornfield. In H.D.'s version, the daughter, finally, does not have to sacrifice herself to speak the mother, and the mother's power no longer lies in being forgotten. Helen attempts to replace the word *Thetis* with Thetis herself and to show Achilles, still caught in the discourse and the economy of the Command, that the "fire of battle" is less dangerous than the refusal to acknowledge the "fire of desire"; he has "bartered the world" not "for a glance" (62) but for "*a memory forgotten*" (304).

Once the oedipal exchange is undone, the semiotic can break through. At the end of the poem, in "a miraculous birth," Helen bears a second child, Euphorion. "*The promised Euphorion is not one child but two. It is 'the child in Chiron's cave' and the 'frail maiden,' stolen by Theseus from Sparta*" (288); it is Achilles and Helen conflated, the phantom and the Command. It seems that what Helen has sought all along is this return to childhood: "I am only a daughter; / no, no, I am not a mother" (191); "no, I am not Demeter, / seated before an altar, / your braizer, there, / I am Koré, Persephone" (195). We see that once the son's story has been altered, given back to him, the daughter can detour through the "New Mortal": "I tremble,/" the poet tells us; "I feel the same / anger and sudden terror, / that I sensed Achilles felt, / when I named his mother" (299–300).

Her's has not been the oedipal journey culminating in maternity; it has been a return to the preoedipal, despite the danger: "Is it Death to know / this immaculate purity, / security?" (194) This question is never entirely answered, although the poem offers a suggestion, and more important perhaps than what it offers is the form of the offering. In a strange little piece at the end of the poem, the poet creates another "eidolon," this one crafted of words. These last six tercets— the only verse in the epic to be written in italics, the mode of the prose—reactivate the alternately disruptive and soothing rhythm of the wooden doll, the beat, reverberation, ripple, echo, crash, and spray of the sea against the broken shale. H.D. has managed to transform the "token" into meter suffused with the mother; the power of the word *Thetis* has been translated into a cadence in which the mother is no longer named but appears as/in language, embodying the riddle of the old *"infinite loneliness / when one is never alone"* (304).

Epilogue

There is a passage from Jean Rhys's *Smile Please* which might serve as an analogue/epilogue to the passage with which this book began, the story of the little girl who tries to speak the unspeakable.

> Before I could read, almost a baby, I imagined that God, this strange thing or person I heard about, was a book. Sometimes it was a large book standing upright and half open and I could see the print inside but it made no sense to me. Other times the book was smaller and inside were sharp flashing things. The smaller book was, I am sure now, my mother's needle-book, and the sharp flashing things were her needles with the sun on them. [27]

Here, transformed, are the same three characters: the book that is God, the child, and the missing mother. Now, however, there is also a new element: the mother's book. Through the associations of the image Rhys chooses, it is both enticing and dangerous, as we remember from childhood: "Once upon a time a lovely queen sat by a window sewing." This is the mother who vanishes as the story begins, who vanishes, we understand now, *because* the story begins; first wounded by the needle (need I say pricked?), she then, wishing for a daughter, succumbs to childbirth. With Snow White left in the care of an enraged stepmother, the story of "mirror mirror on the wall" can be told within the androcentric economy because it begins with the "right" image—the mirror—taking as the point of departure the loss of the preoedipal mother, whose story, we discover, *cannot* be told.

This is the "great unwritten story" Adrienne Rich calls the "cathexis between mother and daughter—essential, distorted, misused" (*OWB*, 226). "The loss of the daughter to the mother, the mother to the daughter"—before Freud, because of Freud, since Freud—"is the essential female tragedy," Rich writes. "We acknowledge Lear (father-daughter split), Hamlet (son and mother), and Oedipus (son and mother) as great embodiments of the human tragedy; but there is no presently enduring recognition of mother-daughter passion and rapture" (*OWB*, 240).

As we have seen in Jean Rhys's and H.D.'s attempts to rework the brother's story, there is no ready model for the daughter in her relationship with or her loss of the mother. H.D., however, would "re-create the whole of the tragic scene." In the larger movement of Rhys's and H.D.'s work—and they are not the only women through whose work this book could have been written—the mother, while still culturally, theologically, and psychologically forbidden, has nonetheless been inscribed. Rhys offers the mother metonymically, as another kind of text; in place of the book that "makes no sense" to the child, there is the "book" she is "sure" of, the one that is not figurative but literal, the mother's book. Moreover, the needle (we cannot ignore the phallic implications) is not single, unitary, privileged; it is, echoing Irigaray, multiple and based not on difference, the castration paradigm, but on sameness. It is a book of presence, in which the identical object asserts itself over and over again. "Almost a baby," Rhys thinks of print and her mother's sewing needles in the same category; the distinction she makes is that God's book is one you have to imagine while mother's book is present, compelling, flashing in the sun. The child does not, of course, "read" the needles, but as Margaret Homans has so forcefully argued, it is this juxtaposition of the Word with the literal within women's texts that marks them, even though it leaves the "dilemma of the woman writer, caught between her own interest in a literal mother-daughter language and her desire at once to placate and to enter the symbolic realm of literary language" (Homans, *BW*, 38).

One of the major impediments to thinking about the inscription of the mother or of a maternally connoted register to discourse, Alice Jardine observes, is that "throughout the debate, no one has been looking at what women have, in fact, written" (*TF*, 6). Marianne

Hirsch claims in her essay "Mothers and Daughters" that "the story of mother-daughter relationships has been written even if it has not been read, that it constitutes the hidden subtext of many texts. The project to uncover these hidden or disguised plots—much like the discovery of the Minoan-Mycenaean civilizations behind the Greek, to use Freud's metaphor—is an archaeological search for prehistory" (214). Part of the problem is that we are often limited by the notion of "plots"; we read the lovely queen sewing but not the flashing "book" lying on her lap.[1] As we have seen so insistently in Rhys and H.D., however, it is not in the mother's "story" that her power lies but in how she riddles the discourse that denies her.

Another impediment Jardine observes is that the major theorists and writers seem bound to the question of the mother only "as it transpires within a *male* economy" (G, 144), which, we realize, would demand forbidding her as the very premise of invoking her. As a final suggestion, I offer an alternative to the notion of *economy* in at least three of its meanings: (1) frugality; (2) "the disposition or regulation of the parts or functions of any organic whole; an organized system or method"; and (3) its theological meaning, "the divine plan for man." I emphasize that "desire" in Lacanian terms, and especially language *as* desire, is by definition an economy: it is frugal, that is, held back, limited, controlled; it regulates function, that is, "disposes" (of) the primary (incestuous) libidinal urges; and it is divine, that is, spoken through and as the Word. This "economy," which works on a system of exchange, with woman as its object and language as the adjunct with the signifier as the "counter," is premised on the forbidden, and the forbidden, both libidinally and textually, is the mother.

The question, then, becomes this: if we have functioned for centuries out of the economy of the son's desire, what would be the consequences of the daughter's desire? What, indeed, if desire were not the term relevant to the daughter at all? Alice Jardine repeatedly returns in *Gynesis* to the idea of "a breakdown in the symbolic function," a crisis in which "new discourses in formation have fore-

[1]Joan Lidoff writes in her work on Virginia Woolf, "We are learning to look for suppressed plots and images in literature by women. We often find as well a hidden presence in the work of women writers, a buried metaphor of the mother, which shapes the style and content of the work" (45).

grounded . . . a space . . . undulating, folded over upon itself, permeable: the self-contained space of eroticism. If this space is maternal . . . what can be the feminist relationship to this desperate search through the maternal body?" (100).

The relationship, I suggest, is incest, "the acutely interior, un-abashedly incestuous exploration" (Jardine, G, 33) of these spaces and an "incestuous challenge to the symbolic order" (Jones, 248). This incest is neither frugal nor regulated nor divinely planned; it is expansive, unbounded, accessible, pleasurable, dangerous, and disruptive. It is not the incest of Freud, who told only the son's story, for, writes Juliet Mitchell, "it is as though the concept of an Oedipus complex—of a fundamental wish for incest—was so radical that if one was to argue at all for the child's incestuous desires then at least these had better be for the parent of the opposite sex" (10). Further, in terms of a specificity of women's writing, "incest" and "desire" are not extensions of each other but different expressions, different modes; desire is an oedipal construct based on the premise of the forbidden, becoming operative only after the mirror stage, which presages the entry into language and culture where the child will finally learn the prohibition of the mother. Incest, on the other hand, is preoedipal, formulated not on severance and lack and prohibition but on presence, on the literal. Incest, then, precedes desire, for earliest relation to the mother *is* incestuous in the sense that the infant's experience is undenied access to her body, both internally (prenatally) and externally. Incest, in the sense that I am using it here, is not a desire but a memory.

Margaret Homans, thinking through Nancy Chodorow, founds the daughter's version of the son's story not on abandonment of the mother but on extended preoedipal relation with her, which, maintains Homans, "has important consequences for the writing of daughters, for the ways women rewrite the story of language" (13) and, I would add, the language in which they write it. Because of this carry-over of the semiotic attachment, the daughter "speaks two languages at once" (Homans, BW, 13).

Homans stresses the "literal" in the work of nineteenth-century women as a "matrilinear language," or what I would call a "matri-line," working within the dominant discourse, exemplified, for her, in Elizabeth Gaskell's "Lizzie Leigh." This story, Homans writes, "suggests not so much that a nonsymbolic language shared between mothers and daughters survives from childhood, or that women's linguistic practices are wholly absorbed within the paternal order, but rather that in the interplay between these seemingly contradictory possibilities exists a language that is specific to mothers and daughters and also, importantly, capable of providing pleasure to them" (BW, 226).

The story centers on a "fallen" daughter, Lizzie Leigh, who is disowned by her father when he learns of her pregnancy. News of it, significantly, comes to him when the family discovers Lizzie has not received a letter they have sent. Lizzie's mother, Anne, however, does not accept "the rigid duplication of patriarchal words, and the linear passage of a letter from sender to receiver that comes to stand for this" (BW, 227–28); when her husband dies several years after declaring Lizzie dead, the mother sets out in search of her daughter. Through a series of complicated plot twists, Anne discovers the woman, Susan, who has been raising Lizzie's infant. When Anne appears, Susan shows her a packet of baby clothes that were left with the child and a letter saying, "Call her Anne." Mrs. Leigh confirms the child's identity partly through the coincidence of the name but mainly through the clothes; she recognizes one of the dresses as cut from a gown that she and Lizzie had bought together. Homans finds it significant that "these signs' correct interpretation must wait for the arrival of the original referent both of the name and of the message of the fabric." Moreover, she continues, "if a sign signifies only in the presence of what it signifies, especially where the referent is a mother, it undoes and refuses the symbolic economy that stipulates the absence of a referent, especially where the referent is a mother. This kind of sign making suggests that mother and daughter could communicate with one another both as women and within the order of written language" (BW, 229).

Homans has made important contributions to the study of reading the mother; she writes thematically, however, out of the realm of literal/figurative and nature/culture, leaving the inscription of sexuality and the body for the most part in the background. We don't see in modernism what Homans sees in nineteenth-century women's texts, the "pleasure" mothers and daughters take in their encoded language. Pleasure in the twentieth century is no longer a shared experience but a textual event.

H.D. and Rhys are gatekeepers, in a sense, standing between the nineteenth century and a space where the literal and figurative collapse, where the boundaries between "name" and "fabric" (or name and eidolon) blur, where "the unsettled and questionable subject of poetic language (for whom the word is never uniquely sign) maintains itself at the cost of reactivating [the] repressed instinctual, maternal element" (Kristeva, *DL*, 136). According to Kristeva:

> If it is true that the prohibition of incest constitutes, at the same time, language as communicative code and women as exchange objects in order for society to be established, *poetic language would be* for its questionable subject-in-process, the *equivalent of incest:* it is within the economy of signification itself that the questionable subject-in-process appropriates to itself this archaic, instinctual, and maternal territory; thus it simultaneously prevents the word from becoming mere sign and the mother from becoming an object like any other—forbidden. [*DL*, 136]

The project of Rhys and H.D. is to break the boundaries of the forbidden, working toward the incestuous *language* of the daughter, which depends not just on the mother's name or her artifacts but on access to her body, its rhythms, scansions, screams, and snorts. To rupture the code, linguistic or cultural, by the reinsertion of the mother *is* incest; woman's language, then, relies on the "unspoken" as well as the "unspeakable."

The preverbal "story," the forbidden story, to which Rhys and H.D. repeatedly return, manifests itself through sounds and images outside (androcentric) discourse: mothers, babies, blood; chants, singing, shouts; eyes, paintings, hallucinations; oceans, moons, floods, and flames. Back through infancy, madness, childbirth, riddles, curses, and song, the writing daughter gasps for memory so that she might, at last, inscribe her utterance, free herself from the myths that have intended to "destory" and destroy her.

> No one who survives to speak
> new language, has avoided this:
> the cutting-away of an old force that held her
> rooted to an old ground

the pitch of utter loneliness
where she herself and all creation
seem equally dispersed, weightless, her being a cry
to which no echo comes or can ever come.

But in fact we were always like this,
rootless, dismembered: knowing it makes the difference.
Birth stripped our birthright from us,
tore us from a woman, from women, from ourselves
so early on
and the whole chorus throbbing at our ears
like midges, told us nothing, nothing
of origins, nothing we needed
to know, nothing that could re-member us.

Only: that it is unnatural,
the homesickness for a woman, for ourselves,
for that acute joy at the shadow her head and arms
cast on a wall, her heavy or slender
thighs on which we lay, flesh against flesh,
eyes steady on the face of love; smell of her milk, her sweat,
terror of her disappearance, all fused in this hunger
for the element they have called most dangerous, to be
lifted breathtaken on her breast, to rock within her
—even if beaten back, stranded again, to apprehend
in a sudden brine-clear thought
trembling like the tiny, orbed, endangered
egg-sac of a new world:
This is what she was to me . . .

[Rich, *DCL*, 75–76]

Bibliography

Primary Sources

Bowen, Stella. *Drawn from Life: Reminiscences*. London: Collins, 1941.
Brontë, Charlotte. *Jane Eyre*. Ed. Richard Dunn. New York: W. W. Norton, 1971.
Browning, Robert. "Popularity." *Robert Browning's Poetry*. Ed. James F. Loucks. New York: W. W. Norton, 1979: 215–17.
Doolittle, Hilda. "Asphodel." Unpublished typescript. Collection of American Literature, Beinecke Rare Book and Manuscript Library, Yale University, New Haven, Conn.
——. *Bid Me to Live (A Madrigal)*. New York: Dial Press, 1960.
——. *Collected Poems, 1912–1944*. Ed. Louis L. Martz. New York: New Directions, 1983.
——. "Compassionate Friendship." Unpublished typescript. Collection of American Literature, Beinecke Rare Book and Manuscript Library, Yale University, New Haven, Conn.
——. *End to Torment: A Memoir of Ezra Pound*. New York: New Directions, 1979.
——. "The Gift." Unpublished typescript. Collection of American Literature, Beinecke Rare Book and Manuscript Library, Yale University, New Haven, Conn.
——. *The Gift*. New York: New Directions, 1982.
——. *Hedylus*. 1928; rpt. Redding Ridge, Conn.: Black Swan Books, 1980.
——. *Helen in Egypt*. New York: New Directions, 1961.
——. *HERmione*. New York: New Directions, 1981.
——. Letter to Viola Jordan, 30 July 1941. Collection of American Literature, Beinecke Rare Book and Manuscript Library, Yale University, New Haven, Conn.
——. "Paint It To-Day." Unpublished typescript. Collection of American Literature, Beinecke Rare Book and Manuscript Library, Yale University, New Haven, Conn.
——. "Paint It To-Day." *Contemporary Literature* 27 (Winter 1986): 444–74.
——. *Palimpsest*. 1926; rpt. Carbondale: Southern Illinois University Press, 1968.

——. *Tribute to Freud.* 1956; rpt. New York: McGraw-Hill, 1975.

——. *Trilogy.* 1944, 1945, 1946; rpt. New York: New Directions, 1973.

Pound, Ezra. *Selected Poems of Ezra Pound.* New York: New Directions, 1957.

Rhys, Jean. *After Leaving Mr. Mackenzie.* 1930; rpt. New York: Perennial Library, Harper & Row, 1982.

——. *Good Morning, Midnight.* 1939; rpt. New York: Vintage Books, 1974.

——. *The Letters of Jean Rhys.* Ed. Francis Wyndham and Diana Melly. New York: Viking, 1984.

——. *Quartet.* 1969; rpt. New York: Vintage Books, 1974.

——. *Smile Please: An Unfinished Autobiography.* 1979; rpt. Harmondsworth, Eng.: Penguin, 1981.

——. *Voyage in the Dark.* 1934; rpt. New York: W. W. Norton, 1982.

——. *Voyage in the Dark,* original ending. Unpublished typescript. Department of Rare Books and Special Collections, McFarlin Library, University of Tulsa, Tulsa, Okla.

——. *Wide Sargasso Sea.* New York: Popular Library, 1966.

Stein, Gertrude. *Tender Buttons: Selected Writings of Gertrude Stein.* Ed. Carl Van Vechten. New York: Vintage Books, 1972.

Williams, William Carlos. "A Letter from William Carlos Williams to Norman Homes Pearson concerning Hilda Doolittle and Her Mother and Father (11 July 1955)," *William Carlos Williams Newsletter* 2, no. 2 (1976): 2.

Critical Works

Abel, Elizabeth. "Women and Schizophrenia: The Fiction of Jean Rhys." *Contemporary Literature* 20 (Spring 1979): 155–77.

Abel, Elizabeth, Marianne Hirsch, and Elizabeth Langland, eds. *The Voyage In: Fictions of Female Development.* Hanover, N.H.: University Press of New England, 1983.

Angier, Carole. *Jean Rhys.* Harmondsworth, Eng.: Penguin, 1985.

Baer, Elizabeth R. "The Sisterhood of Jane Eyre and Antoinette Cosway." *The Voyage In: Fictions of Female Development.* Ed. Elizabeth Abel, Marianne Hirsch, and Elizabeth Langland. Hanover, N.H.: University Press of New England, 1983: 131–48.

Barthes, Roland. *Camera Lucida.* Trans. Richard Howard. New York: Hill and Wang, 1981.

——. "From Work to Text." *Perspectives in Post-structuralist Criticism.* Ed. Josué V. Harari. Ithaca: Cornell University Press, 1979.

Benstock, Shari. *Women of the Left Bank: Paris, 1900–1940.* Austin: University of Texas Press, 1986.

Blanchot, Maurice. *The Gaze of Orpheus.* Ed. P. Adams Sitney. Trans. Lydia Davis. Barrytown, N.Y.: Station Hill Press, 1981.

Bodenheimer, Rosemarie. "Jane Eyre in Search of Her Story." *Papers on Language and Literature* 16 (Fall 1980): 387–402.

Brown, Nancy Hemond. "Jean Rhys and *Voyage in the Dark.*" *London Magazine* 25 (April/May 1985): 40–59.

Burke, Carolyn Greenstein. "Report from Paris: Women's Writing and the Women's Movement." *Signs* 3 (1978): 843–55.

Chessman, Harriet S. "Women and Language in the Fiction of Elizabeth Bowen." *Twentieth Century Literature* 29 (Spring 1983): 69–85.

Chevigny, Bell Gale. "Daughters Writing: Toward a Theory of Women's Biography." *Feminist Studies* 9 (Spring 1983): 79–102.

Chodorow, Nancy. *The Reproduction of Mothering: Pychoanalysis and the Sociology of Gender.* Berkeley: University of California Press, 1979.

Cixous, Hélène. "Castration or Decapitation?" Trans. Annette Kuhn. *Signs* 7 (Autumn 1981): 41–55.

———. "The Laugh of the Medusa." Trans. Keith Cohen and Paula Cohen. *New French Feminisms.* Ed. Elaine Marks and Isabelle de Courtivron. Amherst, Mass.: University of Massachusetts Press, 1980: 245–64.

———. *Vivre l'orange.* Paris: Editions des Femmes, 1979.

Crowder, Diane Griffin. "Amazons and Mothers: Monique Wittig, Hélène Cixous, and Theories of Women's Writing." *Contemporary Literature* 24 (1983): 114–43.

Davidson, Arnold. *Jean Rhys.* New York: Frederick Ungar, 1985.

Davidson, Cathy N., and E. M. Broner, eds. *The Lost Tradition: Mothers and Daughters in Literature.* New York: Frederick Ungar, 1980.

Derrida, Jacques. *Dissemination.* Trans. Barbara Johnson. Chicago: University of Chicago Press, 1981.

———. *Le Seminaire,* book 20: *Encore.* Paris: Seuil, 1975.

DeShazer, Mary K. "'A Primary Intensity between Women': H.D. and the Female Muse." *H.D.: Woman and Poet.* Ed. Michael King. Orono, Me.: National Poetry Foundation, 1986: 157–71.

Dinnerstein, Dorothy. *The Mermaid and the Minotaur: Sexual Arrangements and Human Malaise.* New York: Harper & Row, 1976.

DuPlessis, Rachel Blau. "Family, Sexes, Psyche: An Essay on H.D. and the Muse of the Woman Writer." *Montemora* 6 (1979): 137–56.

———. *H.D.: The Career of That Struggle.* Bloomington: Indiana University Press, 1986.

———. "Language Acquisition." *Iowa Review* 16 (Fall 1986): 252–83.

———. "Romantic Thralldom in H.D." *Contemporary Literature* 20 (Spring 1979): 178–203.

———. *Writing beyond the Ending: Narrative Strategies of Twentieth-Century Women Writers.* Bloomington: Indiana University Press, 1985.

DuPlessis, Rachel Blau, and Susan Stanford Friedman, "'Woman is Perfect': H.D.'s Debate with Freud." *Feminist Studies* 7 (Fall 1981): 417–30.

Eagleton, Terry. *Literary Theory: An Introduction.* Minneapolis: University of Minnesota Press, 1983.

Eisenstein, Hester, and Alice Jardine, eds. *The Future of Difference.* Boston: G. K. Hall, 1980.

Erlich, Iza S. "What Happened to Jocasta?" *Bulletin of the Menninger Clinic* 41 (May 1977): 280–84.

Féral, Josette. "Antigone or *The Irony of the Tribe.*" Trans. Alice Jardine and Tom Gora. *Diacritics* 8 (September 1978): 2–14.

——. "Du texte au sujet: Conditions pour une écriture et un discours au féminin." *Revue de l'Université d'Ottawa* 50, 1:39–46.

Freibert, L. M. "From Semblance to Selfhood: The Evolution of Woman in H.D.'s Neo-Epic *Helen in Egypt.*" *Arizona Quarterly* 36 (Summer 1980): 165–75.

Freud, Sigmund. *The Interpretation of Dreams.* Ed. and trans. James Strachey. 1953; rpt. New York: Avon Books, 1965.

Friedman, Susan Stanford. "Gender and Genre Anxiety: Elizabeth Barrett Browning and H.D. as Epic Poets." *Tulsa Studies in Women's Literature,* 5 (Fall 1986): 203–28.

——. " 'I Go Where I Love': An Intertextual Study of H.D. and Adrienne Rich." *Signs* 9 (Winter 1983): 228–45.

——. *Psyche Reborn: The Emergence of H.D.* Bloomington: Indiana University Press, 1981.

Friedman, Susan Stanford, and Rachel Blau DuPlessis. " 'I Had Two Loves Separate': The Sexualities of H.D.'s *Her.*" *Montemora* 8 (1981): 7–30.

Furman, Nelly. "The Politics of Language: Beyond the Gender Principle?" *Making a Difference: Feminist Literary Criticism.* Ed. Gayle Greene and Coppélia Kahn. London: Methuen, 1985: 59–79.

——. "*A Room of One's Own:* Reading Absence." *Women's Language and Style.* Ed. Douglas Butturff and Edmund L. Epstein. Akron, Ohio: University of Akron Press, 1978: 99–105.

Gallop, Jane. *The Daughter's Seduction: Feminism and Psychoanalysis.* Ithaca: Cornell University Press, 1982.

——. "The Father's Seduction." *The (M)other Tongue: Essays in Feminist Psychoanalytic Interpretation.* Ed. Shirley Nelson Garner, Claire Kahane, and Madelon Sprengnether. Ithaca: Cornell University Press, 1985: 33–50.

——. "Reading the Mother Tongue: Psychoanalytic Feminist Criticism." *Critical Inquiry* 13 (Winter 1987): 314–29.

Gallop, Jane, and Carolyn G. Burke. "Psychoanalysis and Feminism in France." *The Future of Difference.* Boston: G. K. Hall, 1980.

Gardiner, Judith Kegan. "Good Morning, Midnight; Good Night, Modernism." *boundary 2* 11 (Fall/Winter 1982–83): 233–51.

——. "On Female Identity and Writing by Women." *Critical Inquiry* 8 (Winter 1981): 347–61.

——. "A Wake for Mother: The Maternal Deathbed in Women's Fiction." *Feminist Studies* 4 (June 1978): 146–65.

Garner, Shirley Nelson, Claire Kahane, and Madelon Sprengnether, eds. *The (M)other Tongue: Essays in Feminist Psychoanalytic Interpretation.* Ithaca: Cornell University Press, 1985.

Gelpi, Albert. "Hilda in Egypt." *Southern Review* 18 (April 1982): 233–50.

——. "Re-membering the Mother: A Reading of H.D.'s *Trilogy.*" *H.D.: Woman and Poet.* Ed. Michael King. Orono, Me.: National Poetry Foundation, 1986: 173–90.

——. "The Thistle and the Serpent." H.D. *Notes on Thought and Vision.* San Francisco: City Lights Books, 1982.

Gilbert, Sandra. "Life's Empty Pack: Notes toward a Literary Daughteronomy." *Critical Inquiry* 11 (March 1985): 355–84.

Gilbert, Sandra, and Susan Gubar. *The Madwoman in the Attic: The Woman Writer and the Nineteenth-Century Literary Imagination*. New Haven, Conn.: Yale University Press, 1979.

——. *No Man's Land: The Place of the Woman Writer in the Twentieth Century*. New Haven, Conn.: Yale University Press, 1988.

——. *Shakespeare's Sisters: Feminist Essays on Women Poets*. Bloomington: Indiana University Press, 1979.

Greenberg, Caren. "Reading Reading: Echo's Abduction of Language." *Women and Language in Literature and Society*. Ed. Sally McConnell-Ginet, Ruth Borker, and Nelly Furman. New York: Praeger, 1980: 300–9.

Greene, Gayle, and Coppélia Kahn, eds. *Making a Difference: Feminist Literary Criticism*. New York: Methuen, 1985.

Gubar, Susan. "The Echoing Spell of H.D.'s *Trilogy*." *Shakespeare's Sisters: Feminist Essays on Women Poets*. Bloomington: Indiana University Press, 1979.

——. "Sapphistries." *Signs* 10 (Autumn 1984): 43–62.

Guest, Barbara. *Herself Defined: The Poet H.D. and Her World*. New York: Doubleday, 1984.

Hermann, Claudine. "Women in Space and Time." *New French Feminisms*. Amherst: University of Massachusetts Press, 1980: 168–73.

Hirsch, Elizabeth. " 'New Eyes': H.D., Modernism, and the Psychoanalysis of Seeing." *Literature and Psychology* 32, no. 3 (1986): 1–10.

Hirsch, Marianne. "Mothers and Daughters." *Signs* 7 (Autumn 1981): 200–22.

——. "A Mother's Discourse: Incorporation and Repetition in *La Princesse de Cleves*." *Yale French Studies*, No. 62 (1981): 67–87.

Holland, Norman. "H.D. and the 'Blameless Physician.' " *Contemporary Literature* 10 (Autumn 1969): 474–506.

Homans, Margaret. *Bearing the Word: Language and Female Experience in Nineteenth-Century Women's Writing*. Chicago: University of Chicago Press, 1986.

——. " 'Her Very Own Howl': The Ambiguities of Representation in Recent Women's Fiction." *Signs* 9 (Winter 1983): 186–205.

——. *Women Writers and Poetic Identity*. Princeton: Princeton University Press, 1980.

Irigaray, Luce. *Speculum of the Other Woman*. Trans. Gillian C. Gill. Ithaca: Cornell University Press, 1985.

——. *This Sex Which Is Not One*. Trans. Catherine Porter. Ithaca: Cornell University Press, 1985.

——. "Women's Exile: Interview with Luce Irigaray." Trans. Couze Venn. *Ideology and Consciousness* 1 (May 1977): 62–76.

Jardine, Alice A. *Gynesis: Configurations of Woman and Modernity*. Ithaca: Cornell University Press, 1985.

——. "Opaque Texts and Transparent Contexts: The Political Difference of Julia Kristeva." *The Poetics of Gender*. Ed. Nancy K. Miller. New York: Columbia University Press, 1986: 96–116.

——. "Pre-texts for the Transatlantic Feminist." *Yale French Studies* 62 (1981): 220–36.

——. "Theories of the Feminine: Kristeva." *Enclitic* 4 (Fall 1980): 5–15.

Jaynes, Julian. *The Origin of Consciousness in the Breakdown of the Bicameral Mind*. Boston: Houghton Mifflin, 1982.

Jones, Ann Rosalind. "Inscribing Femininity: French Theories of the Feminine." *Making a Difference: Feminist Literary Criticism.* Ed. Gayle Greene and Coppélia Kahn. London: Methuen, 1985: 80–112.

———. "Writing the Body: Towards an Understanding of *L'Ecriture Féminine.*" *Feminist Studies* 7 (Summer 1981): 247–63.

Keefe, Robert. *Charlotte Brontë's World of Death.* Austin: University of Texas Press, 1979.

Kelly, L. Duin. "Jane Eyre's Paintings and Bewick's *History of British Birds.*" *Notes and Queries* 29 (June 1982): 23–32.

King, Michael, ed. *H.D.: Woman and Poet.* Orono, Me.: National Poetry Foundation, 1986.

Kloepfer, Deborah Kelly. "Fishing the Murex Up: Sense and Resonance in H.D.'s *Palimpsest.*" *Contemporary Literature* 27 (Winter 1986): 553–73.

———. "Flesh Made Word: Maternal Inscription in H.D." *Sagetrieb* 3 (Spring 1984): 27–48.

———. "Mother as Muse and Desire: The Sexual Poetics of H.D.'s *Trilogy.*" *H.D.: Woman and Poet.* Ed. Michael King. Orono, Me.: National Poetry Foundation, 1986: 191–206.

———. "*Voyage in the Dark:* Jean Rhys's Masquerade for the Mother." *Contemporary Literature* 26 (Winter 1985): 443–59.

Kristeva, Julia. *Desire in Language: A Semiotic Approach to Literature and Art.* Trans. Thomas Gora, Alice Jardine, and Leon S. Roudiez. Ed. Leon S. Roudiez. New York: Columbia University Press, 1980.

———. *Revolution in Poetic Language.* Trans. Margaret Waller. New York: Columbia University Press, 1984.

Langford, Thomas. "Prophetic Imagination and the Unity of *Jane Eyre.*" *Studies in the Novel* 6 (Summer 1974): 228–35.

———. "The Three Pictures in *Jane Eyre.*" *Victorian Newsletter* 31 (Spring 1967): 47–48.

Lee, Hermione. "Emblems and Engimas in *Jane Eyre.*" *English* 30 (Autumn 1981): 233–55.

Lévi-Strauss, Claude. "The Scope of Anthropology." *Structural Anthropology.* Trans. Monique Layton. New York: Basic Books, 1976: 23–32.

Lidoff, Joan. "Virginia Woolf's Feminine Sentence: The Mother-Daughter World of *To the Lighthouse.*" *Literature and Psychology* 32, no. 3 (1986): 43–59.

McConnell-Ginet, Sally, Ruth Borker, and Nelly Furman, eds. *Women and Language in Literature and Society.* New York: Praeger, 1980.

McLaughlin, M. B. "Past or Future Mindscapes: Pictures in *Jane Eyre.*" *Victorian Newsletter* 41 (Spring 1972): 22–24.

Marks, Elaine, and Isabelle de Courtivron, eds. *New French Feminisms: An Anthology.* Amherst: University of Massachusetts Press, 1980.

Mathis, Mary S., and Michael King. "An Annotated Bibliography of Works about H.D., 1969–1985." *H.D.: Woman and Poet.* Ed. Michael King. Orono, Me.: National Poetry Foundation, 1986: 393–511.

Mellown, Elgin. "Characters and Themes in the Novels of Jean Rhys." *Contemporary Literature* 13 (Autumn 1972): 458–75.

Miller, Nancy K. "Arachnologies: The Woman, the Text, and the Critic." *The Poetics of Gender.* Ed. Miller. New York: Columbia University Press, 1986: 270–95.

———. ed. *The Poetics of Gender.* New York: Columbia University Press, 1986.

Millgate, Jane. "Narrative Distance in *Jane Eyre:* The Relevance of the Pictures." *Modern Language Review* 63 (April 1968): 315–19.

Mitchell, Juliet. "Introduction—I" to Jacques Lacan, *Feminine Sexuality.* Ed. Juliet Mitchell and Jacqueline Rose. Trans. Jacqueline Rose. New York: W. W. Norton, 1983.

Moglen, Helene. *Charlotte Brontë: The Self Conceived.* New York: W. W. Norton, 1976.

Morris, Adalaide. "The Concept of Projection: H.D.'s Visionary Powers." *Contemporary Literature* 24 (Winter 1984): 411–36.

———. "Reading H.D.'s 'Helios and Athene.'" *Extended Outlooks.* Ed. Jane Cooper, Gwen Head, Adalaide Morris, Marcia Southwick. New York: Collier Books, 1982: 155–63.

Moser, Lawrence E., S. J. "From Portrait to Person: A Note on the Surrealistic in *Jane Eyre.*" *Nineteenth-Century Fiction* 20 (December 1965): 275–81.

Nebeker, Helen. *Jean Rhys: Woman in Passage.* Montreal: Eden Press Women's Publications, 1981.

O'Connor, Teresa F. *Jean Rhys: The West Indian Novels.* New York: New York University Press, 1986.

Ostriker, Alicia. *Writing like a Woman.* Ann Arbor: University of Michigan Press, 1983.

Plante, David. *Difficult Women: A Memoir of Three.* New York: Atheneum, 1983.

Porter, Dennis. "Of Heroines and Victims: Jean Rhys and *Jane Eyre.*" *Massachusetts Review* 17 (Autumn 1976): 540–52.

Poston, Carol H. "Childbirth in Literature." *Feminist Studies* 4 (June 1978): 19–31.

Quinn, Vincent. "H.D.'s 'Hermetic Definition': The Poet as Archetypal Mother." *Contemporary Literature* 18 (Winter 1977): 51–61.

Rapaport, Herman. "*Jane Eyre* and the *Mot Tabou.*" *MLN* 94 (December 1979): 1093–1104.

Rich, Adrienne. *Diving into the Wreck: Poems, 1971–1972.* New York: W. W. Norton, 1973.

———. *The Dream of a Common Language: Poems, 1974–1977.* New York: W. W. Norton, 1978.

———. *Of Woman Born: Motherhood as Experience and Institution.* New York: W. W. Norton, 1976.

———. *On Lies, Secrets, and Silence: Selected Prose, 1966–1978.* New York: W. W. Norton, 1979.

Riddel, Joseph N. "H.D. and the Poetics of 'Spiritual Realism.'" *Contemporary Literature* 10 (Autumn 1969): 447–73.

———. "H.D.'s Scene of Writing—Poetry as (and) Analysis." *Studies in the Literary Imagination* 12 (Spring 1979): 41–59.

Robinson, Janice. *H.D.: The Life and Work of an American Poet.* Boston: Houghton Mifflin, 1982.

Rudnytsky, Peter L. *Freud and Oedipus.* New York: Columbia University Press, 1987.

Scharfman, Ronnie. "Mirroring and Mothering in Simone Schwarz-Bart's *Pluie et Vent sur Telumée Miracle* and Jean Rhys' *Wide Sargasso Sea.*" *Yale French Studies* 62 (1981): 88–106.

Schor, Naomi. "*Eugenie Grandet:* Mirrors and Melancholia." *The (M)other Tongue:*

186   Bibliography

Essays in Feminist Psychoanalytic Interpretation. Ed. Shirley Nelson Garner, Claire Kahane, Madelon Sprengnether. Ithaca: Cornell University Press, 1985: 217–37.

Showalter, Elaine. *A Literature of Their Own: British Women Novelists from Brontë to Lessing*. Princeton: Princeton University Press, 1977.

Staley, Thomas F. *Jean Rhys: A Critical Study*. Austin: University of Texas Press, 1979.

Stanton, Domna C. "Difference on Trial: A Critique of the Maternal Metaphor in Cixous, Irigaray, and Kristeva." *The Poetics of Gender*. Ed. Nancy K. Miller. New York: Columbia University Press, 1986: 157–82.

——. "Language and Revolution: The Franco-American Dis-connection." *The Future of Difference*. Boston: G. K. Hall, 1980.

Steadman, Jane W. "Charlotte Brontë and Bewick's *British Birds*." *Brontë Society Transactions* 15, no. 1 (1966): 37.

Stimpson, Catharine R. Foreword to Margaret Homans, *Bearing the Word: Language and Female Experience in Nineteenth-Century Women's Writing*. Chicago: University of Chicago Press, 1986: ix–x.

Suleiman, Susan Rubin. "Writing and Motherhood." *The (M)other Tongue: Essays in Feminist Psychoanalytic Interpretation*. Ed. Shirley Nelson Garner, Claire Kahane, and Madelon Sprengnether. Ithaca: Cornell University Press, 1985: 352–77.

Ulmer, Gregory L. "The Discourse of the Imaginary." *Diacritics* (March 1980): 61–75.

Wagner, Linda Welshimer. "*Helen in Egypt*: A Culmination." *Contemporary Literature* 10 (Autumn 1969): 523–36.

Winnicott, D. W. "Mirror-Role of Mother and Family in Child Development." *The Predicament of the Family*. Ed. Peter Lomas. New York: International University Press, 1967: 26–33.

Wittig, Monique. "One Is Not Born a Woman." *Feminist Issues* 1, no. 2 (1981): 47–54.

Wolfe, Peter. *Jean Rhys*. Twayne's English Author Series, 294. Ed. Kinley E. Roby. Boston: Twayne, 1980.

Yeazell, Ruth Bernard. "More True than Real: Jane Eyre's 'Mysterious Summons.'" *Nineteenth-Century Fiction* 29 (September 1974): 127–43.

Index

Library of Congress Cataloging-in-Publication Data
Kloepfer, Deborah Kelly.
   The unspeakable mother : forbidden discourse in Jean Rhys and H.D.
/ Deborah Kelly Kloepfer.
      p.   cm.—(Reading women writing)
   Bibliography: p.
   Includes index.
   ISBN 0–8014–2306–6 (alk. paper)
      1. Rhys, Jean—Criticism and interpretation.   2. H.D. (Hilda
Doolittle), 1886–1961—Criticism and interpretation.   3. Mothers and
daughters in literature.   4. Feminism and literature—History—20th
century.   5. Women and literature—History—20th century.
I. Title.   II. Series.
PR6035.H96Z76 1989
820.9'355—dc20   89–7182